BILL & TED
GO TO
HELL

Side 1
33⅓
Stereo

SRM 8.84
1.00.001

JOINES & BACHAN
with LAWSON

© Phone Booth
Recording
91725-4

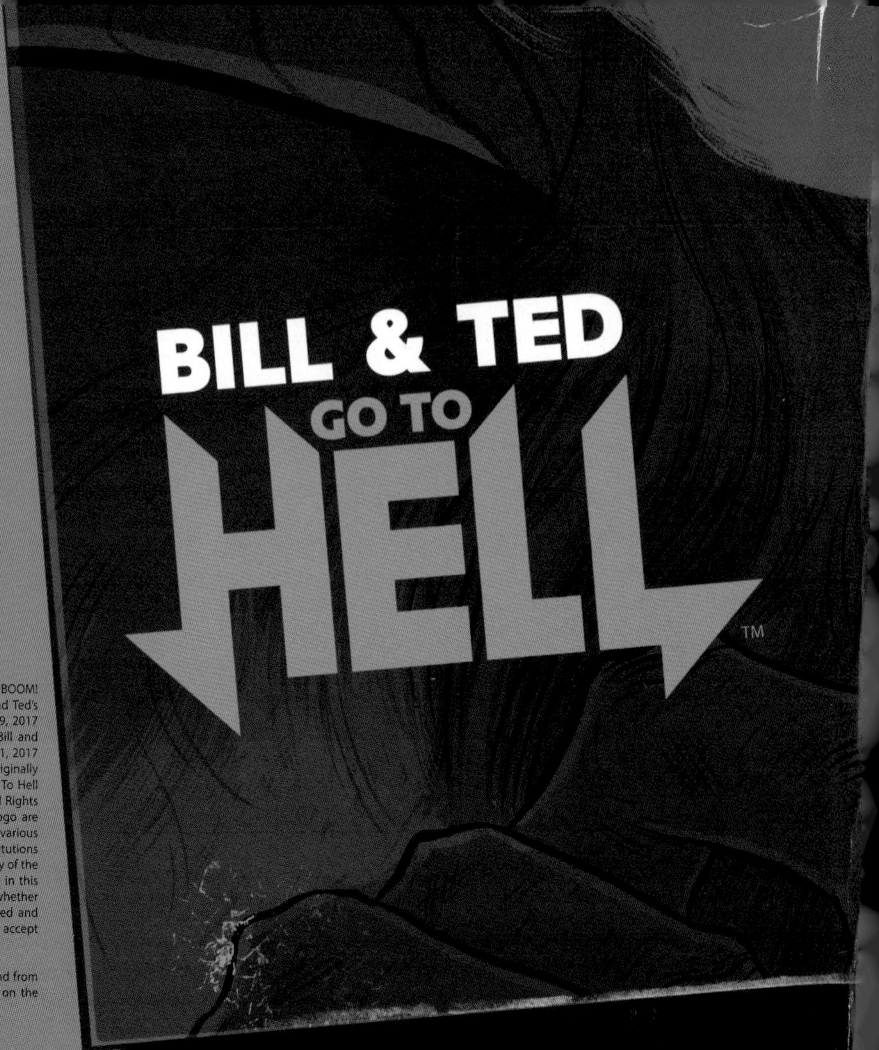
BILL & TED
GO TO
HELL
TM

A catalog record of this book is available from OCLC and from the BOOM! Studios website, www.boom-studios.com, on the Librarians Page.

BOOM! Studios, 5670 Wilshire Boulevard, Suite 450,
Los Angeles, CA 90036-5679. Printed in China. First Printing.

ISBN: 978-1-60886-935-0, eISBN :978-1-61398-606-6

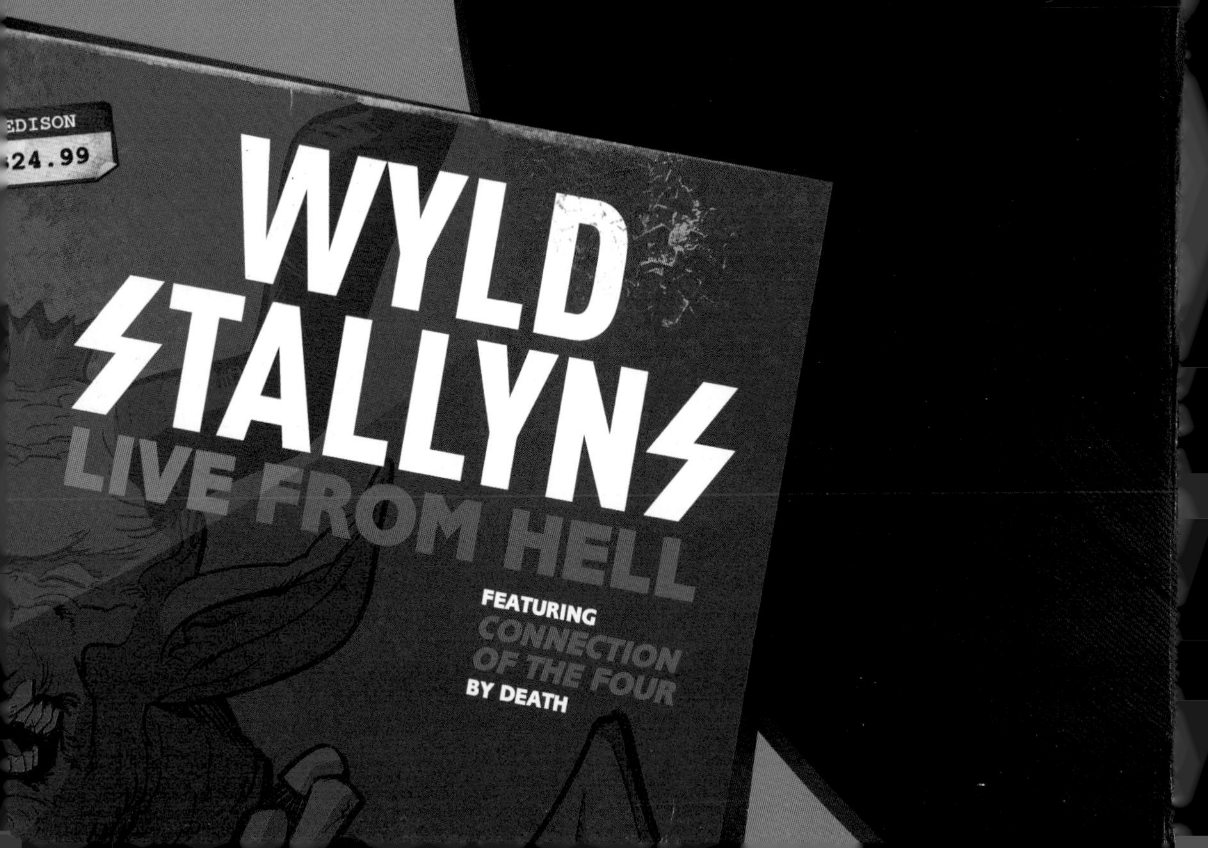
EDISON
24.99
WYLD
STALLYNS
LIVE FROM HELL
FEATURING
CONNECTION
OF THE FOUR
BY DEATH

WRITTEN BY
BRIAN JOINES

ART BY
BACHAN

COLORS BY
JEREMY LAWSON

LETTERS BY
JIM CAMPBELL

COVER
JAMAL CAMPBELL

DESIGNER
SCOTT NEWMAN

ASSOCIATE EDITOR
ALEX GALER

EDITOR
DAFNA PLEBAN

SPECIAL THANKS TO THE MOST EXCELLENT
IAN BRILL
ALEX WINTER
SCOTT KROOPF
BRIAN LYNCH
LINDA KAY

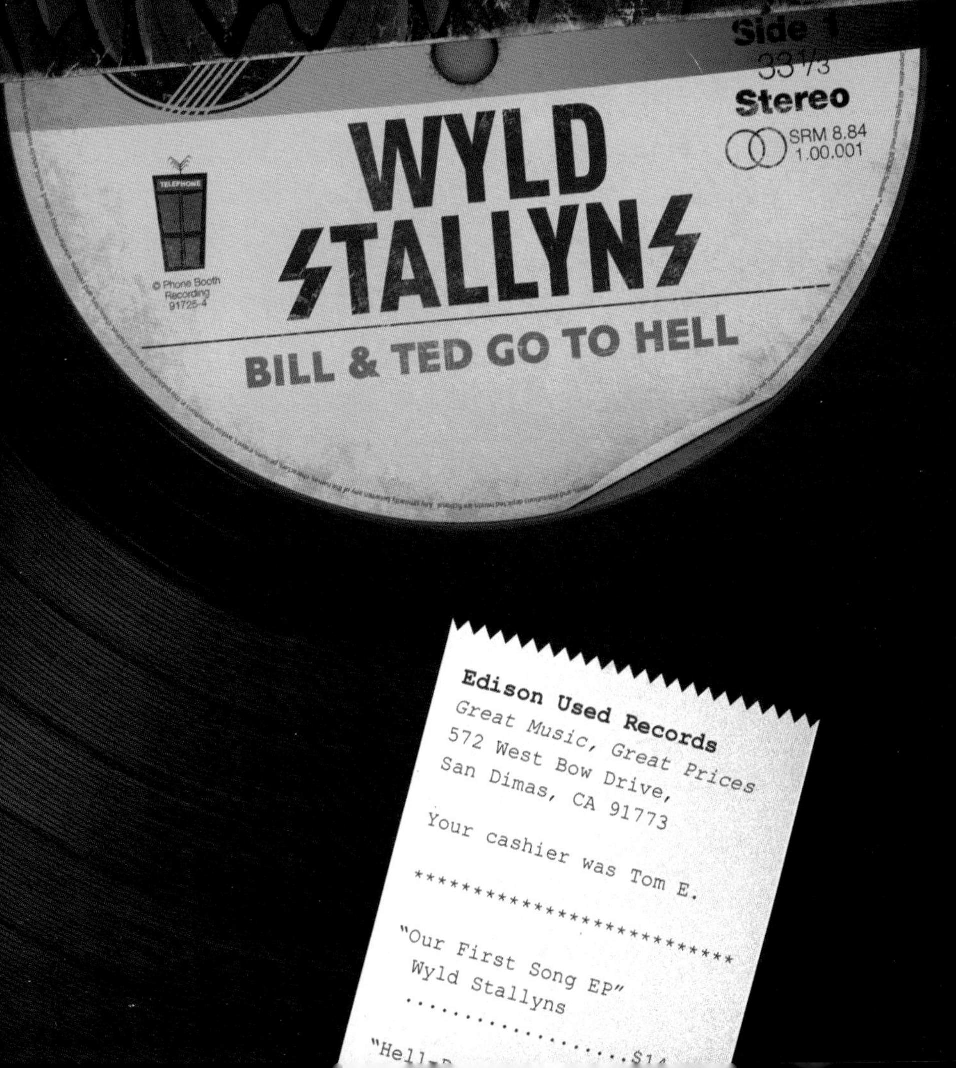
Side 1
33 1/3
Stereo
SRM 8.84
1.00.001
TELEPHONE
© Phone Booth Recording 91725-4
WYLD STALLYNS
BILL & TED GO TO HELL
Edison Used Records
Great Music, Great Prices
572 West Bow Drive,
San Dimas, CA 91773
Your cashier was Tom E.
"Our First Song EP"
Wyld Stallyns

CHAPTER ONE
AFTERLIVING

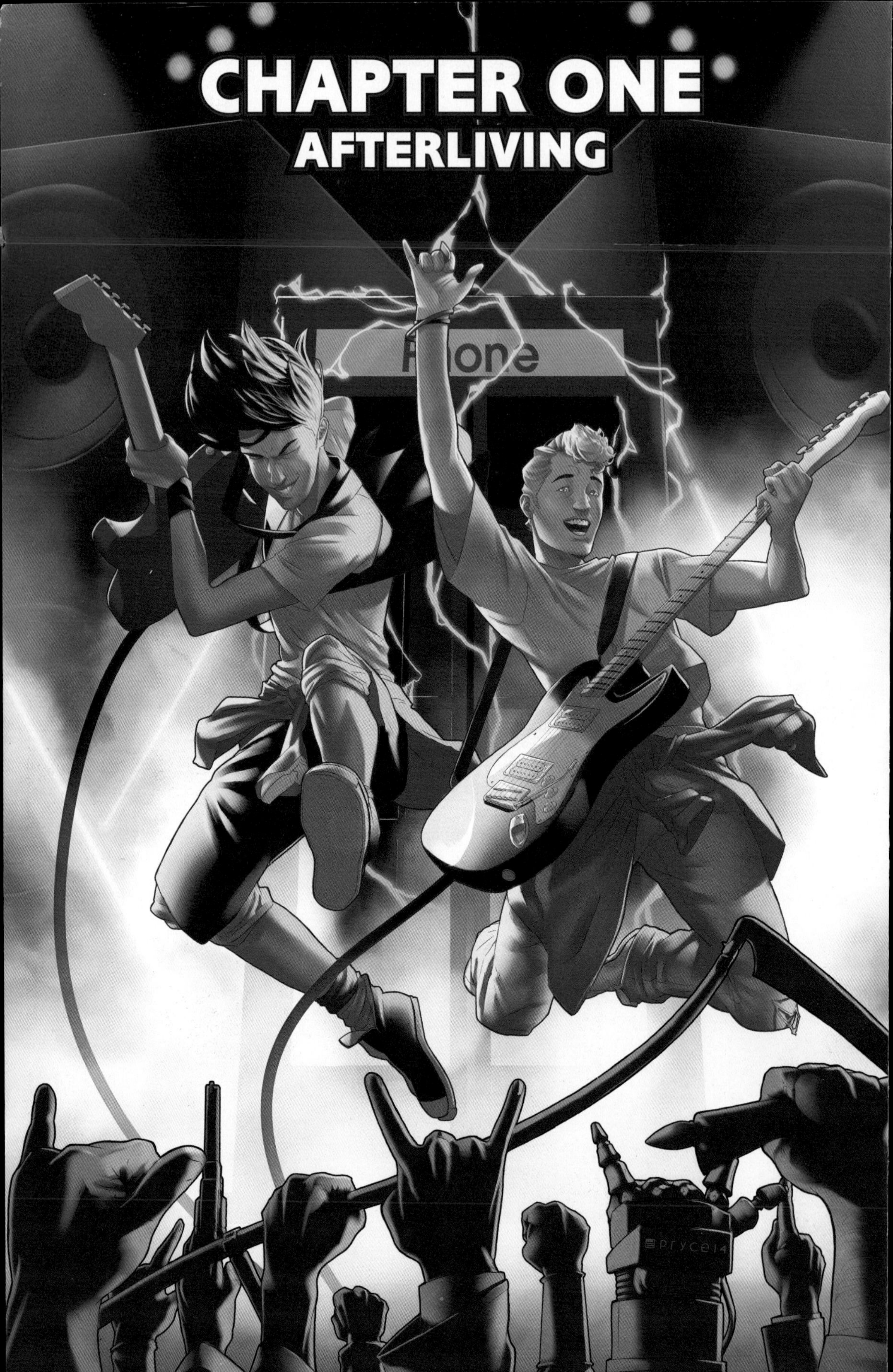

JAMAL CAMPBELL ⚡ ISSUE ONE MAIN COVER

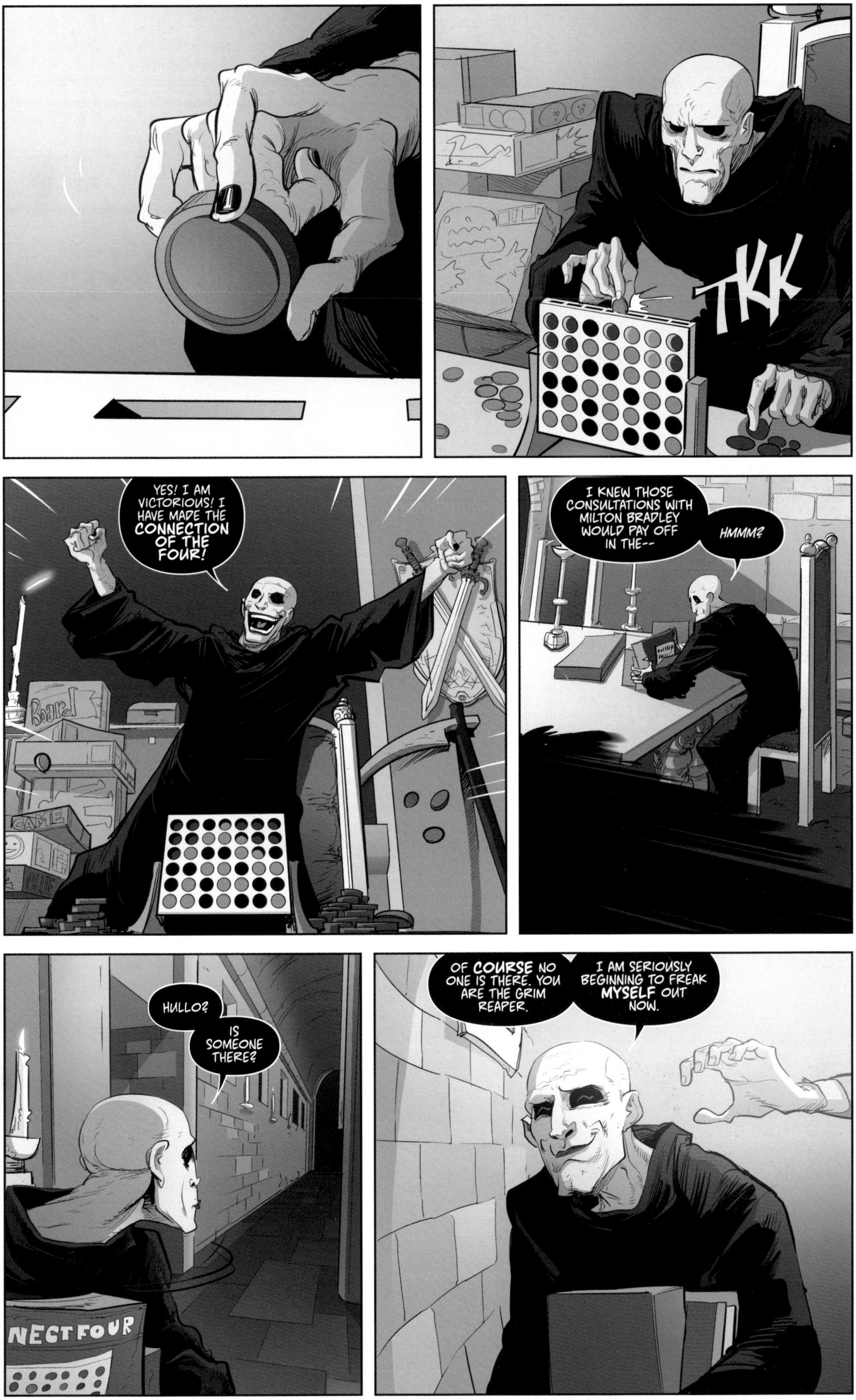
TKK
YES! I AM VICTORIOUS! I HAVE MADE THE CONNECTION OF THE FOUR!
I KNEW THOSE CONSULTATIONS WITH MILTON BRADLEY WOULD PAY OFF IN THE--
HMMM?
HULLO?
IS SOMEONE THERE?
OF COURSE NO ONE IS THERE. YOU ARE THE GRIM REAPER.
I AM SERIOUSLY BEGINNING TO FREAK MYSELF OUT NOW.

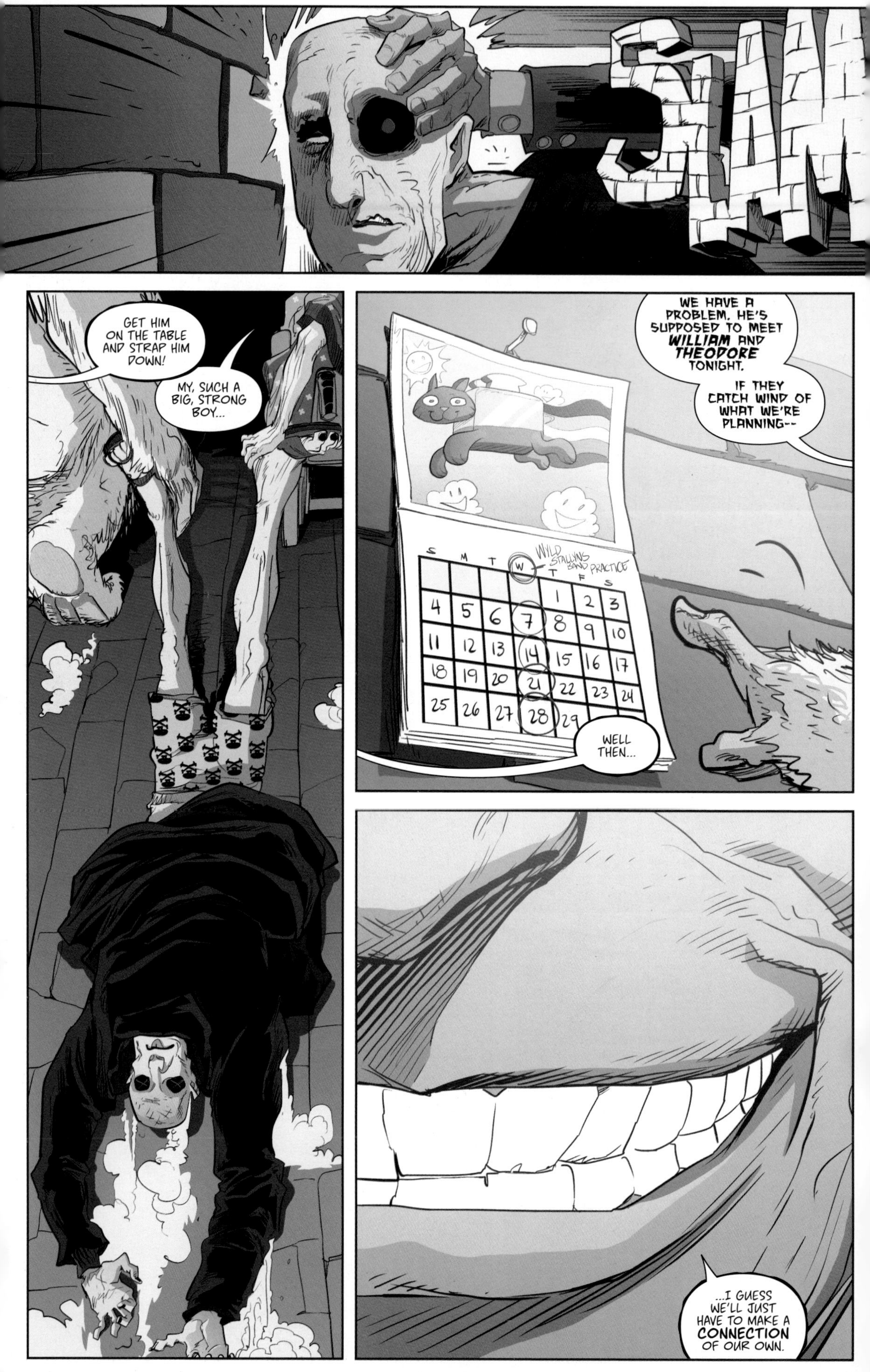
GET HIM ON THE TABLE AND STRAP HIM DOWN!
MY, SUCH A BIG, STRONG BOY...
WE HAVE A PROBLEM. HE'S SUPPOSED TO MEET WILLIAM AND THEODORE TONIGHT.
IF THEY CATCH WIND OF WHAT WE'RE PLANNING--
WYLD STALLYNS BAND PRACTICE
WELL THEN...
...I GUESS WE'LL JUST HAVE TO MAKE A CONNECTION OF OUR OWN.

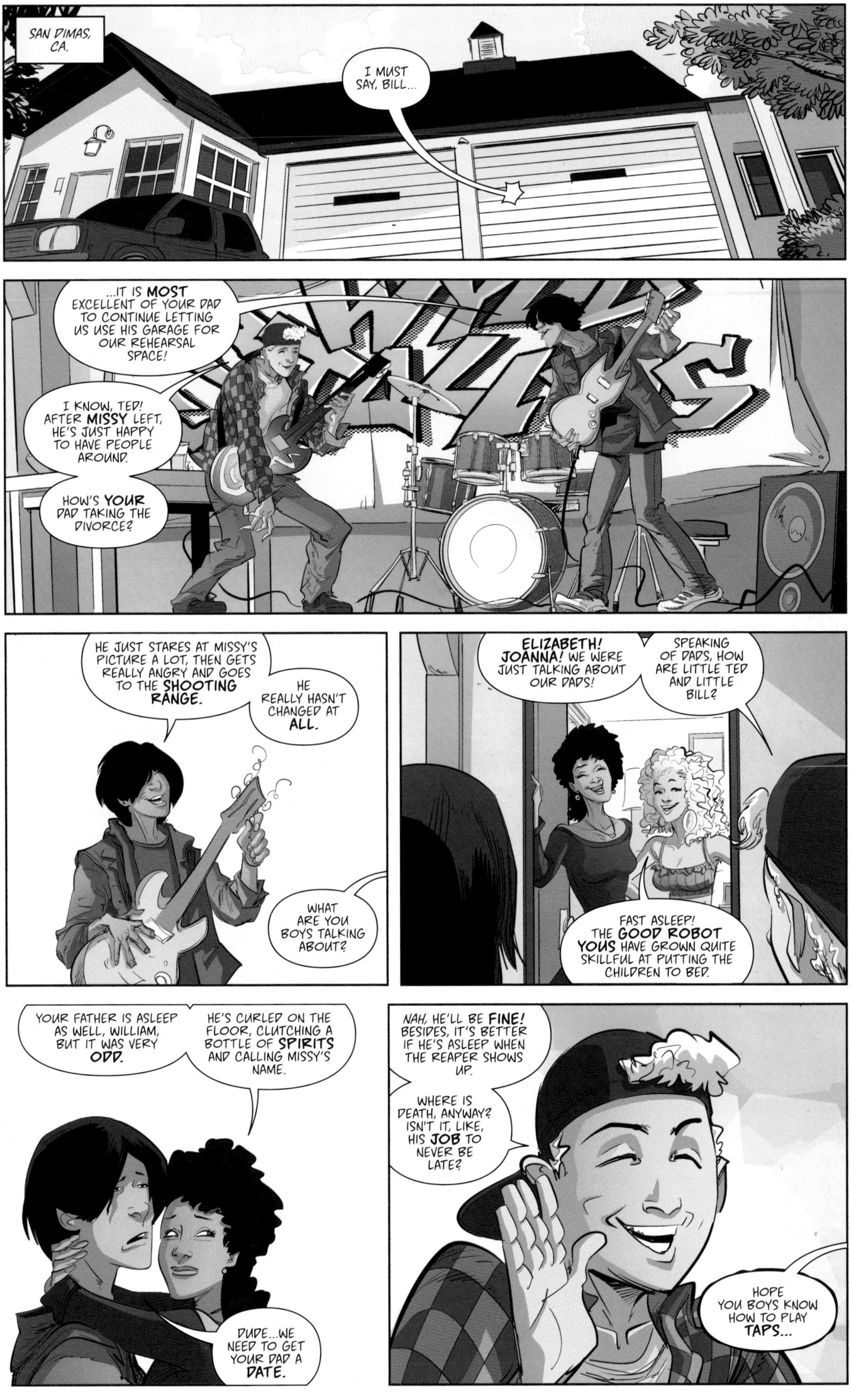
SAN DIMAS, CA.
I MUST SAY, BILL...
...IT IS MOST EXCELLENT OF YOUR DAD TO CONTINUE LETTING US USE HIS GARAGE FOR OUR REHEARSAL SPACE!
I KNOW, TED! AFTER MISSY LEFT, HE'S JUST HAPPY TO HAVE PEOPLE AROUND.
HOW'S YOUR DAD TAKING THE DIVORCE?
HE JUST STARES AT MISSY'S PICTURE A LOT, THEN GETS REALLY ANGRY AND GOES TO THE SHOOTING RANGE.
HE REALLY HASN'T CHANGED AT ALL.
WHAT ARE YOU BOYS TALKING ABOUT?
ELIZABETH! JOANNA! WE WERE JUST TALKING ABOUT OUR DADS!
SPEAKING OF DADS, HOW ARE LITTLE TED AND LITTLE BILL?
FAST ASLEEP! THE GOOD ROBOT YOUS HAVE GROWN QUITE SKILLFUL AT PUTTING THE CHILDREN TO BED.
YOUR FATHER IS ASLEEP AS WELL, WILLIAM, BUT IT WAS VERY ODD.
HE'S CURLED ON THE FLOOR, CLUTCHING A BOTTLE OF SPIRITS AND CALLING MISSY'S NAME.
DUDE...WE NEED TO GET YOUR DAD A DATE.
NAH, HE'LL BE FINE! BESIDES, IT'S BETTER IF HE'S ASLEEP WHEN THE REAPER SHOWS UP.
WHERE IS DEATH, ANYWAY? ISN'T IT, LIKE, HIS JOB TO NEVER BE LATE?
HOPE YOU BOYS KNOW HOW TO PLAY TAPS...

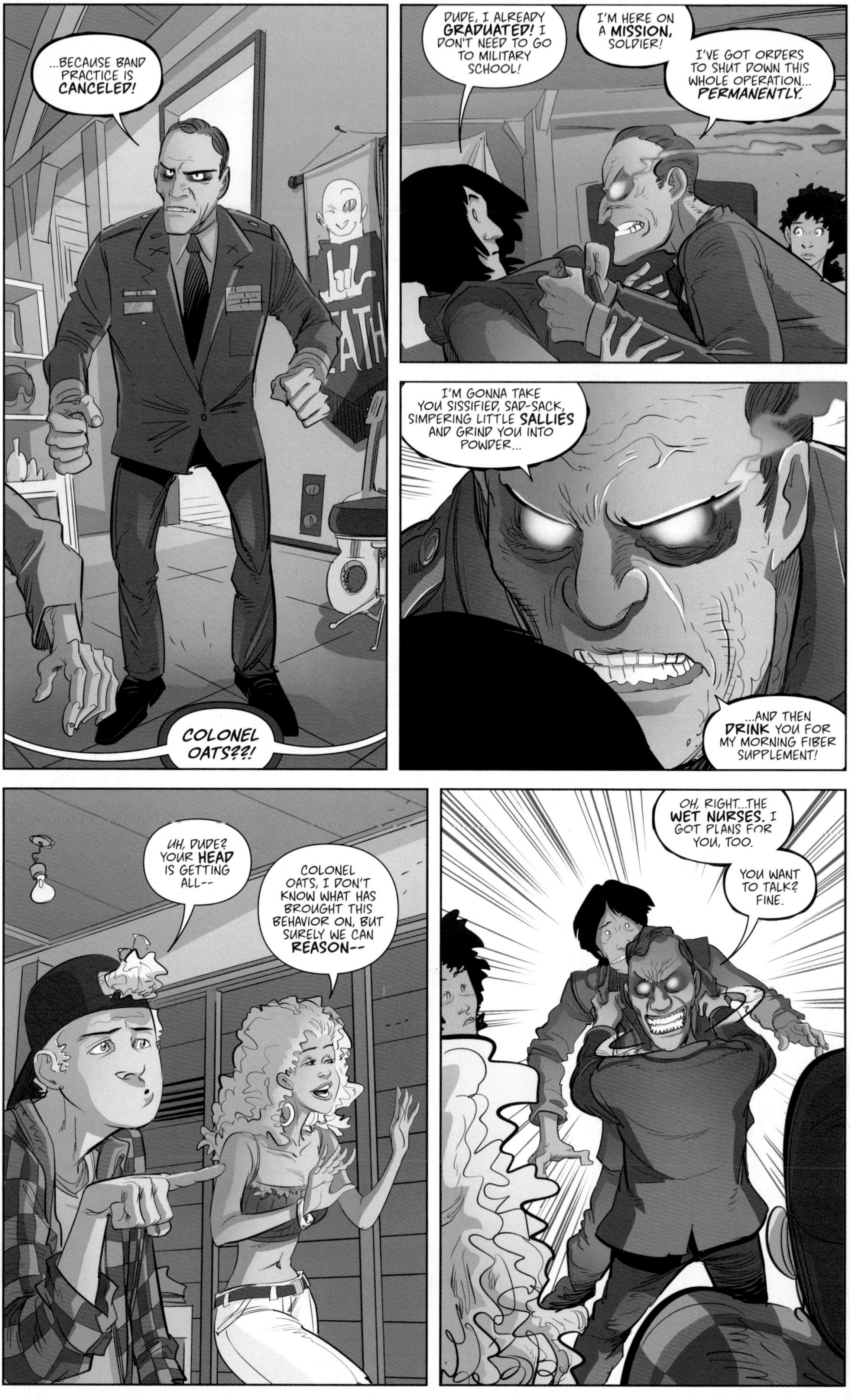
...BECAUSE BAND PRACTICE IS CANCELED!
COLONEL OATS?!?!
DUDE, I ALREADY GRADUATED! I DON'T NEED TO GO TO MILITARY SCHOOL!
I'M HERE ON A MISSION, SOLDIER!
I'VE GOT ORDERS TO SHUT DOWN THIS WHOLE OPERATION... PERMANENTLY.
I'M GONNA TAKE YOU SISSIFIED, SAD-SACK, SIMPERING LITTLE SALLIES AND GRIND YOU INTO POWDER...
...AND THEN DRINK YOU FOR MY MORNING FIBER SUPPLEMENT!
UH, DUDE? YOUR HEAD IS GETTING ALL--
COLONEL OATS, I DON'T KNOW WHAT HAS BROUGHT THIS BEHAVIOR ON, BUT SURELY WE CAN REASON--
OH, RIGHT...THE WET NURSES. I GOT PLANS FOR YOU, TOO.
YOU WANT TO TALK? FINE.

IT CAN BE YOUR **LAST** WORDS!

TED!

ZZZZ-ZZZZ...

YOU MILITANT **DILLHOLE!** IF YOU'VE HURT TED I'LLLLL**KKKK**--!!

YOU'LL DO **NOTHING,** "BILL S. PRESTON, ESQUIRE."

LOOK AT YOU. DO YOU EVEN KNOW WHAT AN ESQUIRE **IS?**

IT'S FROM THE DAYS OF ROYALTY, RESERVED ONLY FOR **GENTLEMEN.**

AND YOU'RE NO GENTLEMAN, PRESTON...

SILKY BOYS CAN'T BE GENTLEM--

DON'T SPEAK TO **US** OF A TIME OF ROYALTY! WE'RE **FROM** A TIME OF ROYALTY!

QUITE RIGHT! AND BASED ON YOUR BEHAVIOR...

...IT'S OBVIOUS WHO THE **TRUE** GENTLEMEN ARE HERE!

TAKE A LOOK, PRESTON!

THUD

THU

THESE GALS ARE MORE OF A MAN THAN YOU'LL EVER BE! THEY'LL **THRIVE** AT MY ACADEMY.

AND SO WILL THEIR **SONS.**

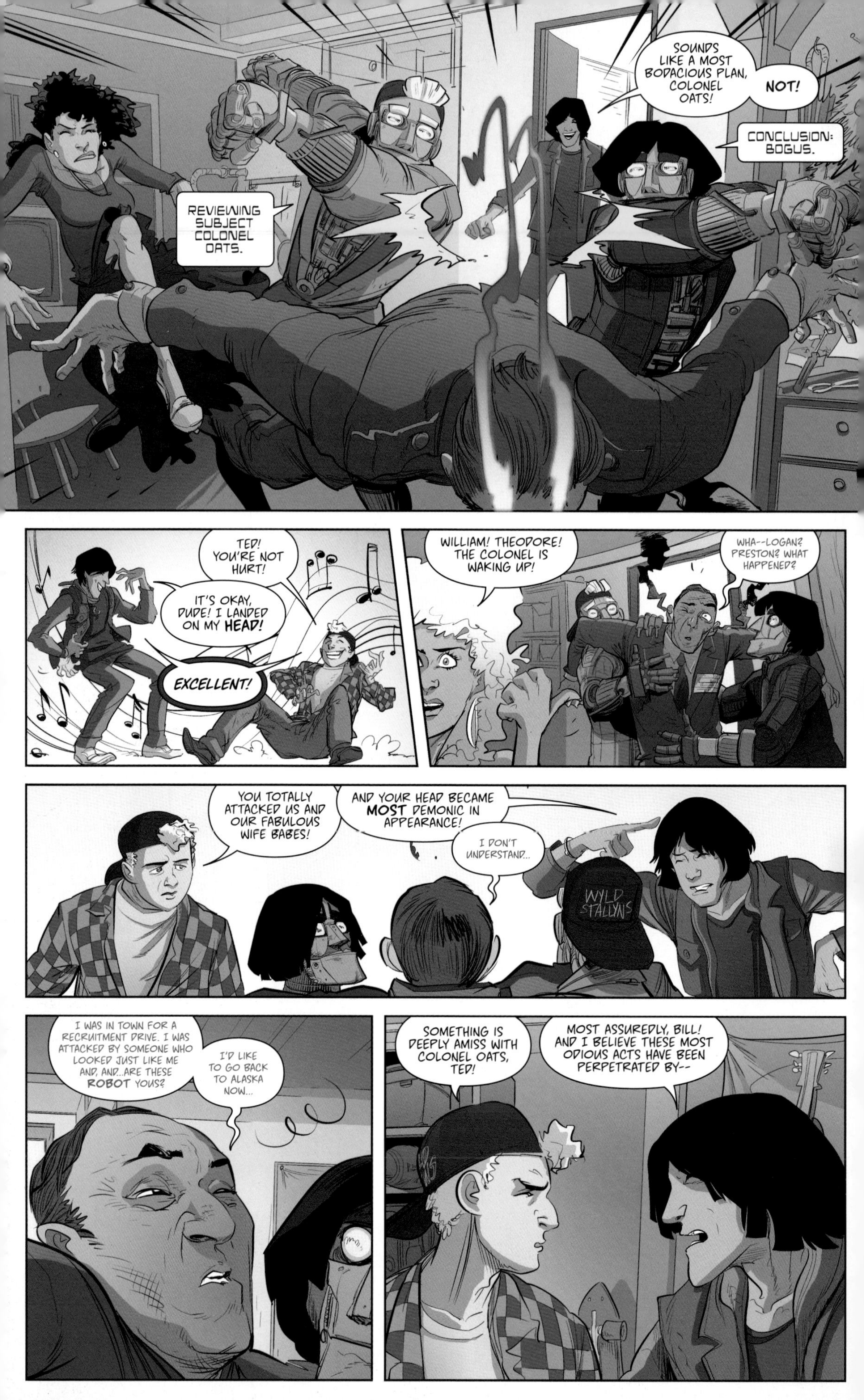
REVIEWING SUBJECT COLONEL OATS.
SOUNDS LIKE A MOST BODACIOUS PLAN, COLONEL OATS!
NOT!
CONCLUSION: BOGUS.
TED! YOU'RE NOT HURT!
IT'S OKAY, DUDE! I LANDED ON MY HEAD!
EXCELLENT!
WILLIAM! THEODORE! THE COLONEL IS WAKING UP!
WHA--LOGAN? PRESTON? WHAT HAPPENED?
YOU TOTALLY ATTACKED US AND OUR FABULOUS WIFE BABES!
AND YOUR HEAD BECAME MOST DEMONIC IN APPEARANCE!
I DON'T UNDERSTAND...
WYLD STALLYNS
I WAS IN TOWN FOR A RECRUITMENT DRIVE. I WAS ATTACKED BY SOMEONE WHO LOOKED JUST LIKE ME AND, AND...ARE THESE ROBOT YOUS?
I'D LIKE TO GO BACK TO ALASKA NOW...
SOMETHING IS DEEPLY AMISS WITH COLONEL OATS, TED!
MOST ASSUREDLY, BILL! AND I BELIEVE THESE MOST ODIOUS ACTS HAVE BEEN PERPETRATED BY--

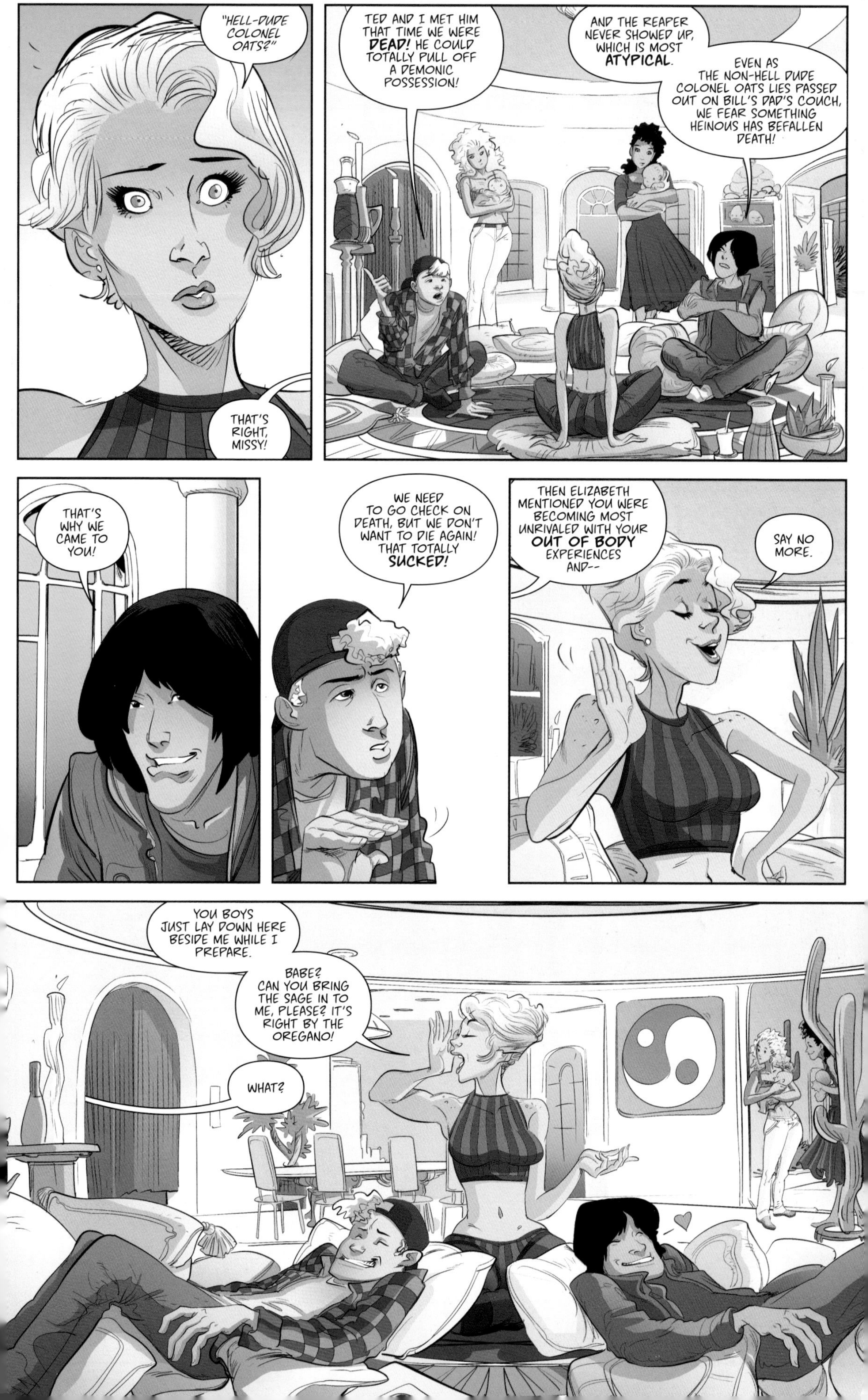
"HELL-DUDE COLONEL OATS?"
THAT'S RIGHT, MISSY!
TED AND I MET HIM THAT TIME WE WERE DEAD! HE COULD TOTALLY PULL OFF A DEMONIC POSSESSION!
AND THE REAPER NEVER SHOWED UP, WHICH IS MOST ATYPICAL.
EVEN AS THE NON-HELL DUDE COLONEL OATS LIES PASSED OUT ON BILL'S DAD'S COUCH, WE FEAR SOMETHING HEINOUS HAS BEFALLEN DEATH!
THAT'S WHY WE CAME TO YOU!
WE NEED TO GO CHECK ON DEATH, BUT WE DON'T WANT TO DIE AGAIN! THAT TOTALLY SUCKED!
THEN ELIZABETH MENTIONED YOU WERE BECOMING MOST UNRIVALED WITH YOUR OUT OF BODY EXPERIENCES AND--
SAY NO MORE.
YOU BOYS JUST LAY DOWN HERE BESIDE ME WHILE I PREPARE.
BABE? CAN YOU BRING THE SAGE IN TO ME, PLEASE? IT'S RIGHT BY THE OREGANO!
WHAT?

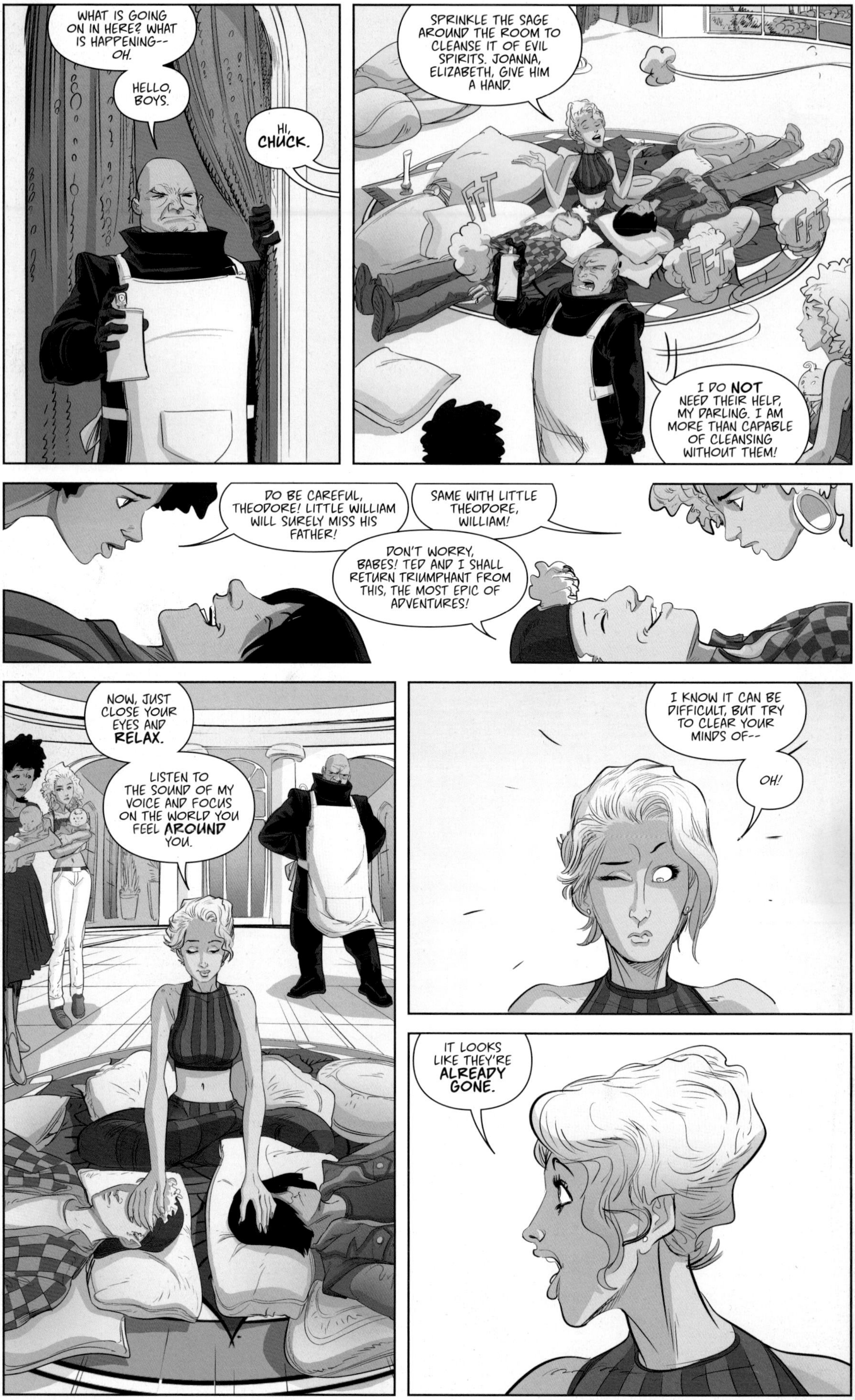

WHAT IS GOING ON IN HERE? WHAT IS HAPPENING-- OH.
HELLO, BOYS.
HI, CHUCK.
SPRINKLE THE SAGE AROUND THE ROOM TO CLEANSE IT OF EVIL SPIRITS. JOANNA, ELIZABETH, GIVE HIM A HAND.
FFT
FFT
FFT
I DO NOT NEED THEIR HELP, MY DARLING. I AM MORE THAN CAPABLE OF CLEANSING WITHOUT THEM!
DO BE CAREFUL, THEODORE! LITTLE WILLIAM WILL SURELY MISS HIS FATHER!
SAME WITH LITTLE THEODORE, WILLIAM!
DON'T WORRY, BABES! TED AND I SHALL RETURN TRIUMPHANT FROM THIS, THE MOST EPIC OF ADVENTURES!
NOW, JUST CLOSE YOUR EYES AND RELAX.
LISTEN TO THE SOUND OF MY VOICE AND FOCUS ON THE WORLD YOU FEEL AROUND YOU.
I KNOW IT CAN BE DIFFICULT, BUT TRY TO CLEAR YOUR MINDS OF--
OH!
IT LOOKS LIKE THEY'RE ALREADY GONE.

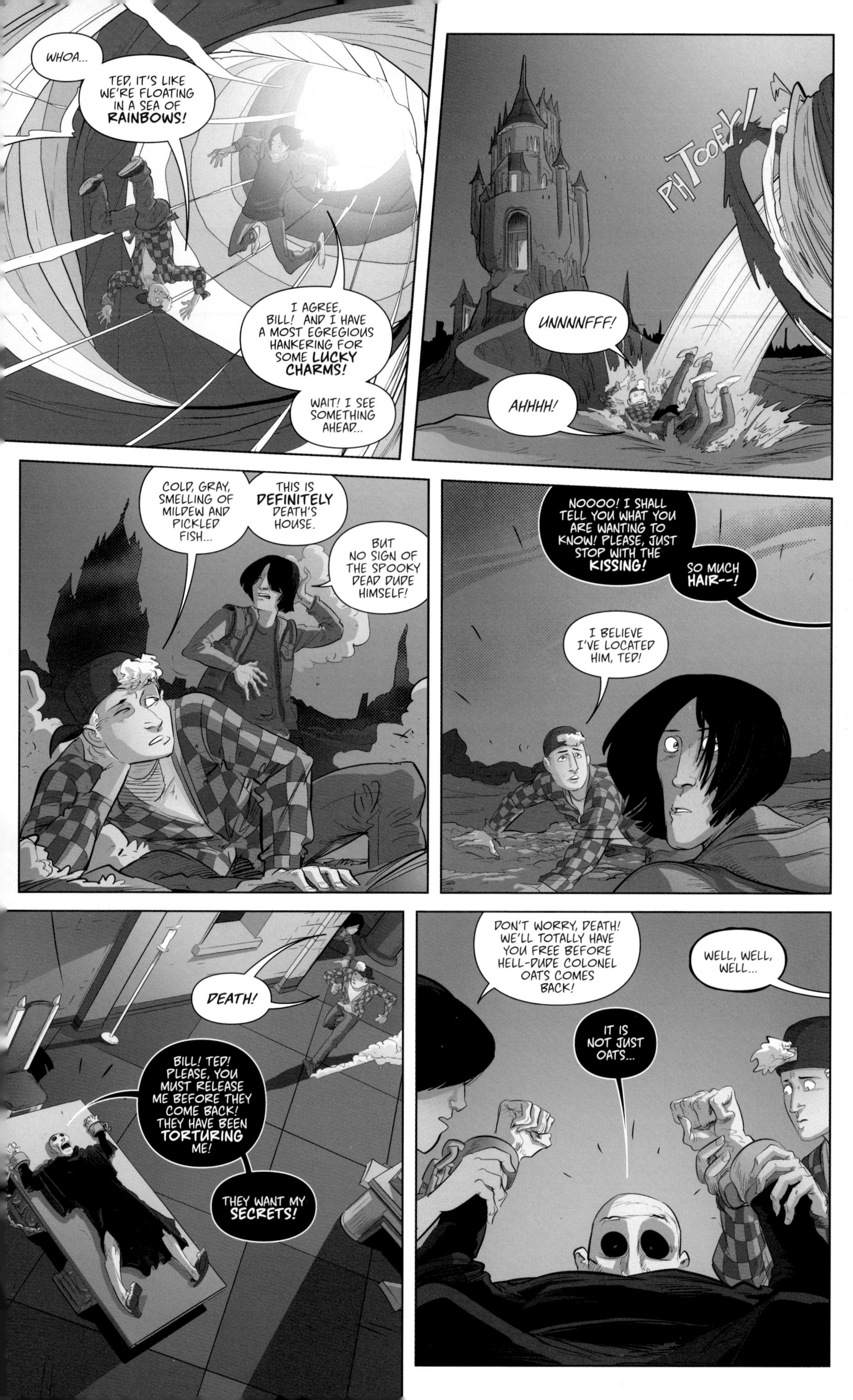
WHOA...
TED, IT'S LIKE WE'RE FLOATING IN A SEA OF RAINBOWS!
I AGREE, BILL! AND I HAVE A MOST EGREGIOUS HANKERING FOR SOME LUCKY CHARMS!
WAIT! I SEE SOMETHING AHEAD...
PHTOOEY!
UNNNNFFF!
AHHHH!
COLD, GRAY, SMELLING OF MILDEW AND PICKLED FISH...
THIS IS DEFINITELY DEATH'S HOUSE.
BUT NO SIGN OF THE SPOOKY DEAD DUDE HIMSELF!
NOOOO! I SHALL TELL YOU WHAT YOU ARE WANTING TO KNOW! PLEASE, JUST STOP WITH THE KISSING!
SO MUCH HAIR--!
I BELIEVE I'VE LOCATED HIM, TED!
DEATH!
BILL! TED! PLEASE, YOU MUST RELEASE ME BEFORE THEY COME BACK! THEY HAVE BEEN TORTURING ME!
THEY WANT MY SECRETS!
DON'T WORRY, DEATH! WE'LL TOTALLY HAVE YOU FREE BEFORE HELL-DUDE COLONEL OATS COMES BACK!
IT IS NOT JUST OATS...
WELL, WELL, WELL...

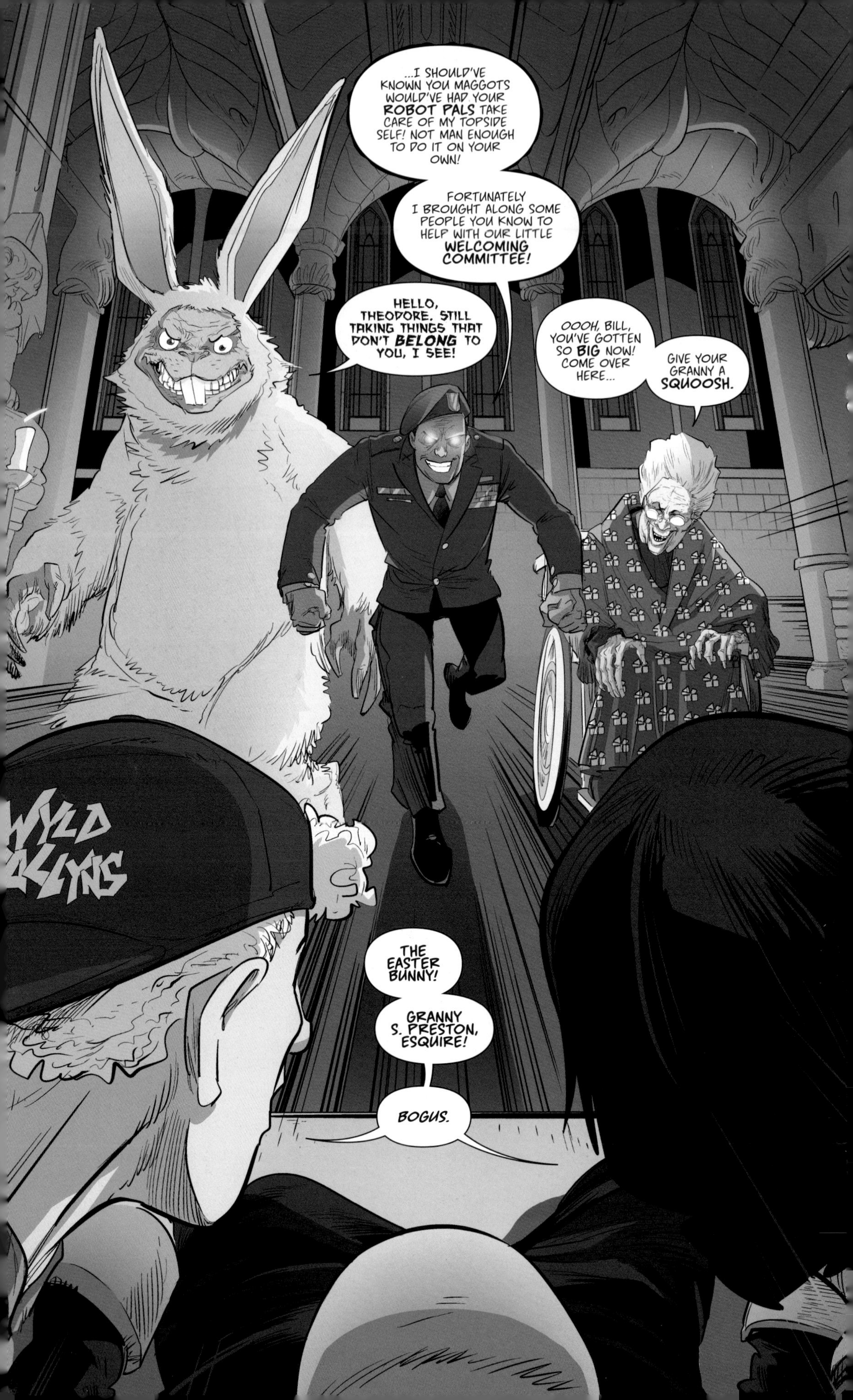
...I SHOULD'VE KNOWN YOU MAGGOTS WOULD'VE HAD YOUR ROBOT PALS TAKE CARE OF MY TOPSIDE SELF! NOT MAN ENOUGH TO DO IT ON YOUR OWN!
FORTUNATELY I BROUGHT ALONG SOME PEOPLE YOU KNOW TO HELP WITH OUR LITTLE WELCOMING COMMITTEE!
HELLO, THEODORE. STILL TAKING THINGS THAT DON'T BELONG TO YOU, I SEE!
OOOH, BILL, YOU'VE GOTTEN SO BIG NOW! COME OVER HERE...
GIVE YOUR GRANNY A SQUOOSH.
WYLD STALLYNS
THE EASTER BUNNY!
GRANNY S. PRESTON, ESQUIRE!
BOGUS.

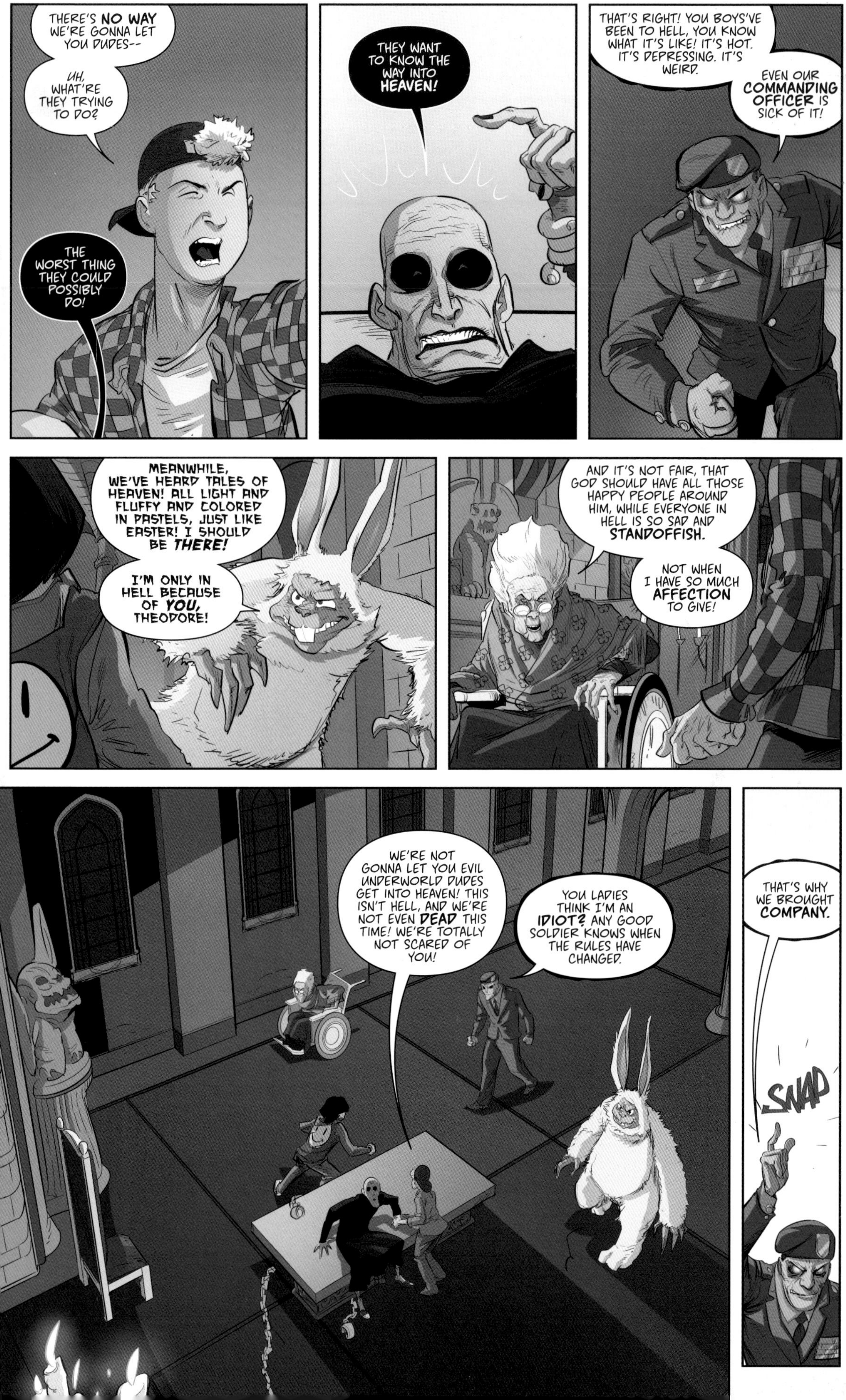
THERE'S NO WAY WE'RE GONNA LET YOU DUDES--
UH, WHAT'RE THEY TRYING TO DO?
THE WORST THING THEY COULD POSSIBLY DO!
THEY WANT TO KNOW THE WAY INTO HEAVEN!
THAT'S RIGHT! YOU BOYS'VE BEEN TO HELL, YOU KNOW WHAT IT'S LIKE! IT'S HOT. IT'S DEPRESSING. IT'S WEIRD.
EVEN OUR COMMANDING OFFICER IS SICK OF IT!
MEANWHILE, WE'VE HEARD TALES OF HEAVEN! ALL LIGHT AND FLUFFY AND COLORED IN PASTELS, JUST LIKE EASTER! I SHOULD BE THERE!
I'M ONLY IN HELL BECAUSE OF YOU, THEODORE!
AND IT'S NOT FAIR, THAT GOD SHOULD HAVE ALL THOSE HAPPY PEOPLE AROUND HIM, WHILE EVERYONE IN HELL IS SO SAD AND STANDOFFISH.
NOT WHEN I HAVE SO MUCH AFFECTION TO GIVE!
WE'RE NOT GONNA LET YOU EVIL UNDERWORLD DUDES GET INTO HEAVEN! THIS ISN'T HELL, AND WE'RE NOT EVEN DEAD THIS TIME! WE'RE TOTALLY NOT SCARED OF YOU!
YOU LADIES THINK I'M AN IDIOT? ANY GOOD SOLDIER KNOWS WHEN THE RULES HAVE CHANGED.
THAT'S WHY WE BROUGHT COMPANY.
SNAP

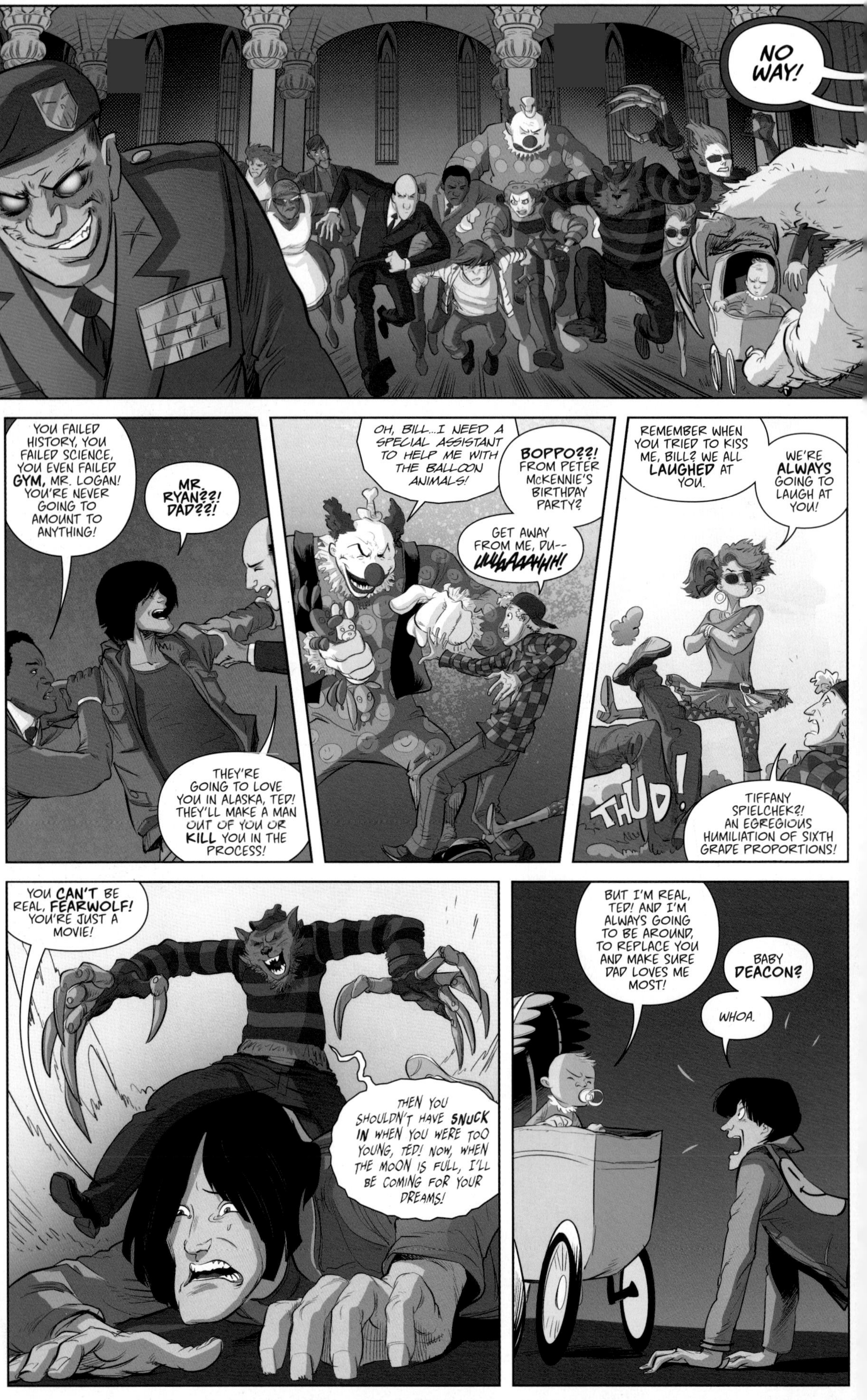
NO WAY!
YOU FAILED HISTORY, YOU FAILED SCIENCE, YOU EVEN FAILED GYM, MR. LOGAN! YOU'RE NEVER GOING TO AMOUNT TO ANYTHING!
MR. RYAN??! DAD??!
THEY'RE GOING TO LOVE YOU IN ALASKA, TED! THEY'LL MAKE A MAN OUT OF YOU OR KILL YOU IN THE PROCESS!
OH, BILL...I NEED A SPECIAL ASSISTANT TO HELP ME WITH THE BALLOON ANIMALS!
BOPPO??! FROM PETER McKENNIE'S BIRTHDAY PARTY?
GET AWAY FROM ME, DU-- UUUAAAAHHH!
REMEMBER WHEN YOU TRIED TO KISS ME, BILL? WE ALL LAUGHED AT YOU.
WE'RE ALWAYS GOING TO LAUGH AT YOU!
THUD!
TIFFANY SPIELCHEK?! AN EGREGIOUS HUMILIATION OF SIXTH GRADE PROPORTIONS!
YOU CAN'T BE REAL, FEARWOLF! YOU'RE JUST A MOVIE!
THEN YOU SHOULDN'T HAVE SNUCK IN WHEN YOU WERE TOO YOUNG, TED! NOW, WHEN THE MOON IS FULL, I'LL BE COMING FOR YOUR DREAMS!
BUT I'M REAL, TED! AND I'M ALWAYS GOING TO BE AROUND, TO REPLACE YOU AND MAKE SURE DAD LOVES ME MOST!
BABY DEACON?
WHOA.

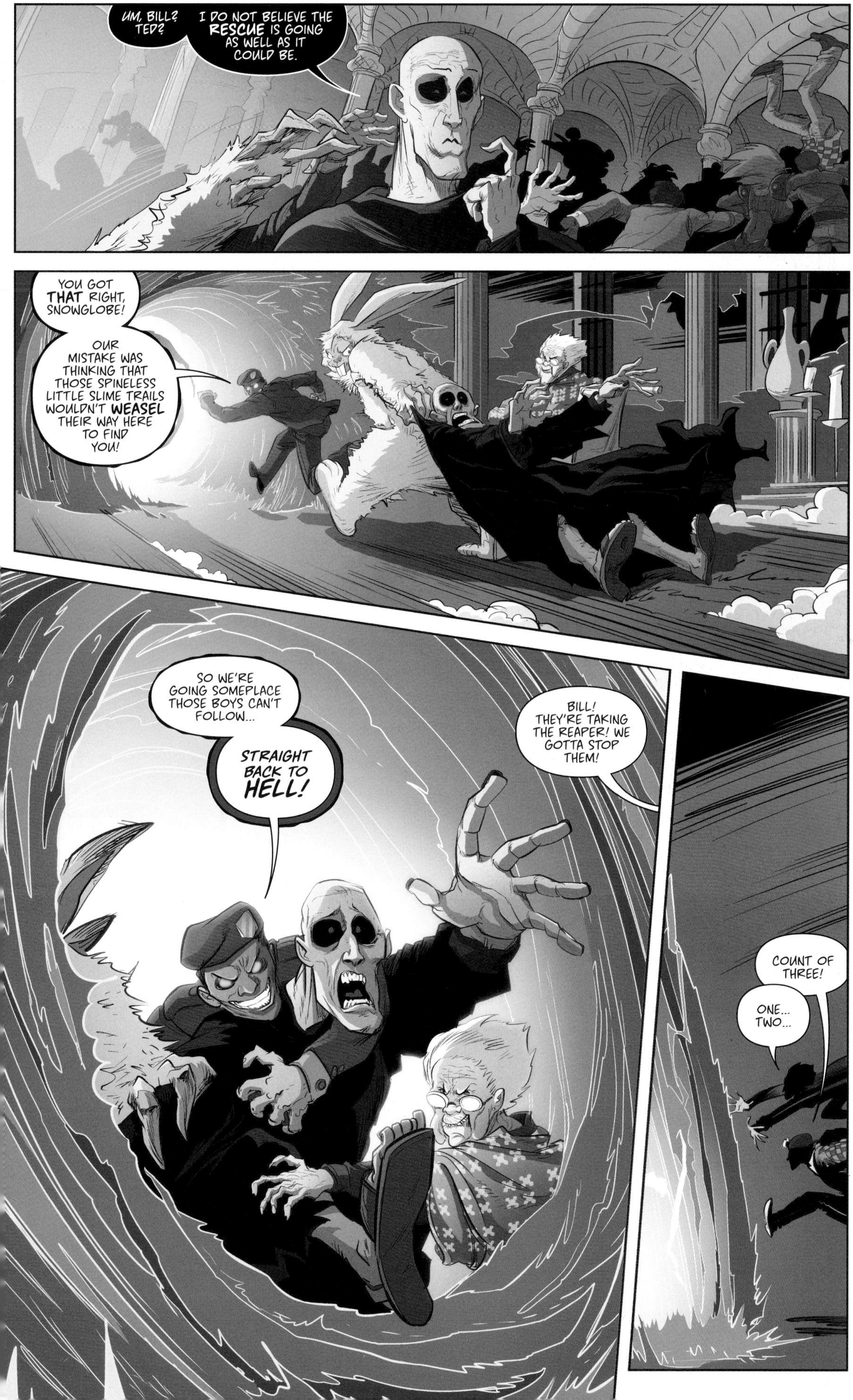
UM, BILL? TED?
I DO NOT BELIEVE THE RESCUE IS GOING AS WELL AS IT COULD BE.
YOU GOT THAT RIGHT, SNOWGLOBE!
OUR MISTAKE WAS THINKING THAT THOSE SPINELESS LITTLE SLIME TRAILS WOULDN'T WEASEL THEIR WAY HERE TO FIND YOU!
SO WE'RE GOING SOMEPLACE THOSE BOYS CAN'T FOLLOW...
STRAIGHT BACK TO HELL!
BILL! THEY'RE TAKING THE REAPER! WE GOTTA STOP THEM!
COUNT OF THREE!
ONE... TWO...

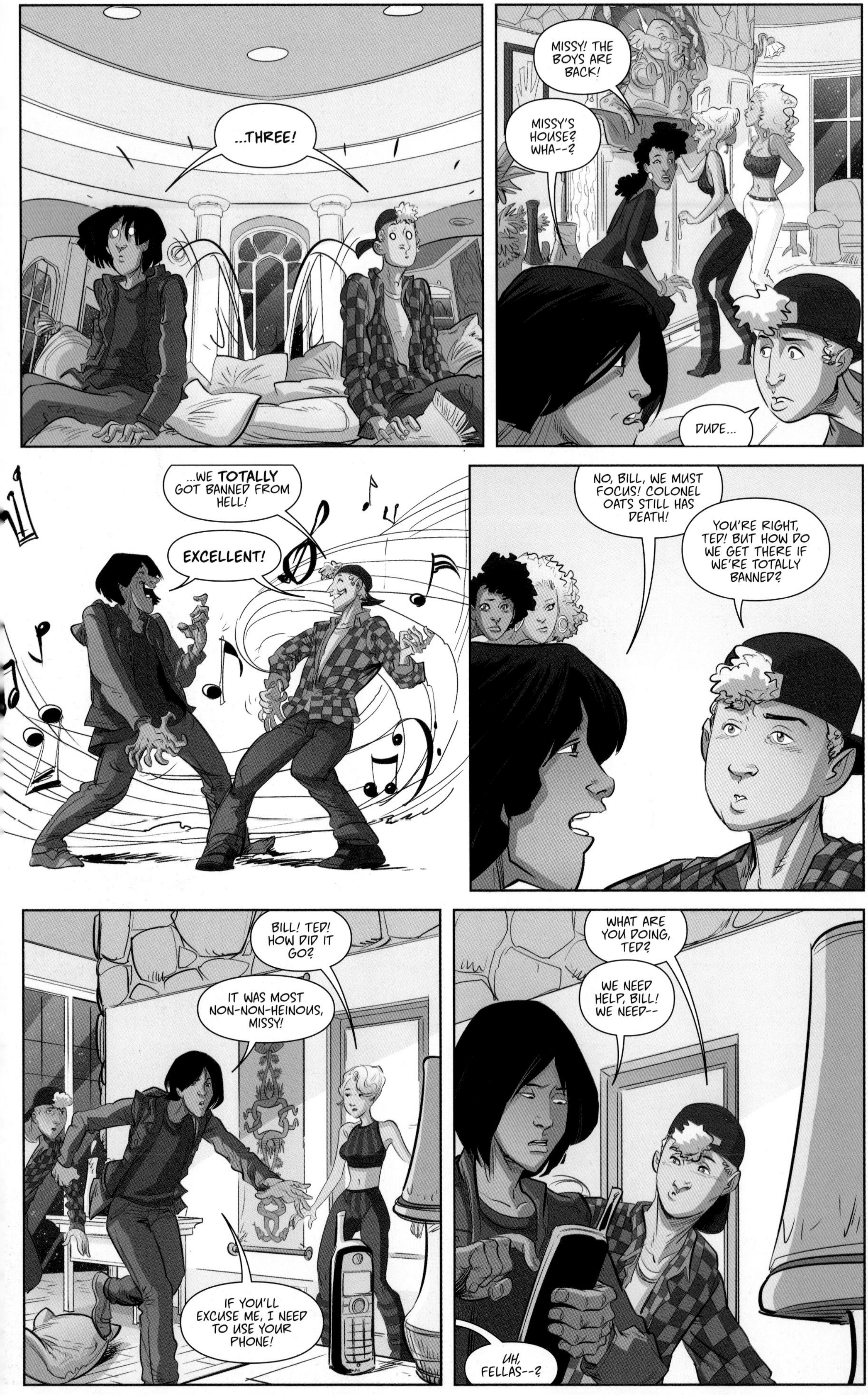
...THREE!
MISSY! THE BOYS ARE BACK!
MISSY'S HOUSE? WHA--?
DUDE...
...WE **TOTALLY** GOT BANNED FROM HELL!
EXCELLENT!
NO, BILL, WE MUST FOCUS! COLONEL OATS STILL HAS DEATH!
YOU'RE RIGHT, TED! BUT HOW DO WE GET THERE IF WE'RE TOTALLY BANNED?
BILL! TED! HOW DID IT GO?
IT WAS MOST NON-NON-HEINOUS, MISSY!
IF YOU'LL EXCUSE ME, I NEED TO USE YOUR PHONE!
WHAT ARE YOU DOING, TED?
WE NEED HELP, BILL! WE NEED--
UH, FELLAS--?

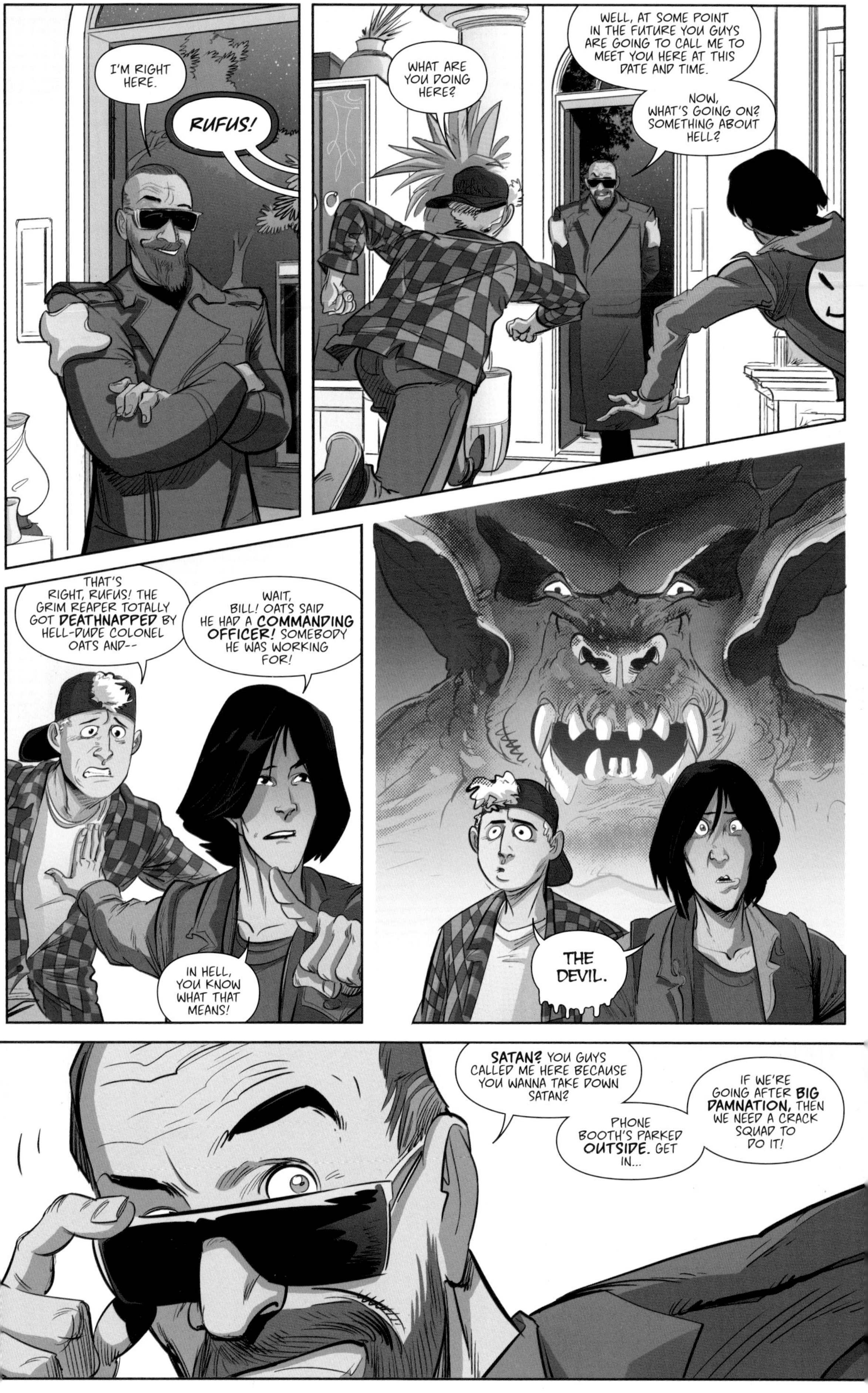

I'M RIGHT HERE.
RUFUS!
WHAT ARE YOU DOING HERE?
WELL, AT SOME POINT IN THE FUTURE YOU GUYS ARE GOING TO CALL ME TO MEET YOU HERE AT THIS DATE AND TIME.
NOW, WHAT'S GOING ON? SOMETHING ABOUT HELL?
THAT'S RIGHT, RUFUS! THE GRIM REAPER TOTALLY GOT DEATHNAPPED BY HELL-DUDE COLONEL OATS AND--
WAIT, BILL! OATS SAID HE HAD A COMMANDING OFFICER! SOMEBODY HE WAS WORKING FOR!
IN HELL, YOU KNOW WHAT THAT MEANS!
THE DEVIL.
SATAN? YOU GUYS CALLED ME HERE BECAUSE YOU WANNA TAKE DOWN SATAN?
PHONE BOOTH'S PARKED OUTSIDE. GET IN...
IF WE'RE GOING AFTER BIG DAMNATION, THEN WE NEED A CRACK SQUAD TO DO IT!

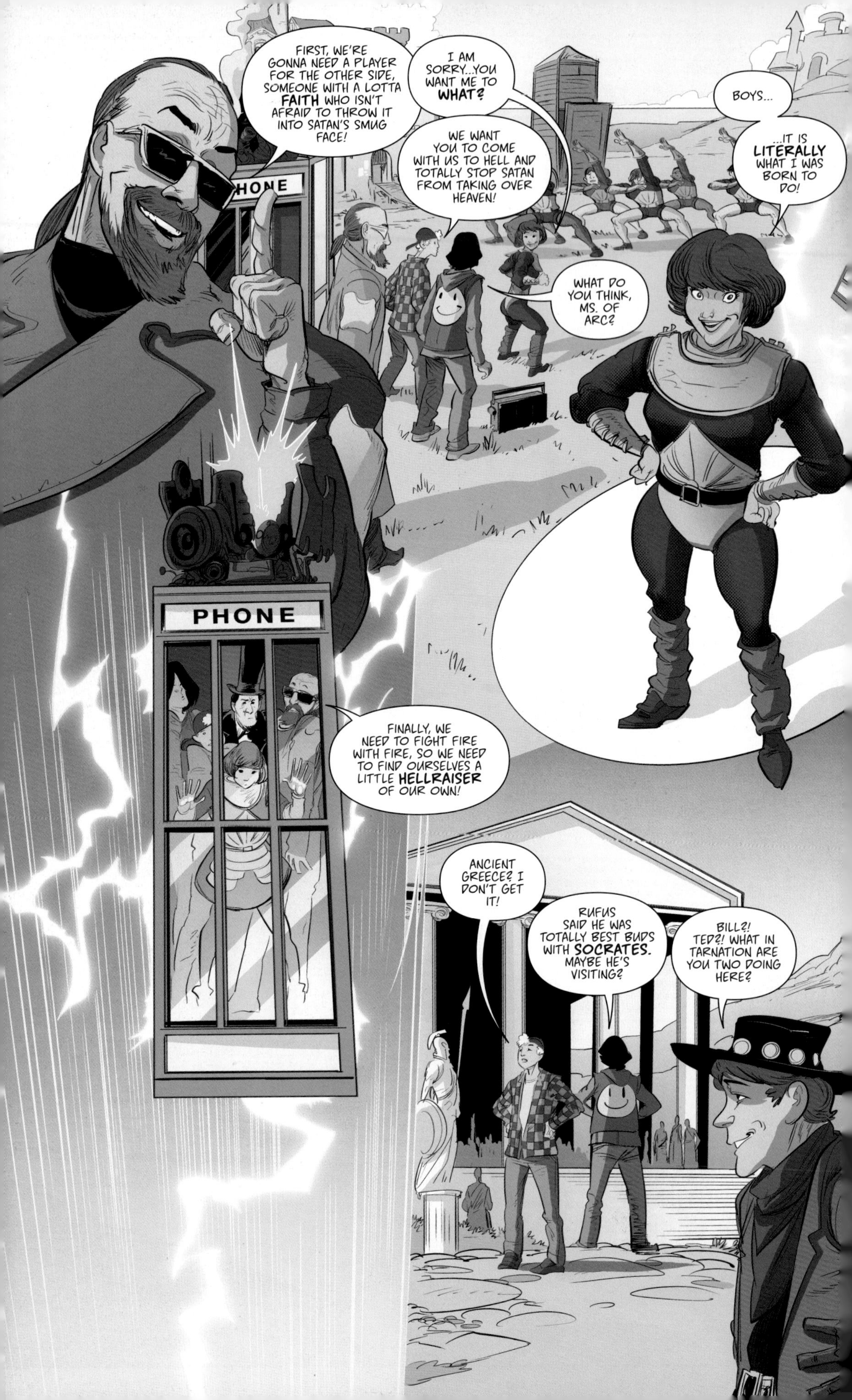

FIRST, WE'RE GONNA NEED A PLAYER FOR THE OTHER SIDE, SOMEONE WITH A LOTTA FAITH WHO ISN'T AFRAID TO THROW IT INTO SATAN'S SMUG FACE!
PHONE
I AM SORRY...YOU WANT ME TO WHAT?
WE WANT YOU TO COME WITH US TO HELL AND TOTALLY STOP SATAN FROM TAKING OVER HEAVEN!
WHAT DO YOU THINK, MS. OF ARC?
BOYS...
...IT IS LITERALLY WHAT I WAS BORN TO DO!
PHONE
FINALLY, WE NEED TO FIGHT FIRE WITH FIRE, SO WE NEED TO FIND OURSELVES A LITTLE HELLRAISER OF OUR OWN!
ANCIENT GREECE? I DON'T GET IT!
RUFUS SAID HE WAS TOTALLY BEST BUDS WITH SOCRATES. MAYBE HE'S VISITING?
BILL?! TED?! WHAT IN TARNATION ARE YOU TWO DOING HERE?

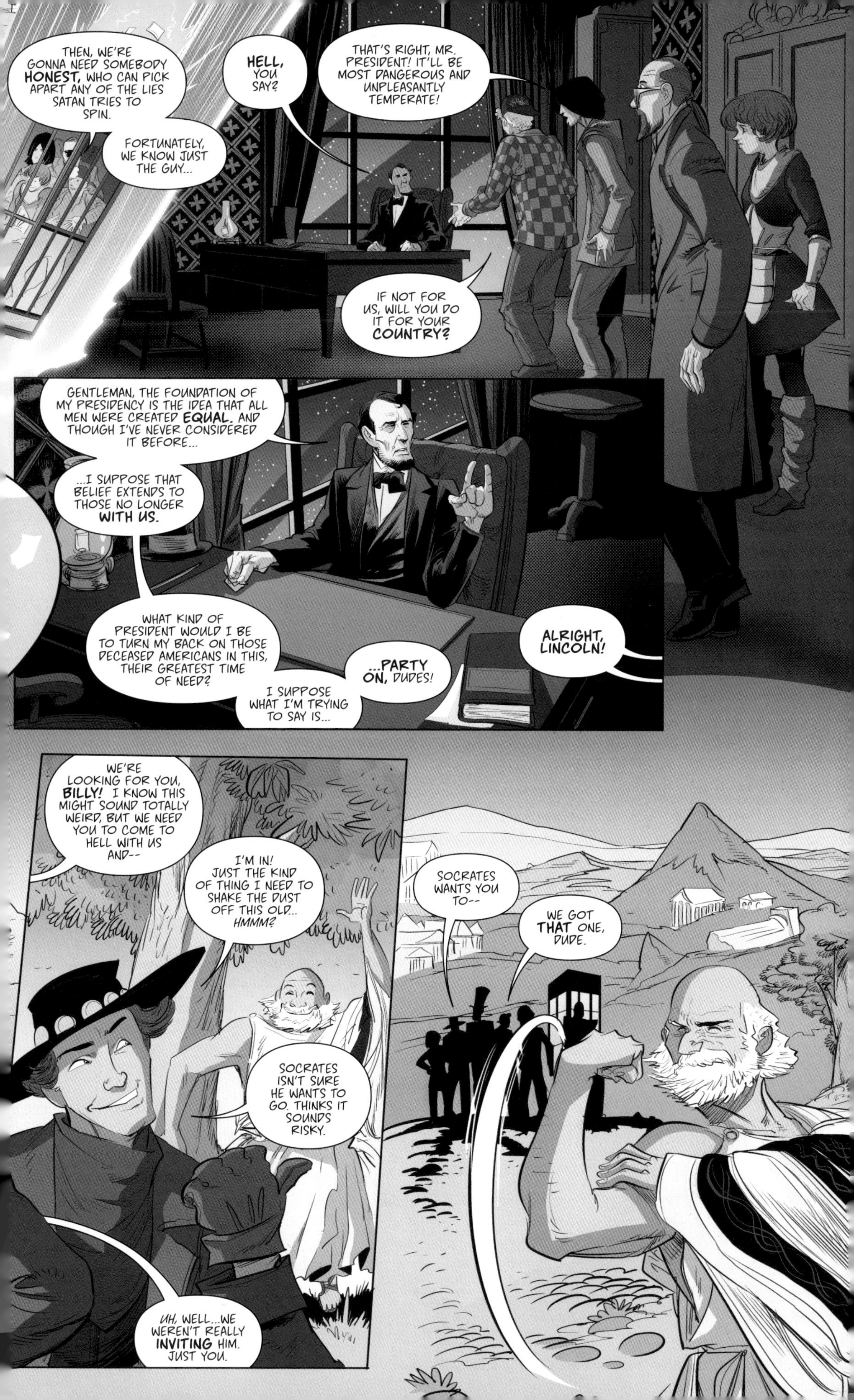
THEN, WE'RE GONNA NEED SOMEBODY **HONEST,** WHO CAN PICK APART ANY OF THE LIES SATAN TRIES TO SPIN.
FORTUNATELY, WE KNOW JUST THE GUY...
HELL, YOU SAY?
THAT'S RIGHT, MR. PRESIDENT! IT'LL BE MOST DANGEROUS AND UNPLEASANTLY TEMPERATE!
IF NOT FOR US, WILL YOU DO IT FOR YOUR **COUNTRY?**
GENTLEMAN, THE FOUNDATION OF MY PRESIDENCY IS THE IDEA THAT ALL MEN WERE CREATED **EQUAL.** AND THOUGH I'VE NEVER CONSIDERED IT BEFORE...
...I SUPPOSE THAT BELIEF EXTENDS TO THOSE NO LONGER **WITH US.**
WHAT KIND OF PRESIDENT WOULD I BE TO TURN MY BACK ON THOSE DECEASED AMERICANS IN THIS, THEIR GREATEST TIME OF NEED?
I SUPPOSE WHAT I'M TRYING TO SAY IS...
...PARTY ON, DUDES!
ALRIGHT, LINCOLN!
WE'RE LOOKING FOR YOU, **BILLY!** I KNOW THIS MIGHT SOUND TOTALLY WEIRD, BUT WE NEED YOU TO COME TO HELL WITH US AND--
I'M IN! JUST THE KIND OF THING I NEED TO SHAKE THE DUST OFF THIS OLD... *HMMM?*
SOCRATES ISN'T SURE HE WANTS TO GO. THINKS IT SOUNDS RISKY.
UH, WELL...WE WEREN'T REALLY **INVITING** HIM. JUST YOU.
SOCRATES WANTS YOU TO--
WE GOT **THAT** ONE, DUDE.

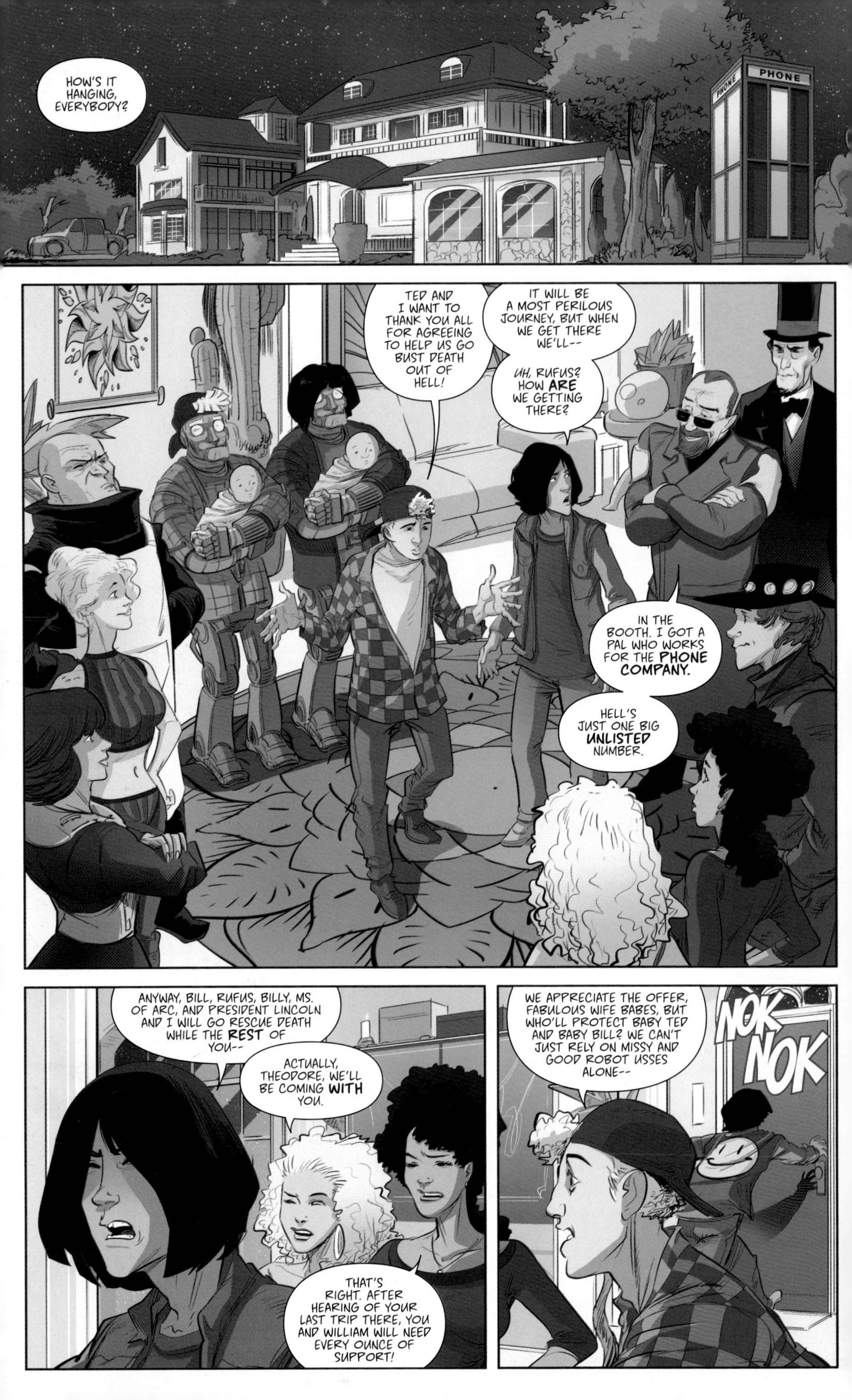
HOW'S IT HANGING, EVERYBODY?
PHONE
TED AND I WANT TO THANK YOU ALL FOR AGREEING TO HELP US GO BUST DEATH OUT OF HELL!
IT WILL BE A MOST PERILOUS JOURNEY, BUT WHEN WE GET THERE WE'LL--
UH, RUFUS? HOW ARE WE GETTING THERE?
IN THE BOOTH. I GOT A PAL WHO WORKS FOR THE PHONE COMPANY.
HELL'S JUST ONE BIG UNLISTED NUMBER.
ANYWAY, BILL, RUFUS, BILLY, MS. OF ARC, AND PRESIDENT LINCOLN AND I WILL GO RESCUE DEATH WHILE THE REST OF YOU--
ACTUALLY, THEODORE, WE'LL BE COMING WITH YOU.
THAT'S RIGHT. AFTER HEARING OF YOUR LAST TRIP THERE, YOU AND WILLIAM WILL NEED EVERY OUNCE OF SUPPORT!
WE APPRECIATE THE OFFER, FABULOUS WIFE BABES, BUT WHO'LL PROTECT BABY TED AND BABY BILL? WE CAN'T JUST RELY ON MISSY AND GOOD ROBOT USSES ALONE--
NOK NOK

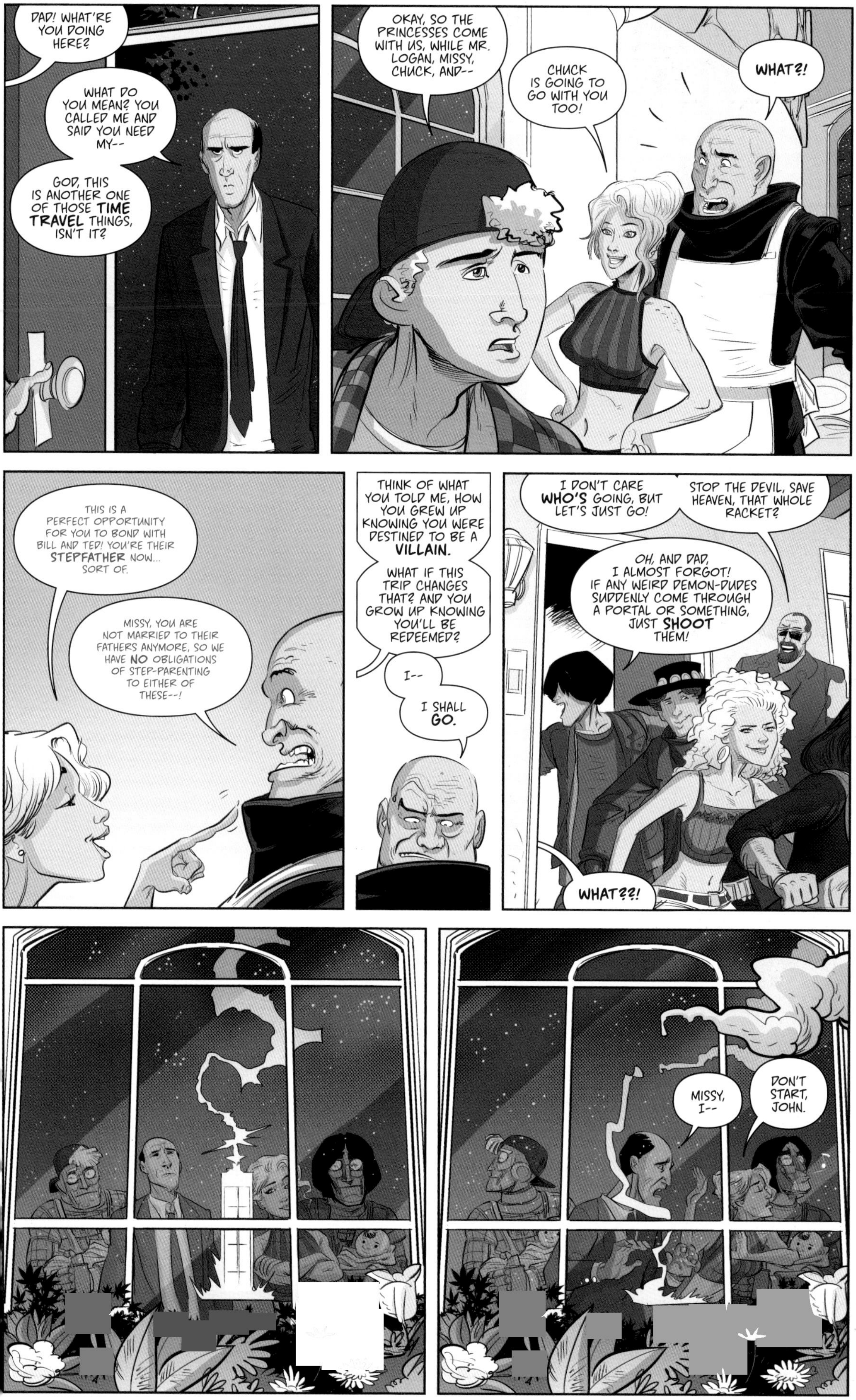
DAD! WHAT'RE YOU DOING HERE?
WHAT DO YOU MEAN? YOU CALLED ME AND SAID YOU NEED MY--
GOD, THIS IS ANOTHER ONE OF THOSE TIME TRAVEL THINGS, ISN'T IT?
OKAY, SO THE PRINCESSES COME WITH US, WHILE MR. LOGAN, MISSY, CHUCK, AND--
CHUCK IS GOING TO GO WITH YOU TOO!
WHAT?!
THIS IS A PERFECT OPPORTUNITY FOR YOU TO BOND WITH BILL AND TED! YOU'RE THEIR STEPFATHER NOW... SORT OF.
MISSY, YOU ARE NOT MARRIED TO THEIR FATHERS ANYMORE, SO WE HAVE NO OBLIGATIONS OF STEP-PARENTING TO EITHER OF THESE--!
THINK OF WHAT YOU TOLD ME, HOW YOU GREW UP KNOWING YOU WERE DESTINED TO BE A VILLAIN.
WHAT IF THIS TRIP CHANGES THAT? AND YOU GROW UP KNOWING YOU'LL BE REDEEMED?
I--
I SHALL GO.
I DON'T CARE WHO'S GOING, BUT LET'S JUST GO!
STOP THE DEVIL, SAVE HEAVEN, THAT WHOLE RACKET?
OH, AND DAD, I ALMOST FORGOT! IF ANY WEIRD DEMON-DUDES SUDDENLY COME THROUGH A PORTAL OR SOMETHING, JUST SHOOT THEM!
WHAT??!
MISSY, I--
DON'T START, JOHN.

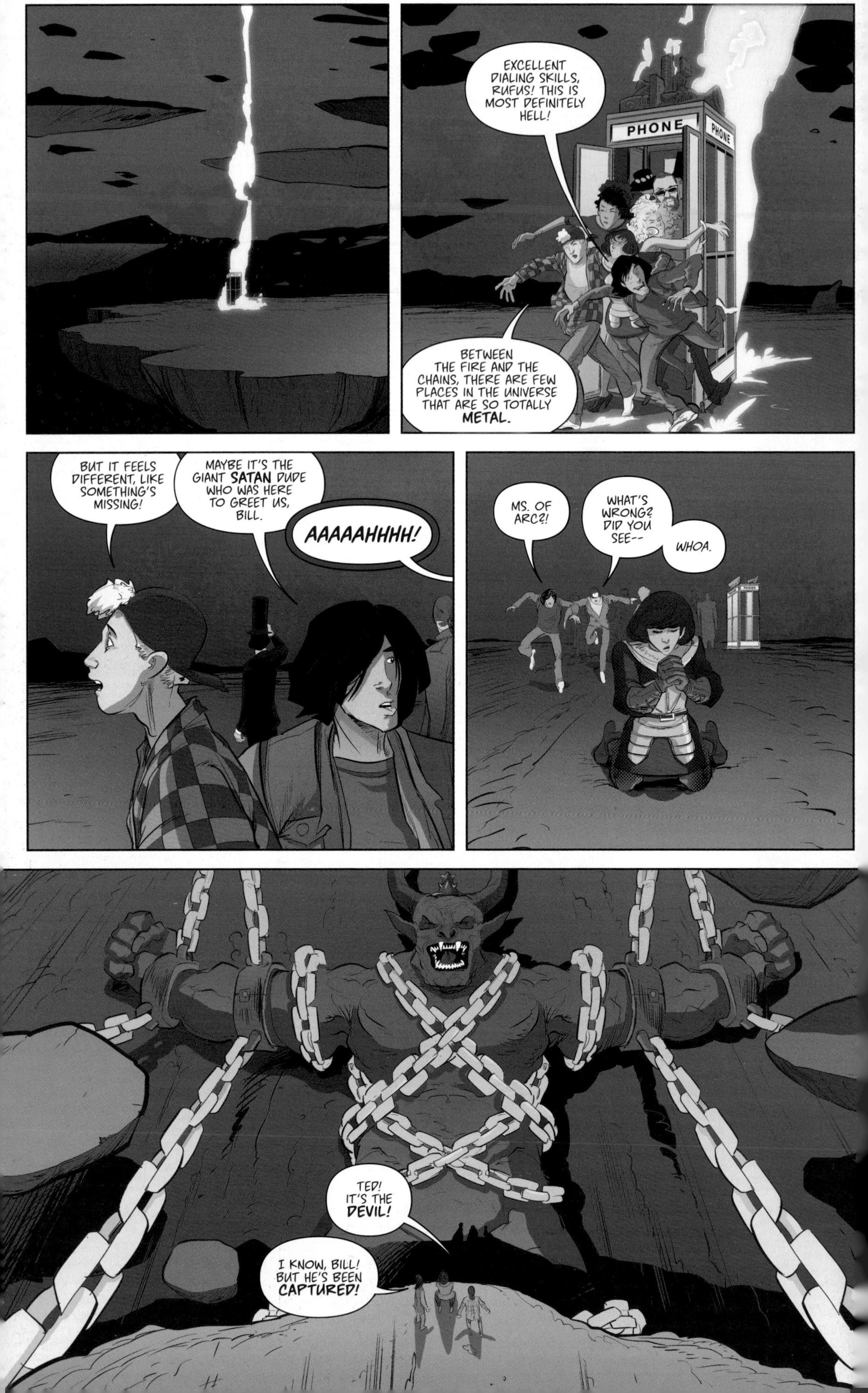

EXCELLENT DIALING SKILLS, RUFUS! THIS IS MOST DEFINITELY HELL!
PHONE
PHONE
BETWEEN THE FIRE AND THE CHAINS, THERE ARE FEW PLACES IN THE UNIVERSE THAT ARE SO TOTALLY **METAL.**
BUT IT FEELS DIFFERENT, LIKE SOMETHING'S MISSING!
MAYBE IT'S THE GIANT **SATAN** DUDE WHO WAS HERE TO GREET US, BILL.
AAAAAHHHH!
MS. OF ARC?!
WHAT'S WRONG? DID YOU SEE--
WHOA.
TED! IT'S THE **DEVIL!**
I KNOW, BILL! BUT HE'S BEEN **CAPTURED!**

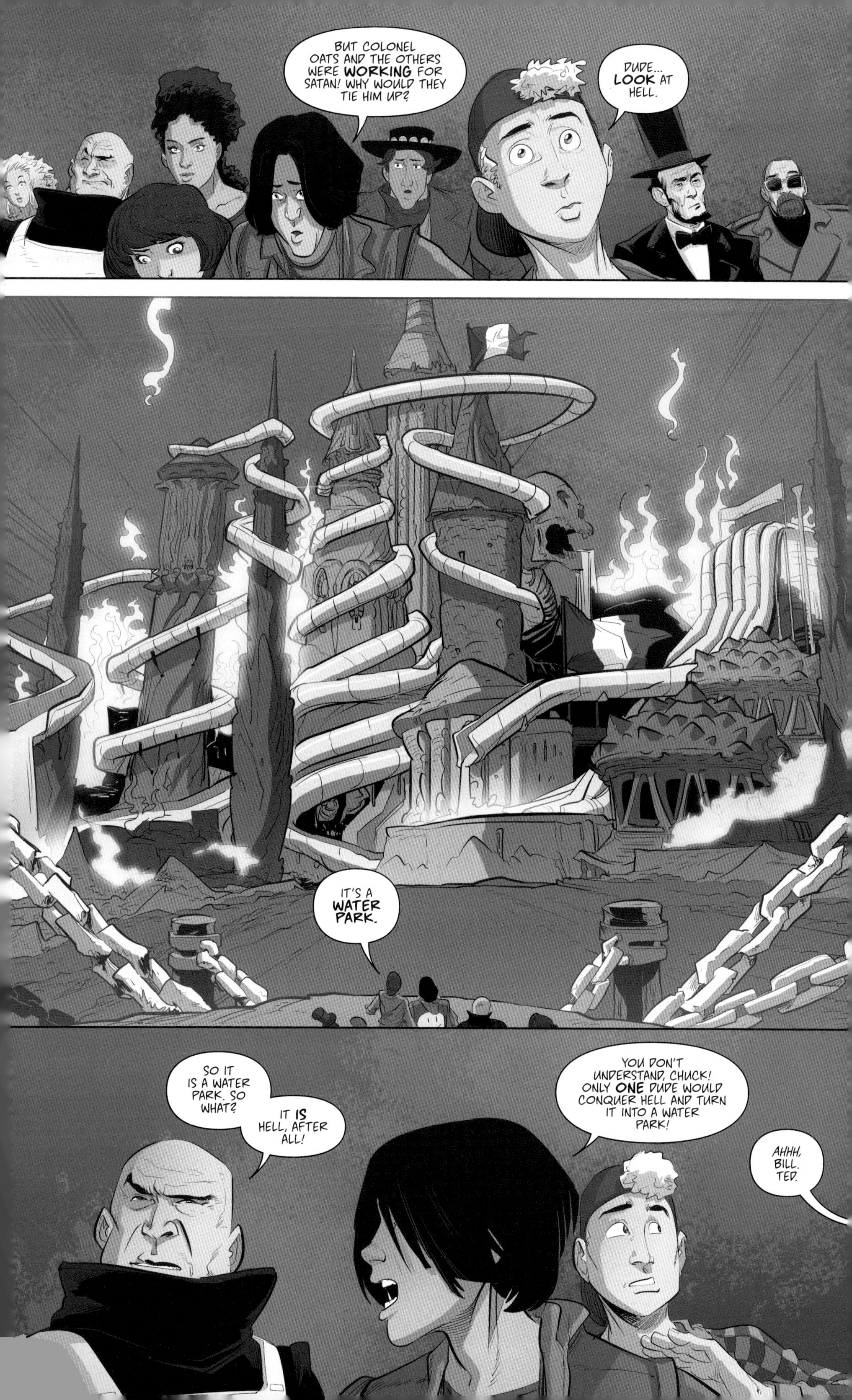
BUT COLONEL OATS AND THE OTHERS WERE WORKING FOR SATAN! WHY WOULD THEY TIE HIM UP?
DUDE... LOOK AT HELL.
IT'S A WATER PARK.
SO IT IS A WATER PARK. SO WHAT?
IT IS HELL, AFTER ALL!
YOU DON'T UNDERSTAND, CHUCK! ONLY ONE DUDE WOULD CONQUER HELL AND TURN IT INTO A WATER PARK!
AHHH, BILL. TED.

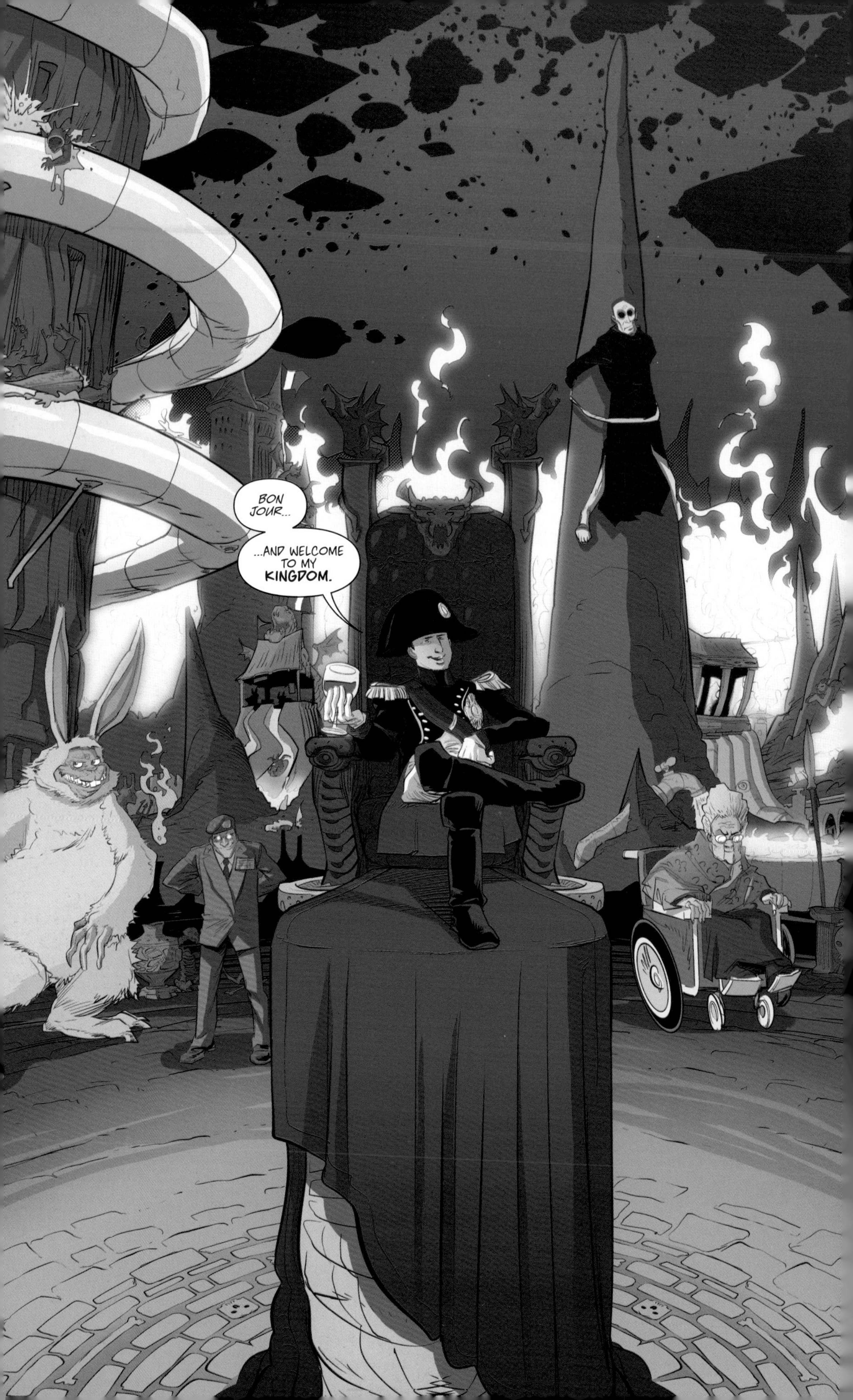
BON JOUR...
...AND WELCOME TO MY KINGDOM.

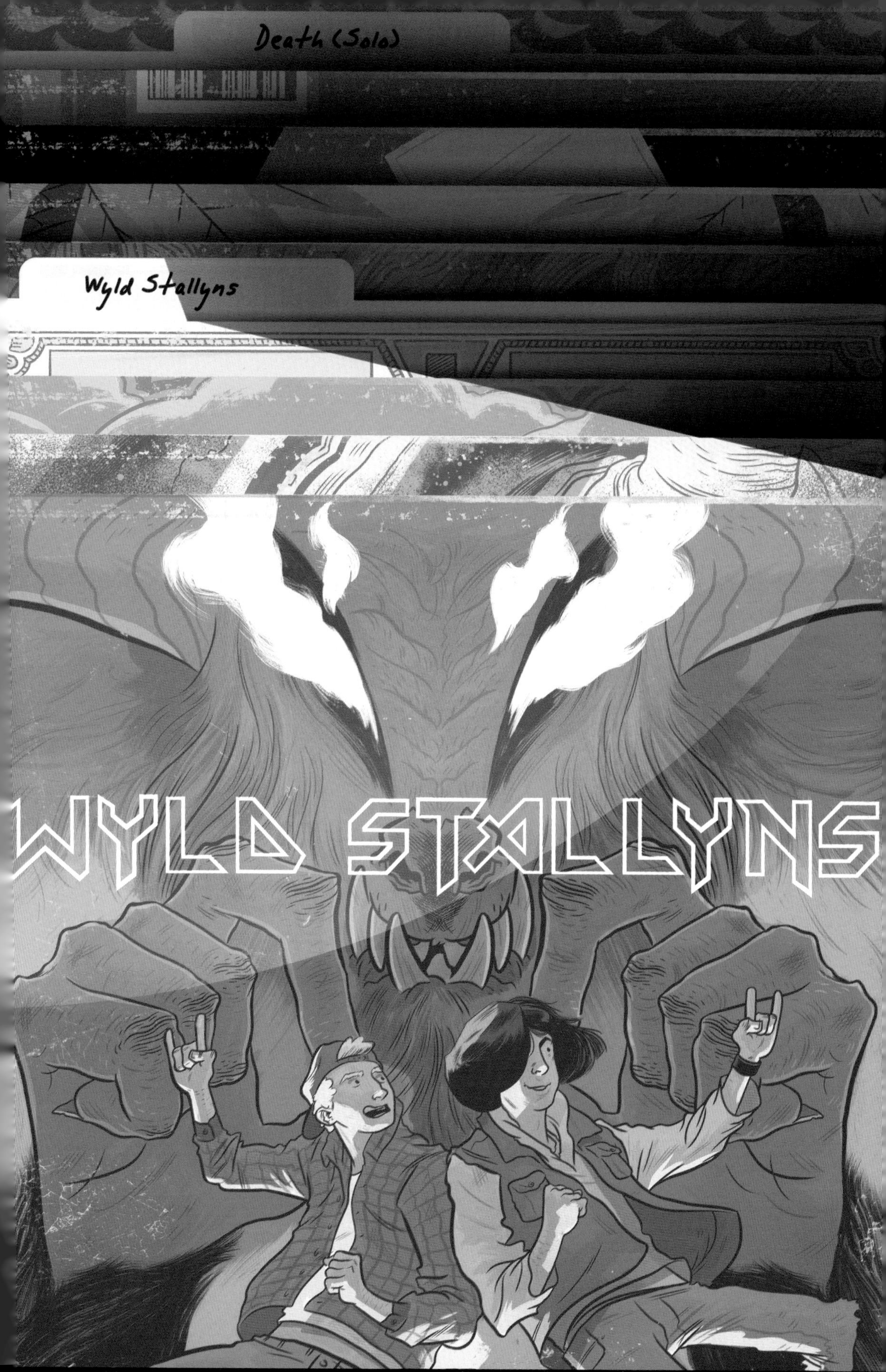
Death (Solo)
Wyld Stallyns
WYLD STALLYNS

LOGAN FAERBER ⚡ ISSUE ONE SUBSCRIPTION ALBUM COVER

CHAPTER TWO
MOST EPICALLY GAULED

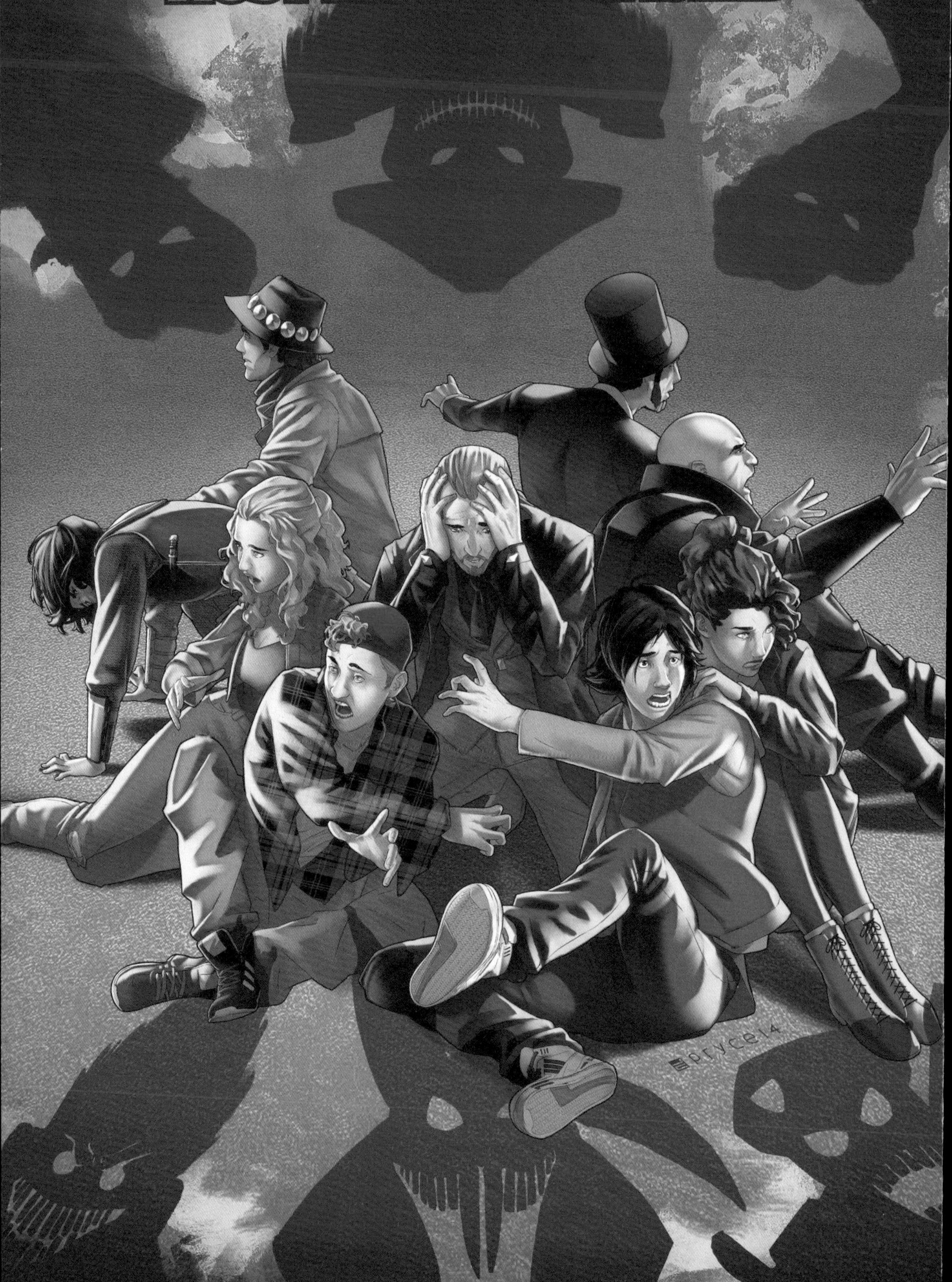

JAMAL CAMPBELL ⚡ ISSUE TWO MAIN COVER

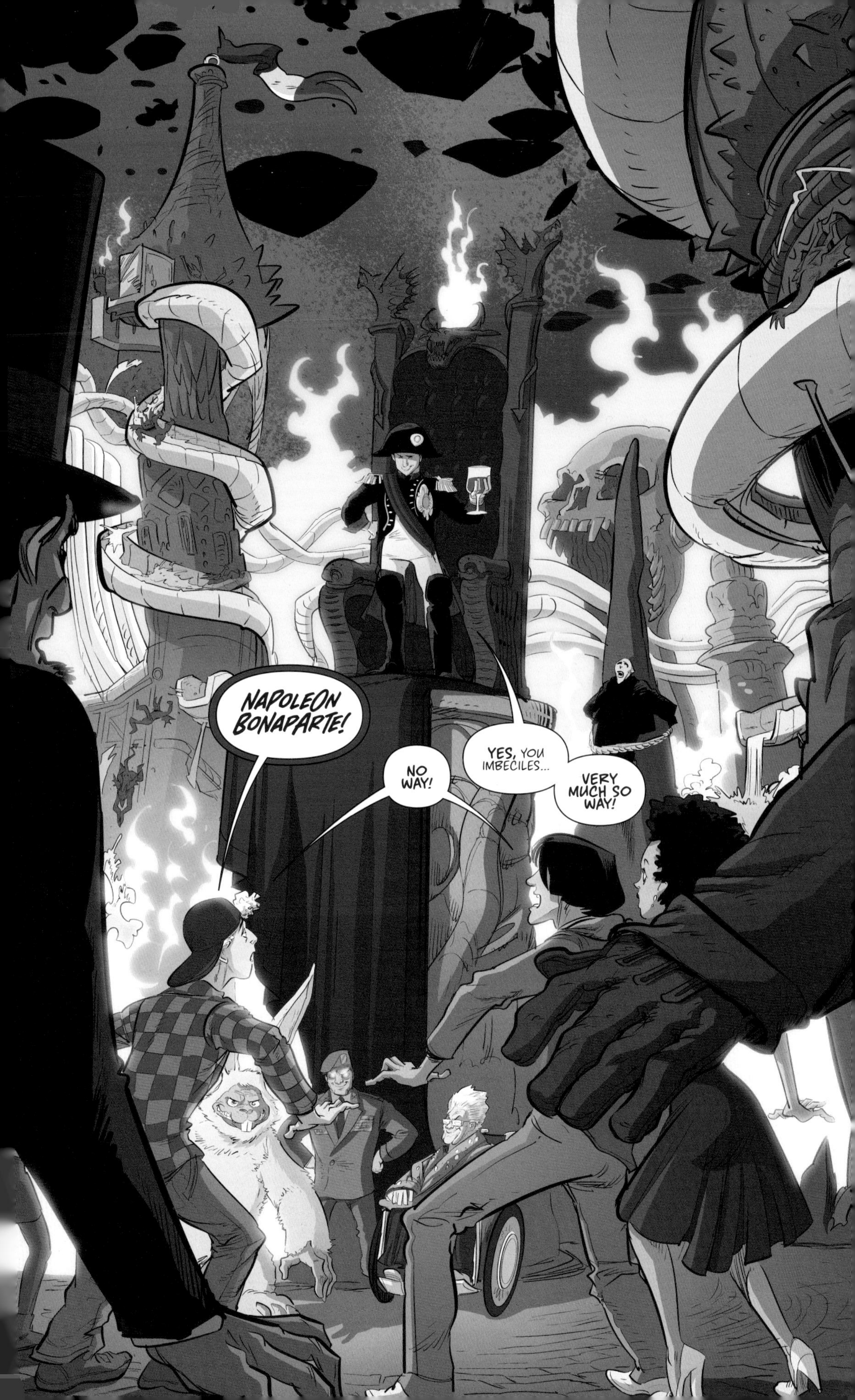
NAPOLEON BONAPARTE!
NO WAY!
YES, YOU IMBECILES...
VERY MUCH SO WAY!

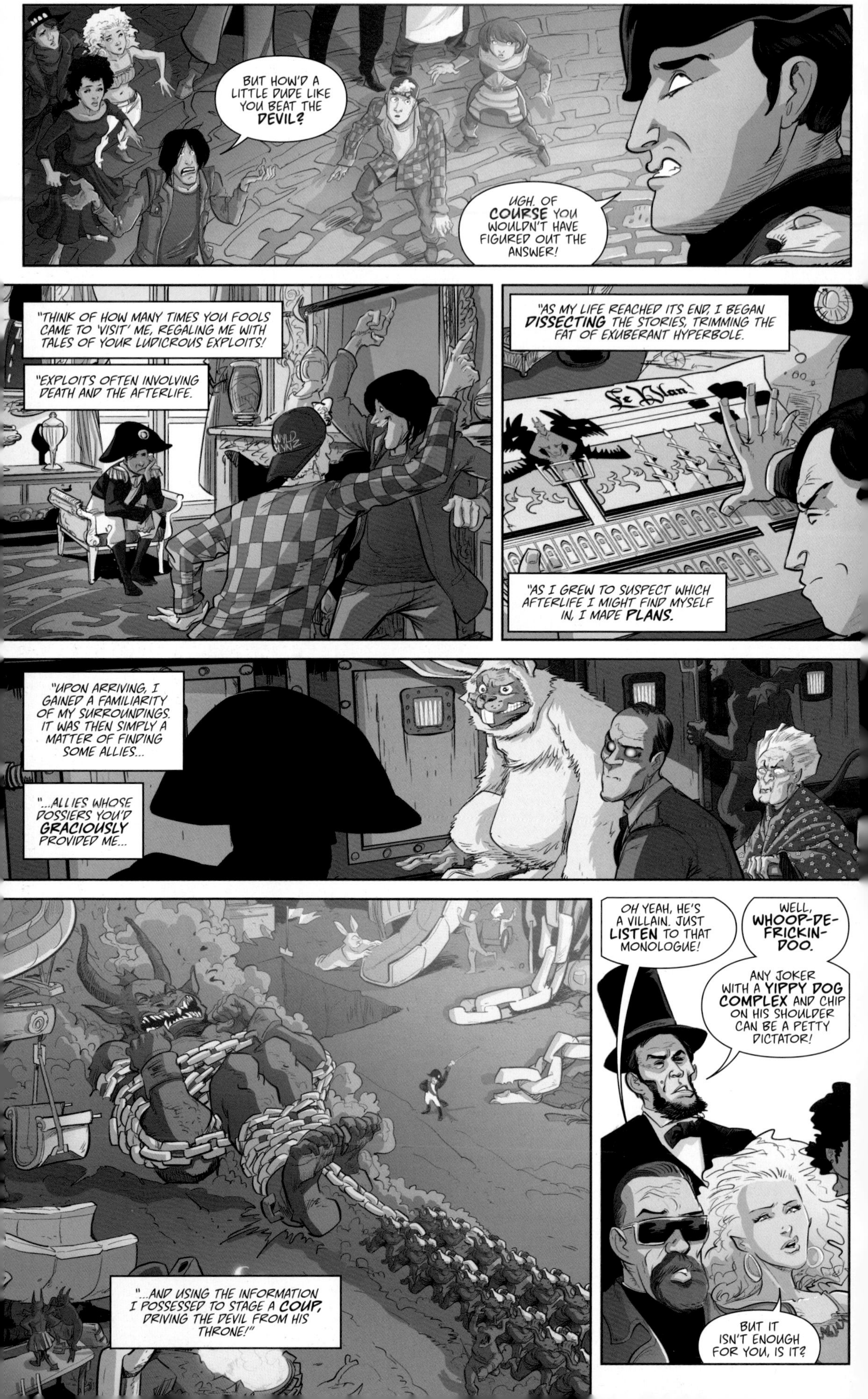

BUT HOW'D A LITTLE DUDE LIKE YOU BEAT THE **DEVIL?**
UGH. OF **COURSE** YOU WOULDN'T HAVE FIGURED OUT THE ANSWER!
"THINK OF HOW MANY TIMES YOU FOOLS CAME TO 'VISIT' ME, REGALING ME WITH TALES OF YOUR LUDICROUS EXPLOITS!
"EXPLOITS OFTEN INVOLVING DEATH AND THE AFTERLIFE.
"AS MY LIFE REACHED ITS END, I BEGAN **DISSECTING** THE STORIES, TRIMMING THE FAT OF EXUBERANT HYPERBOLE.
"AS I GREW TO SUSPECT WHICH AFTERLIFE I MIGHT FIND MYSELF IN, I MADE **PLANS.**
"UPON ARRIVING, I GAINED A FAMILIARITY OF MY SURROUNDINGS. IT WAS THEN SIMPLY A MATTER OF FINDING SOME ALLIES...
"...ALLIES WHOSE DOSSIERS YOU'D **GRACIOUSLY** PROVIDED ME...
"...AND USING THE INFORMATION I POSSESSED TO STAGE A **COUP,** DRIVING THE DEVIL FROM HIS THRONE!"
OH YEAH, HE'S A VILLAIN. JUST **LISTEN** TO THAT MONOLOGUE!
WELL, **WHOOP-DE-FRICKIN-DOO.**
ANY JOKER WITH A **YIPPY DOG COMPLEX** AND CHIP ON HIS SHOULDER CAN BE A PETTY DICTATOR!
BUT IT ISN'T ENOUGH FOR YOU, IS IT?

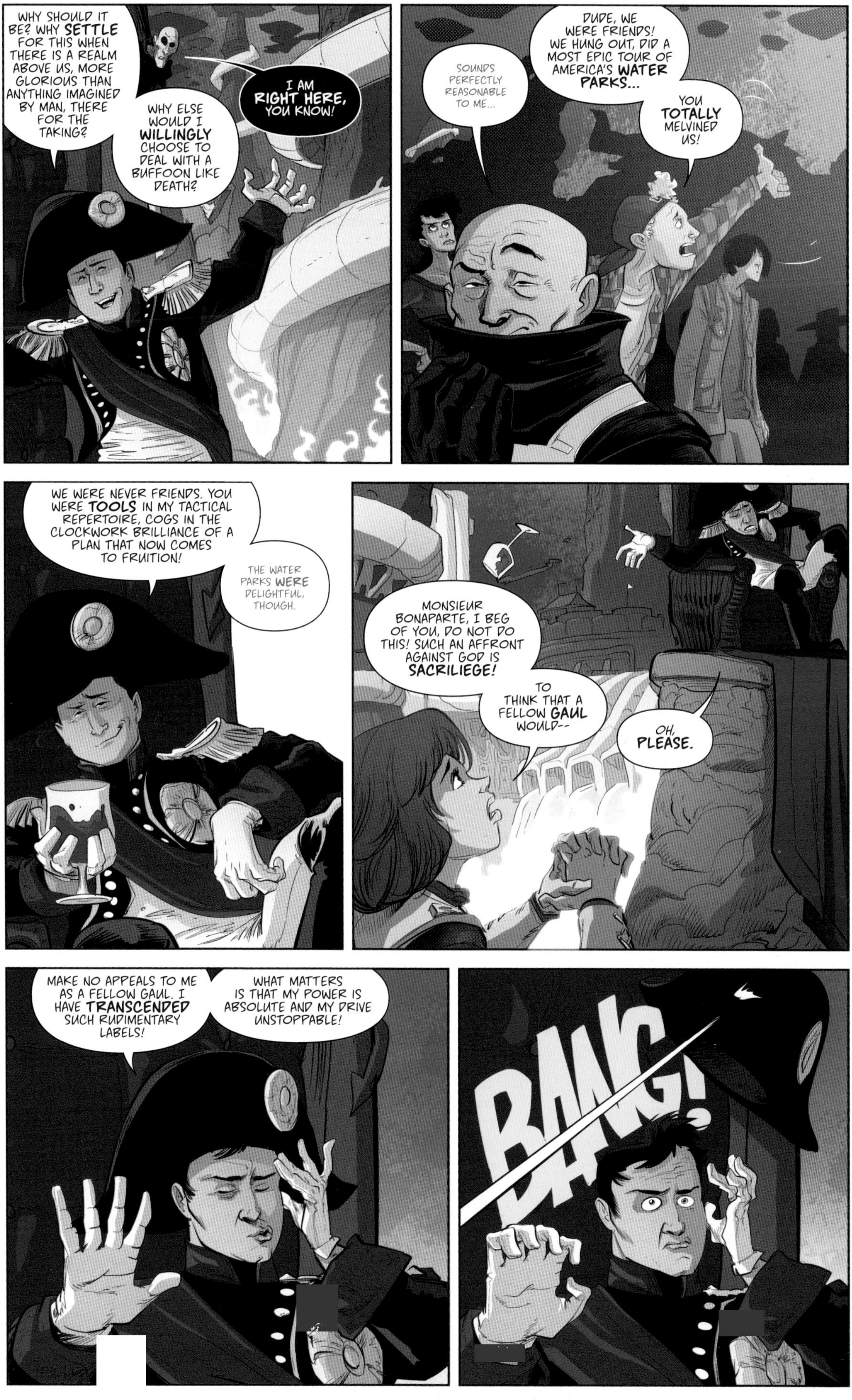
WHY SHOULD IT BE? WHY SETTLE FOR THIS WHEN THERE IS A REALM ABOVE US, MORE GLORIOUS THAN ANYTHING IMAGINED BY MAN, THERE FOR THE TAKING?
WHY ELSE WOULD I WILLINGLY CHOOSE TO DEAL WITH A BUFFOON LIKE DEATH?
I AM RIGHT HERE, YOU KNOW!
SOUNDS PERFECTLY REASONABLE TO ME...
DUDE, WE WERE FRIENDS! WE HUNG OUT, DID A MOST EPIC TOUR OF AMERICA'S WATER PARKS...
YOU TOTALLY MELVINED US!
WE WERE NEVER FRIENDS. YOU WERE TOOLS IN MY TACTICAL REPERTOIRE, COGS IN THE CLOCKWORK BRILLIANCE OF A PLAN THAT NOW COMES TO FRUITION!
THE WATER PARKS WERE DELIGHTFUL, THOUGH.
MONSIEUR BONAPARTE, I BEG OF YOU, DO NOT DO THIS! SUCH AN AFFRONT AGAINST GOD IS SACRILIEGE!
TO THINK THAT A FELLOW GAUL WOULD--
OH, PLEASE.
MAKE NO APPEALS TO ME AS A FELLOW GAUL. I HAVE TRANSCENDED SUCH RUDIMENTARY LABELS!
WHAT MATTERS IS THAT MY POWER IS ABSOLUTE AND MY DRIVE UNSTOPPABLE!
BANG!

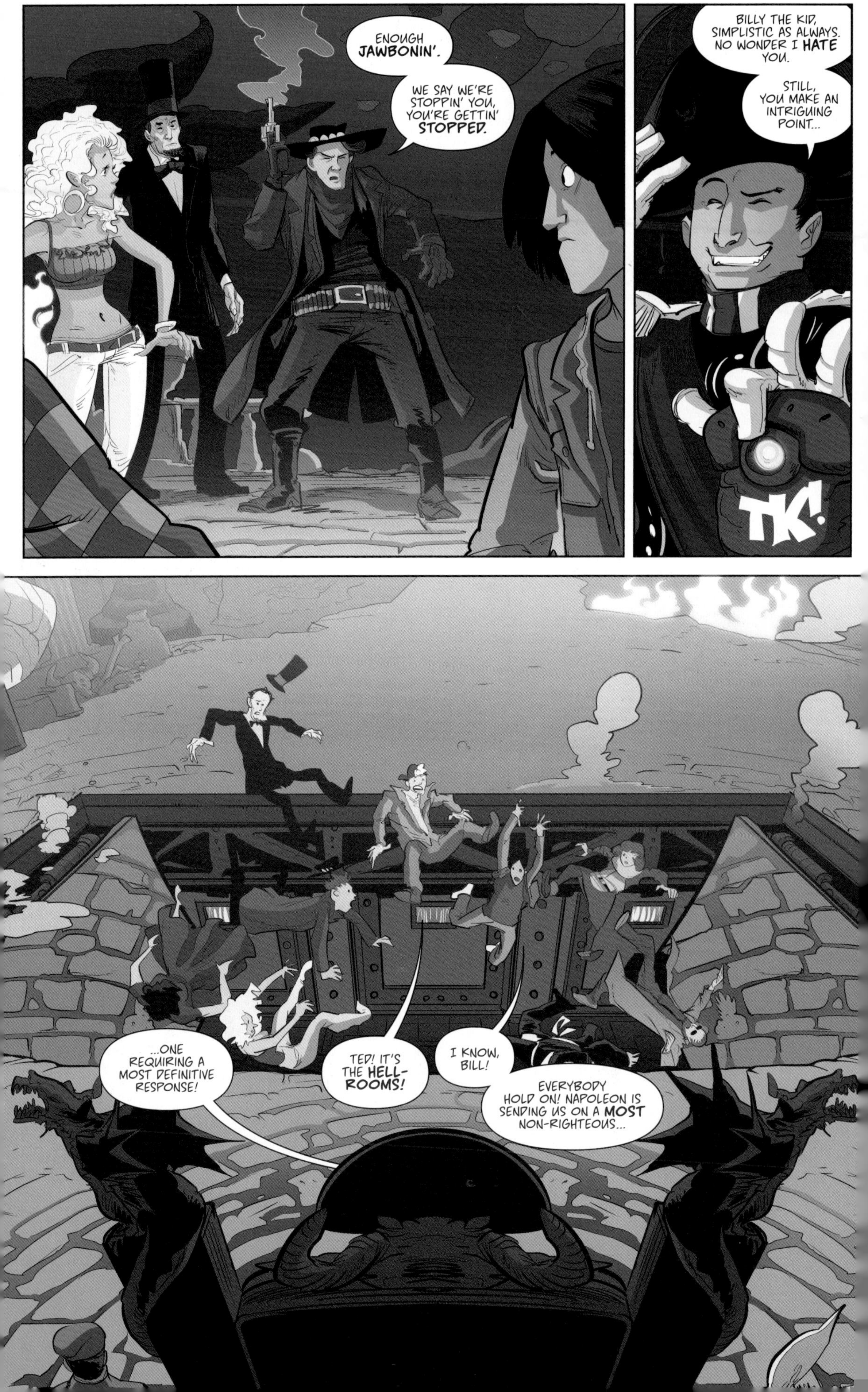
ENOUGH JAWBONIN'.
WE SAY WE'RE STOPPIN' YOU, YOU'RE GETTIN' STOPPED.
BILLY THE KID, SIMPLISTIC AS ALWAYS. NO WONDER I HATE YOU.
STILL, YOU MAKE AN INTRIGUING POINT...
TK!
...ONE REQUIRING A MOST DEFINITIVE RESPONSE!
TED! IT'S THE HELL-ROOMS!
I KNOW, BILL!
EVERYBODY HOLD ON! NAPOLEON IS SENDING US ON A MOST NON-RIGHTEOUS...

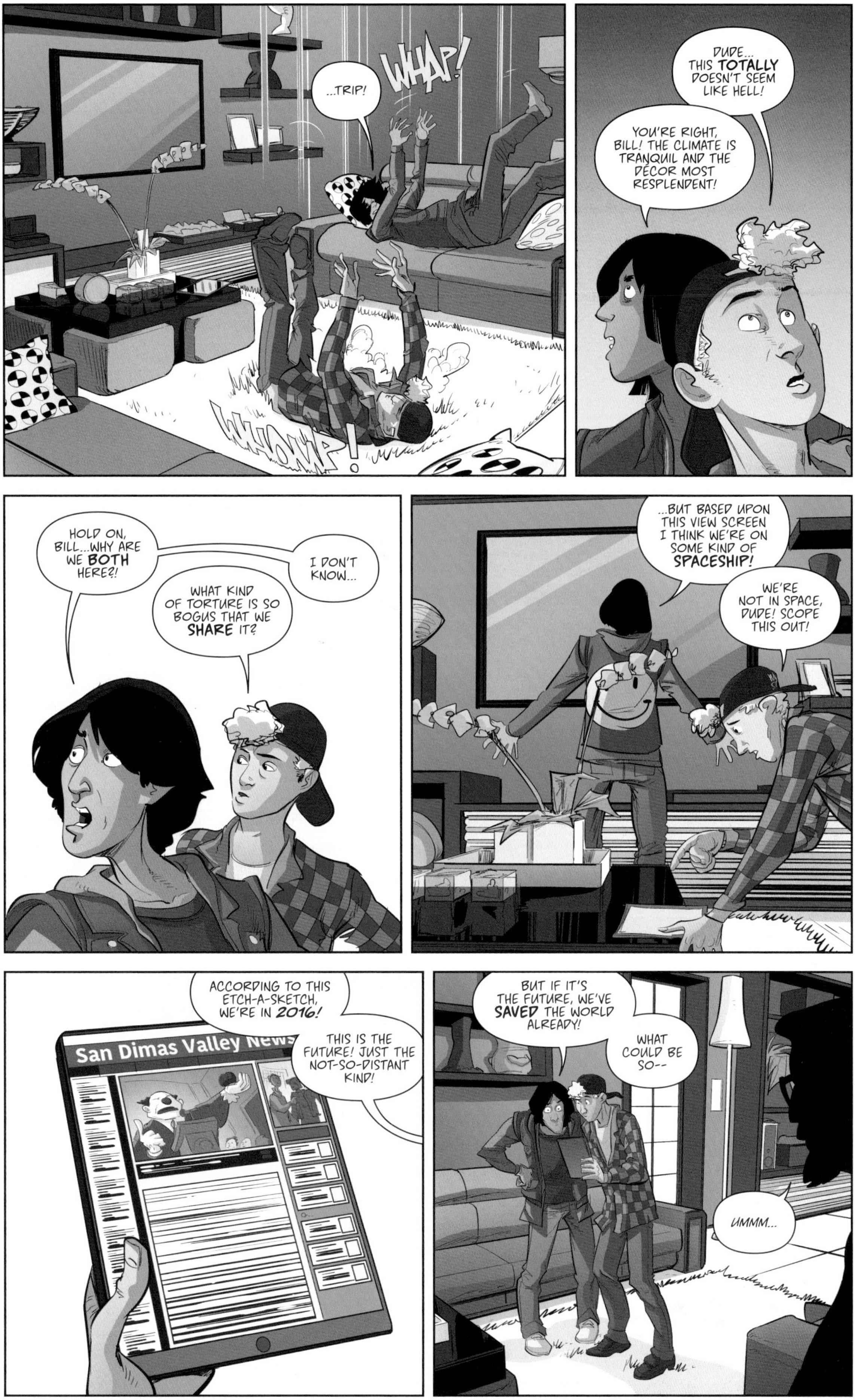
...TRIP!
WHAP!
WHOMP!
DUDE... THIS TOTALLY DOESN'T SEEM LIKE HELL!
YOU'RE RIGHT, BILL! THE CLIMATE IS TRANQUIL AND THE DÉCOR MOST RESPLENDENT!
HOLD ON, BILL...WHY ARE WE BOTH HERE?!
I DON'T KNOW...
WHAT KIND OF TORTURE IS SO BOGUS THAT WE SHARE IT?
...BUT BASED UPON THIS VIEW SCREEN I THINK WE'RE ON SOME KIND OF SPACESHIP!
WE'RE NOT IN SPACE, DUDE! SCOPE THIS OUT!
ACCORDING TO THIS ETCH-A-SKETCH, WE'RE IN 2016!
San Dimas Valley News
THIS IS THE FUTURE! JUST THE NOT-SO-DISTANT KIND!
BUT IF IT'S THE FUTURE, WE'VE SAVED THE WORLD ALREADY!
WHAT COULD BE SO--
UMMM...

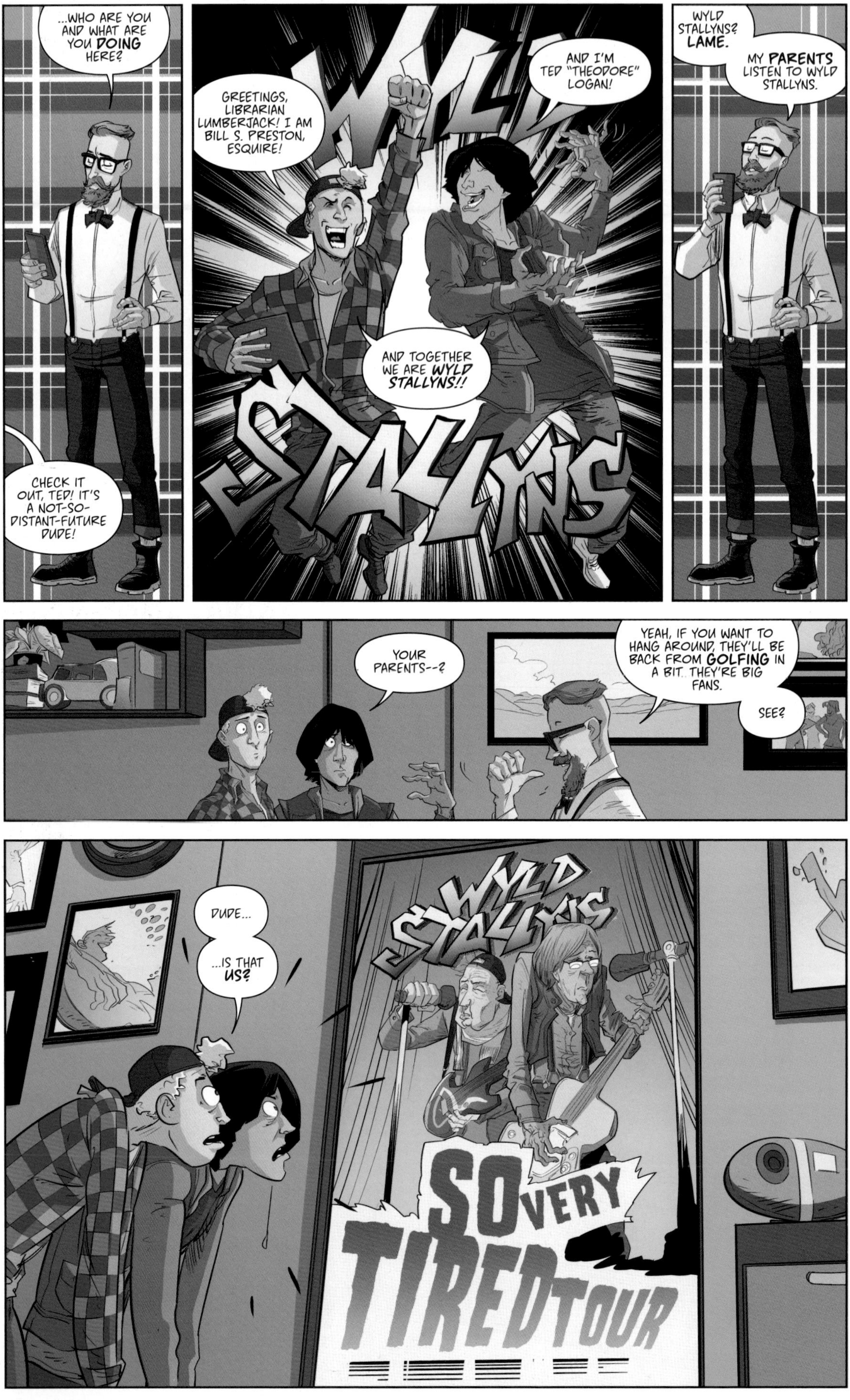
...WHO ARE YOU AND WHAT ARE YOU DOING HERE?
CHECK IT OUT, TED! IT'S A NOT-SO-DISTANT-FUTURE DUDE!
WYLD
GREETINGS, LIBRARIAN LUMBERJACK! I AM BILL S. PRESTON, ESQUIRE!
AND I'M TED "THEODORE" LOGAN!
AND TOGETHER WE ARE WYLD STALLYNS!!
STALLYNS
WYLD STALLYNS? LAME.
MY PARENTS LISTEN TO WYLD STALLYNS.
YOUR PARENTS--?
YEAH, IF YOU WANT TO HANG AROUND, THEY'LL BE BACK FROM GOLFING IN A BIT. THEY'RE BIG FANS.
SEE?
DUDE...
...IS THAT US?
WYLD STALLYNS
SO VERY TIRED TOUR

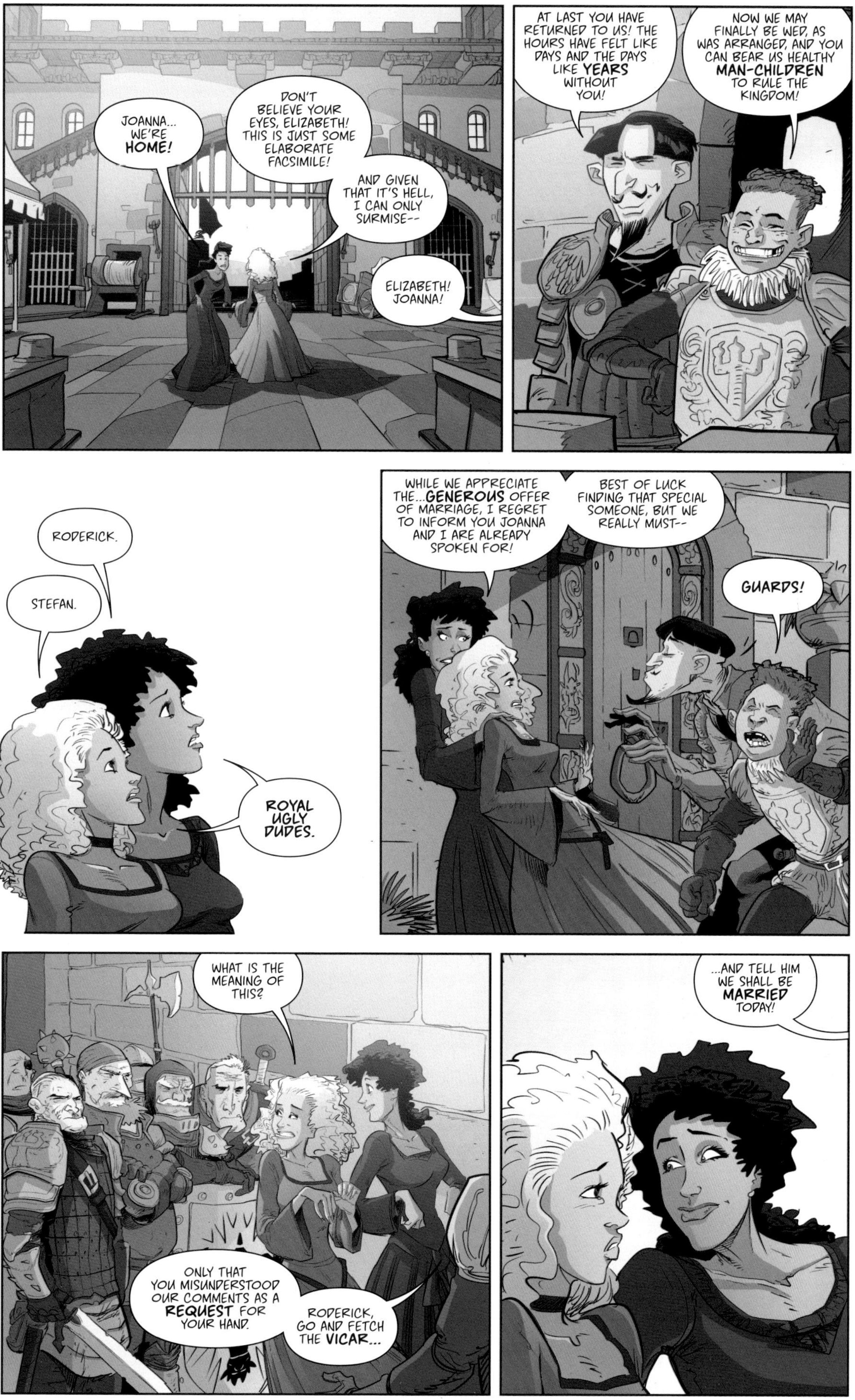
JOANNA... WE'RE **HOME!**
DON'T BELIEVE YOUR EYES, ELIZABETH! THIS IS JUST SOME ELABORATE FACSIMILE!
AND GIVEN THAT IT'S HELL, I CAN ONLY SURMISE--
ELIZABETH! JOANNA!
AT LAST YOU HAVE RETURNED TO US! THE HOURS HAVE FELT LIKE DAYS AND THE DAYS LIKE **YEARS** WITHOUT YOU!
NOW WE MAY FINALLY BE WED, AS WAS ARRANGED, AND YOU CAN BEAR US HEALTHY **MAN-CHILDREN** TO RULE THE KINGDOM!
RODERICK.
STEFAN.
ROYAL UGLY DUDES.
WHILE WE APPRECIATE THE...**GENEROUS** OFFER OF MARRIAGE, I REGRET TO INFORM YOU JOANNA AND I ARE ALREADY SPOKEN FOR!
BEST OF LUCK FINDING THAT SPECIAL SOMEONE, BUT WE REALLY MUST--
GUARDS!
WHAT IS THE MEANING OF THIS?
ONLY THAT YOU MISUNDERSTOOD OUR COMMENTS AS A **REQUEST** FOR YOUR HAND.
RODERICK, GO AND FETCH THE **VICAR...**
...AND TELL HIM WE SHALL BE **MARRIED** TODAY!

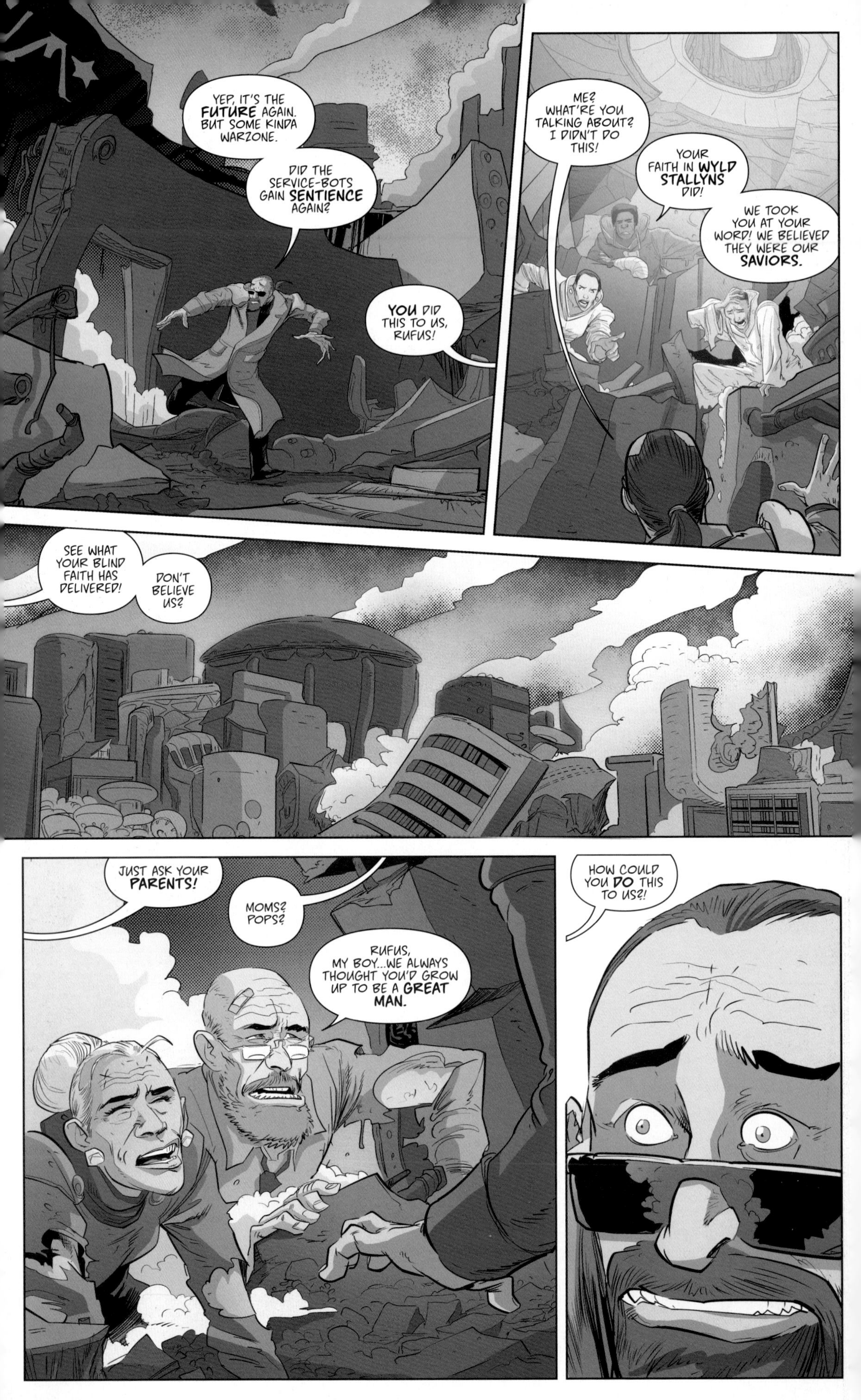

YEP, IT'S THE FUTURE AGAIN. BUT SOME KINDA WARZONE.
DID THE SERVICE-BOTS GAIN SENTIENCE AGAIN?
YOU DID THIS TO US, RUFUS!
ME? WHAT'RE YOU TALKING ABOUT? I DIDN'T DO THIS!
YOUR FAITH IN WYLD STALLYNS DID!
WE TOOK YOU AT YOUR WORD! WE BELIEVED THEY WERE OUR SAVIORS.
SEE WHAT YOUR BLIND FAITH HAS DELIVERED!
DON'T BELIEVE US?
JUST ASK YOUR PARENTS!
MOMS? POPS?
RUFUS, MY BOY...WE ALWAYS THOUGHT YOU'D GROW UP TO BE A GREAT MAN.
HOW COULD YOU DO THIS TO US?!

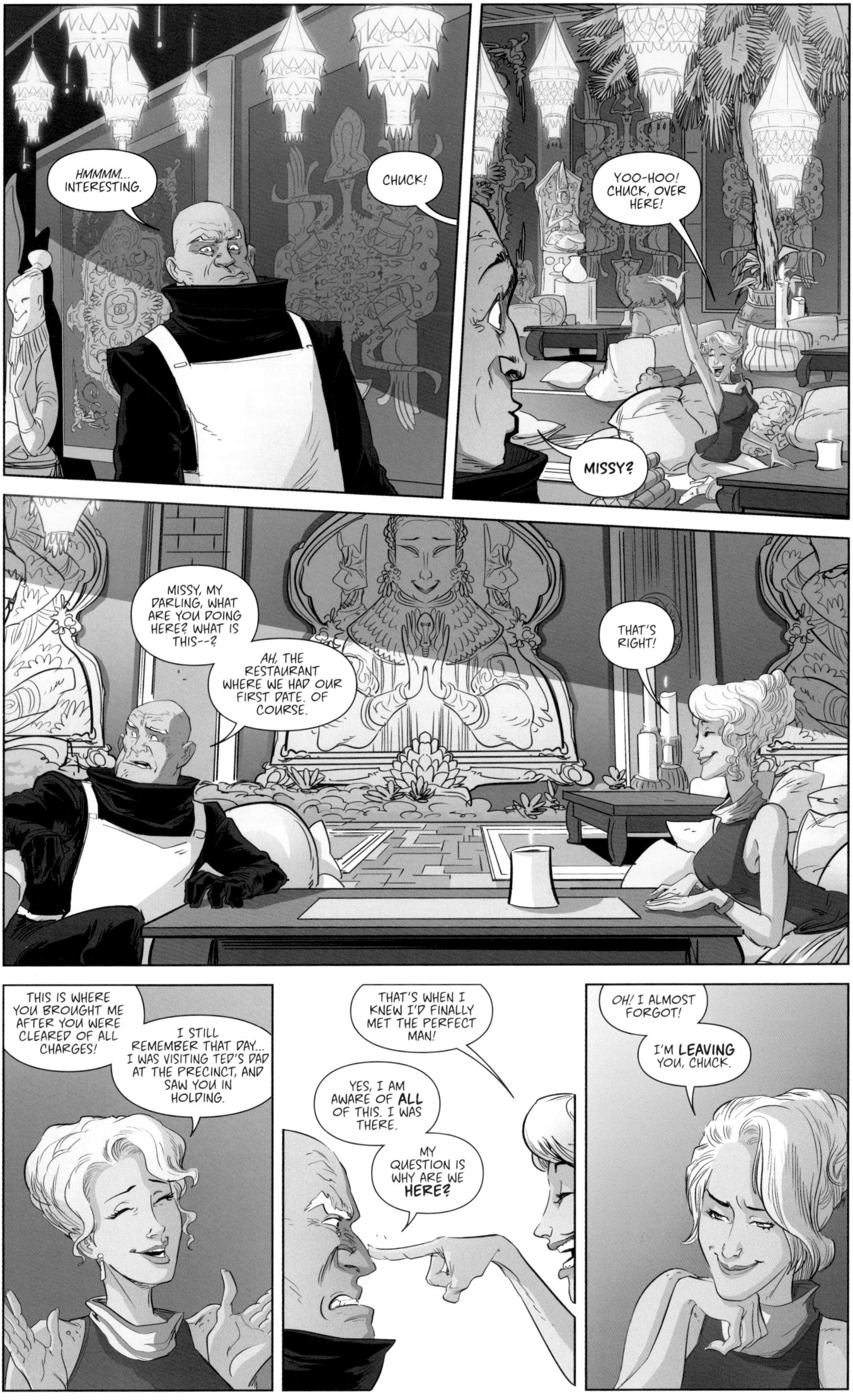
HMMMM... INTERESTING.
CHUCK!
YOO-HOO! CHUCK, OVER HERE!
MISSY?
MISSY, MY DARLING, WHAT ARE YOU DOING HERE? WHAT IS THIS--?
AH, THE RESTAURANT WHERE WE HAD OUR FIRST DATE. OF COURSE.
THAT'S RIGHT!
THIS IS WHERE YOU BROUGHT ME AFTER YOU WERE CLEARED OF ALL CHARGES!
I STILL REMEMBER THAT DAY... I WAS VISITING TED'S DAD AT THE PRECINCT, AND SAW YOU IN HOLDING.
THAT'S WHEN I KNEW I'D FINALLY MET THE PERFECT MAN!
YES, I AM AWARE OF ALL OF THIS. I WAS THERE.
MY QUESTION IS WHY ARE WE HERE?
OH! I ALMOST FORGOT!
I'M LEAVING YOU, CHUCK.

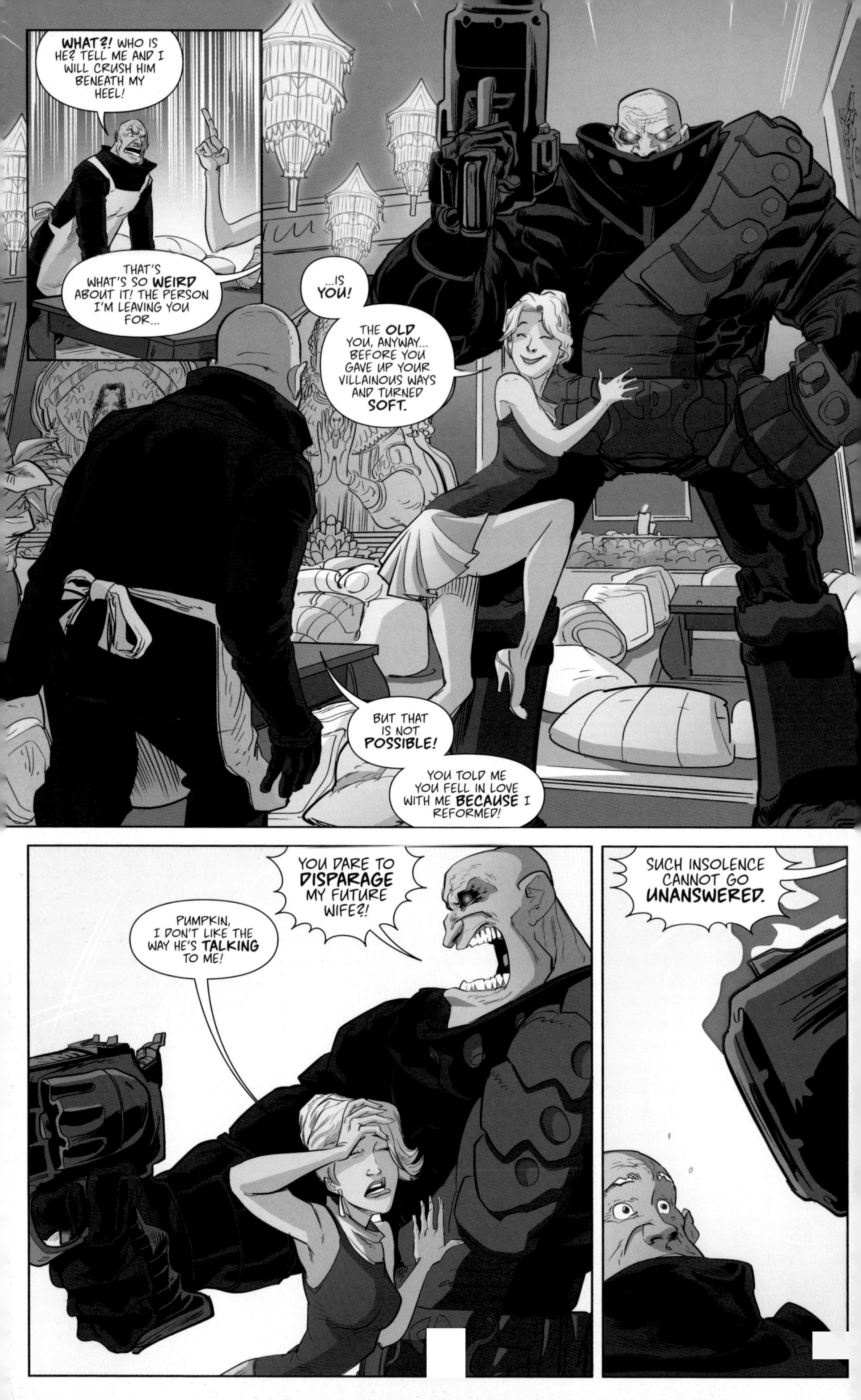

WHAT?! WHO IS HE? TELL ME AND I WILL CRUSH HIM BENEATH MY HEEL!
THAT'S WHAT'S SO WEIRD ABOUT IT! THE PERSON I'M LEAVING YOU FOR...
...IS YOU!
THE OLD YOU, ANYWAY... BEFORE YOU GAVE UP YOUR VILLAINOUS WAYS AND TURNED SOFT.
BUT THAT IS NOT POSSIBLE!
YOU TOLD ME YOU FELL IN LOVE WITH ME BECAUSE I REFORMED!
YOU DARE TO DISPARAGE MY FUTURE WIFE?!
PUMPKIN, I DON'T LIKE THE WAY HE'S TALKING TO ME!
SUCH INSOLENCE CANNOT GO UNANSWERED.

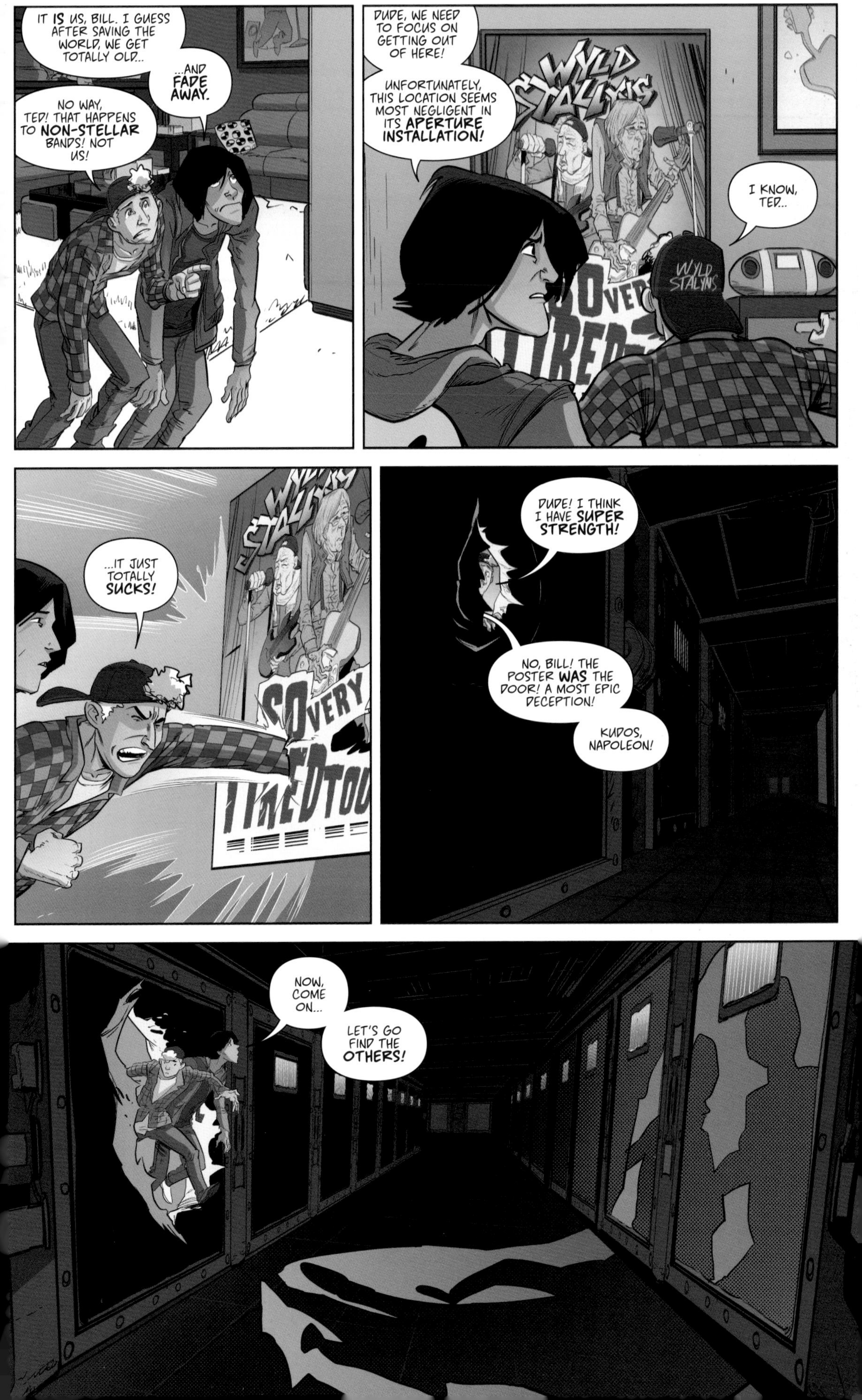
IT IS US, BILL. I GUESS AFTER SAVING THE WORLD, WE GET TOTALLY OLD...
...AND FADE AWAY.
NO WAY, TED! THAT HAPPENS TO NON-STELLAR BANDS! NOT US!
DUDE, WE NEED TO FOCUS ON GETTING OUT OF HERE!
UNFORTUNATELY, THIS LOCATION SEEMS MOST NEGLIGENT IN ITS APERTURE INSTALLATION!
I KNOW, TED...
WYLD STALYNS
...IT JUST TOTALLY SUCKS!
DUDE! I THINK I HAVE SUPER STRENGTH!
NO, BILL! THE POSTER WAS THE DOOR! A MOST EPIC DECEPTION!
KUDOS, NAPOLEON!
NOW, COME ON...
LET'S GO FIND THE OTHERS!

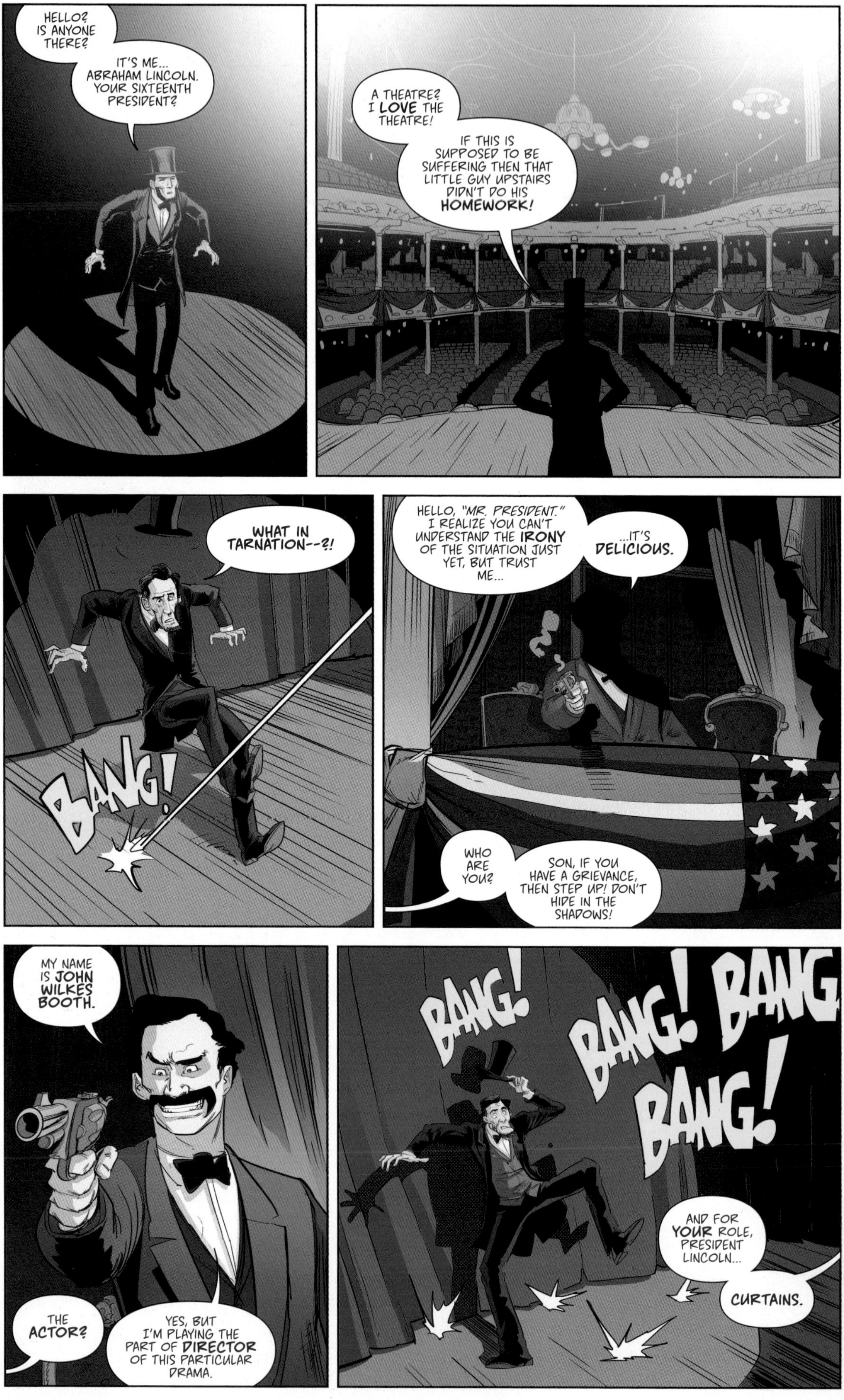
HELLO? IS ANYONE THERE?
IT'S ME... ABRAHAM LINCOLN. YOUR SIXTEENTH PRESIDENT?
A THEATRE? I LOVE THE THEATRE!
IF THIS IS SUPPOSED TO BE SUFFERING THEN THAT LITTLE GUY UPSTAIRS DIDN'T DO HIS HOMEWORK!
WHAT IN TARNATION--?!
BANG!
HELLO, "MR. PRESIDENT." I REALIZE YOU CAN'T UNDERSTAND THE IRONY OF THE SITUATION JUST YET, BUT TRUST ME...
...IT'S DELICIOUS.
WHO ARE YOU?
SON, IF YOU HAVE A GRIEVANCE, THEN STEP UP! DON'T HIDE IN THE SHADOWS!
MY NAME IS JOHN WILKES BOOTH.
THE ACTOR?
YES, BUT I'M PLAYING THE PART OF DIRECTOR OF THIS PARTICULAR DRAMA.
BANG!
BANG! BANG!
BANG!
BANG!
AND FOR YOUR ROLE, PRESIDENT LINCOLN...
CURTAINS.

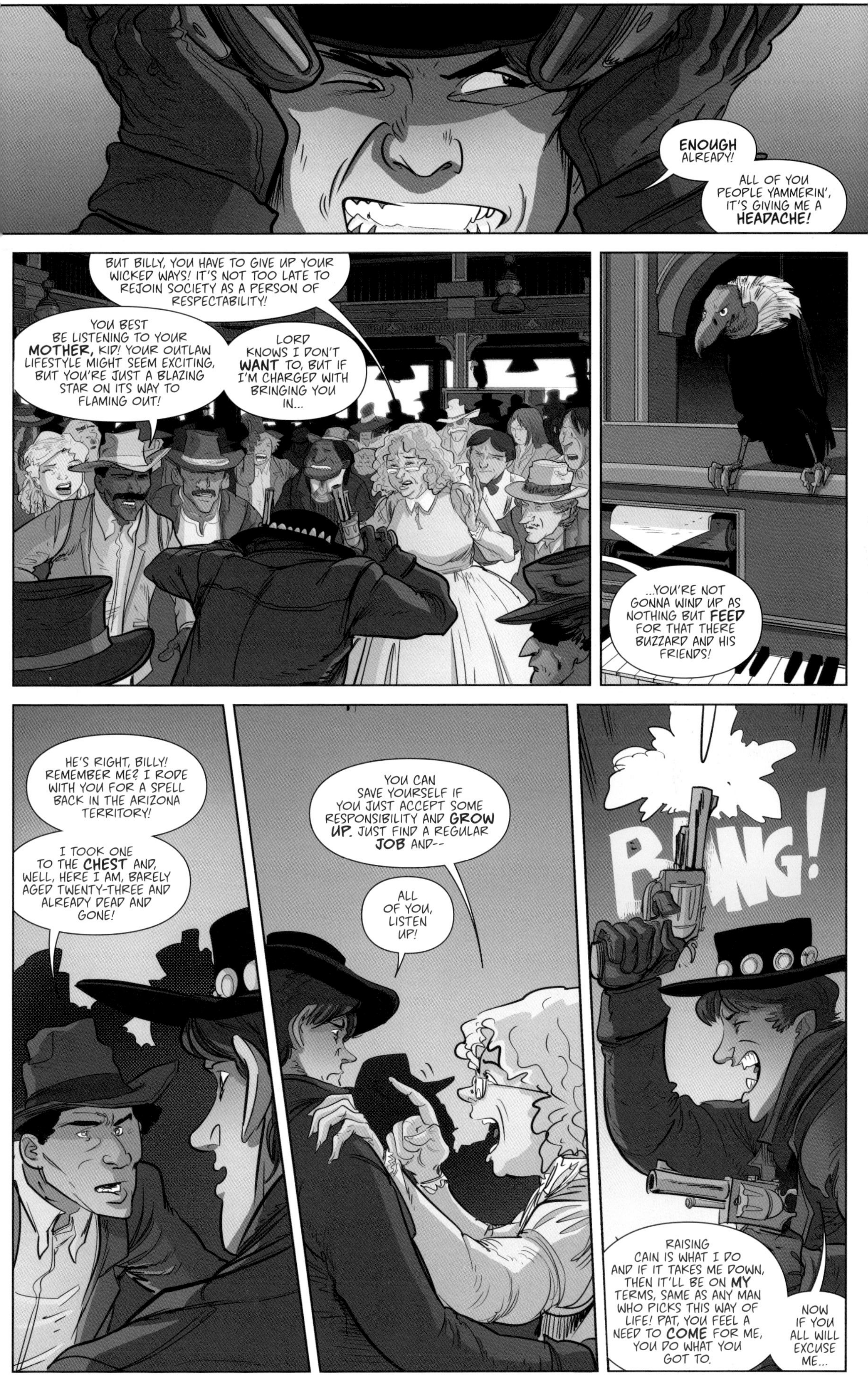

ENOUGH ALREADY!
ALL OF YOU PEOPLE YAMMERIN', IT'S GIVING ME A HEADACHE!
BUT BILLY, YOU HAVE TO GIVE UP YOUR WICKED WAYS! IT'S NOT TOO LATE TO REJOIN SOCIETY AS A PERSON OF RESPECTABILITY!
YOU BEST BE LISTENING TO YOUR MOTHER, KID! YOUR OUTLAW LIFESTYLE MIGHT SEEM EXCITING, BUT YOU'RE JUST A BLAZING STAR ON ITS WAY TO FLAMING OUT!
LORD KNOWS I DON'T WANT TO, BUT IF I'M CHARGED WITH BRINGING YOU IN...
...YOU'RE NOT GONNA WIND UP AS NOTHING BUT FEED FOR THAT THERE BUZZARD AND HIS FRIENDS!
HE'S RIGHT, BILLY! REMEMBER ME? I RODE WITH YOU FOR A SPELL BACK IN THE ARIZONA TERRITORY!
I TOOK ONE TO THE CHEST AND, WELL, HERE I AM, BARELY AGED TWENTY-THREE AND ALREADY DEAD AND GONE!
YOU CAN SAVE YOURSELF IF YOU JUST ACCEPT SOME RESPONSIBILITY AND GROW UP. JUST FIND A REGULAR JOB AND--
ALL OF YOU, LISTEN UP!
BANG!
RAISING CAIN IS WHAT I DO AND IF IT TAKES ME DOWN, THEN IT'LL BE ON MY TERMS, SAME AS ANY MAN WHO PICKS THIS WAY OF LIFE! PAT, YOU FEEL A NEED TO COME FOR ME, YOU DO WHAT YOU GOT TO.
NOW IF YOU ALL WILL EXCUSE ME...

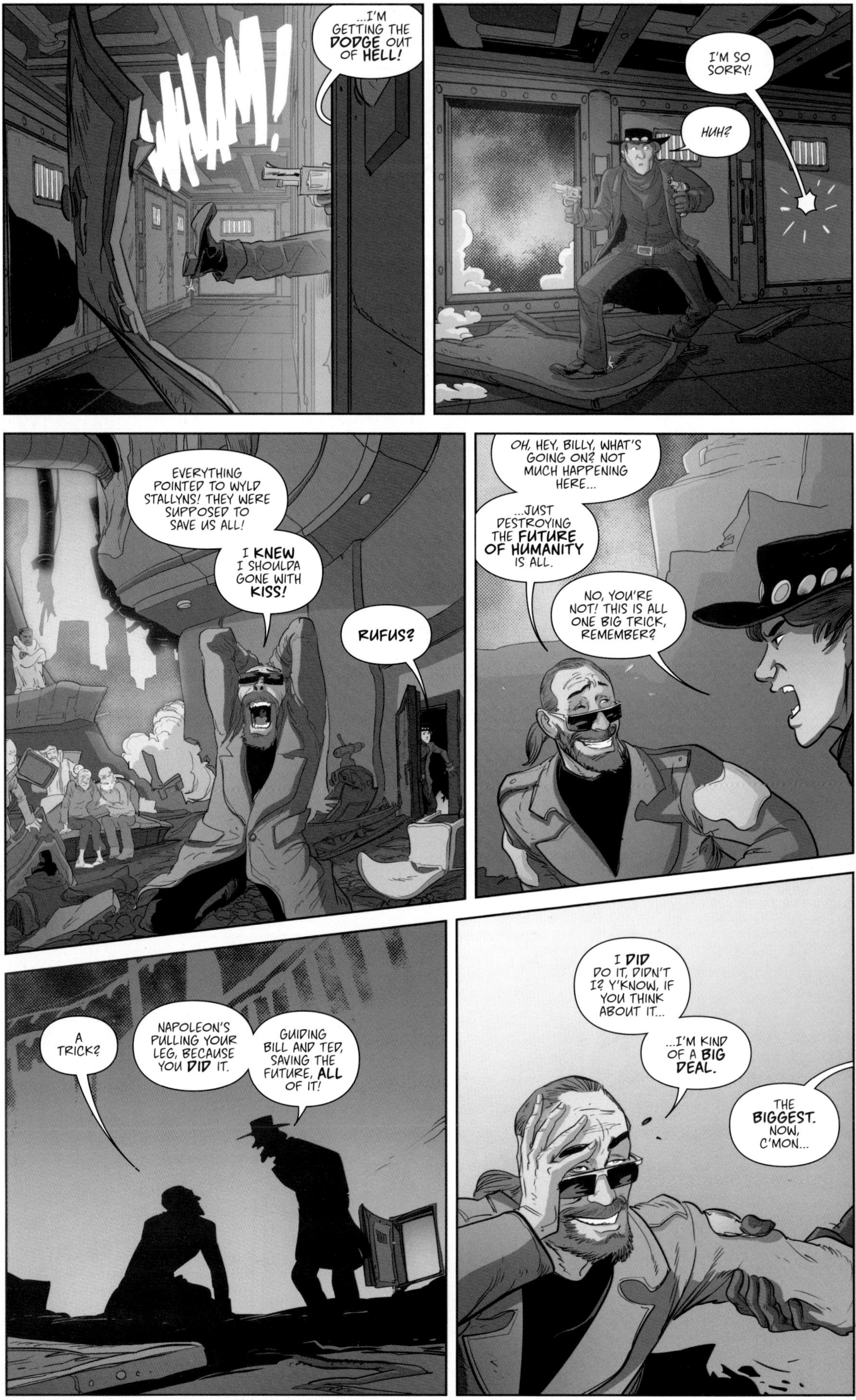
WHAM!
...I'M GETTING THE DODGE OUT OF HELL!
I'M SO SORRY!
HUH?
EVERYTHING POINTED TO WYLD STALLYNS! THEY WERE SUPPOSED TO SAVE US ALL!
I KNEW I SHOULDA GONE WITH KISS!
RUFUS?
OH, HEY, BILLY, WHAT'S GOING ON? NOT MUCH HAPPENING HERE...
...JUST DESTROYING THE FUTURE OF HUMANITY IS ALL.
NO, YOU'RE NOT! THIS IS ALL ONE BIG TRICK, REMEMBER?
A TRICK?
NAPOLEON'S PULLING YOUR LEG, BECAUSE YOU DID IT.
GUIDING BILL AND TED, SAVING THE FUTURE, ALL OF IT!
I DID DO IT, DIDN'T I? Y'KNOW, IF YOU THINK ABOUT IT...
...I'M KIND OF A BIG DEAL.
THE BIGGEST. NOW, C'MON...

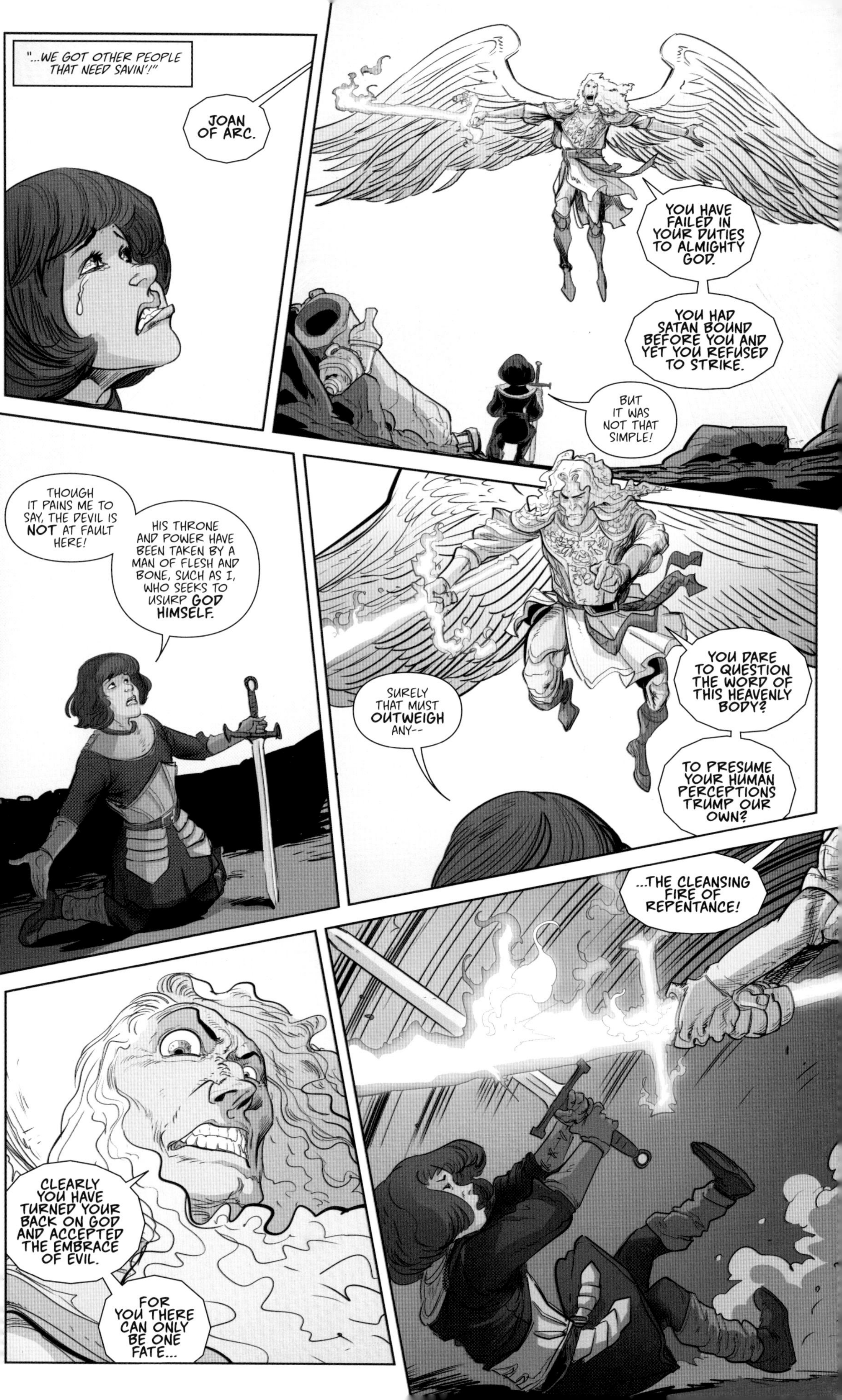
"...WE GOT OTHER PEOPLE THAT NEED SAVIN'!"
JOAN OF ARC.
YOU HAVE FAILED IN YOUR DUTIES TO ALMIGHTY GOD.
YOU HAD SATAN BOUND BEFORE YOU AND YET YOU REFUSED TO STRIKE.
BUT IT WAS NOT THAT SIMPLE!
THOUGH IT PAINS ME TO SAY, THE DEVIL IS NOT AT FAULT HERE!
HIS THRONE AND POWER HAVE BEEN TAKEN BY A MAN OF FLESH AND BONE, SUCH AS I, WHO SEEKS TO USURP GOD HIMSELF.
SURELY THAT MUST OUTWEIGH ANY--
YOU DARE TO QUESTION THE WORD OF THIS HEAVENLY BODY?
TO PRESUME YOUR HUMAN PERCEPTIONS TRUMP OUR OWN?
CLEARLY YOU HAVE TURNED YOUR BACK ON GOD AND ACCEPTED THE EMBRACE OF EVIL.
FOR YOU THERE CAN ONLY BE ONE FATE...
...THE CLEANSING FIRE OF REPENTANCE!

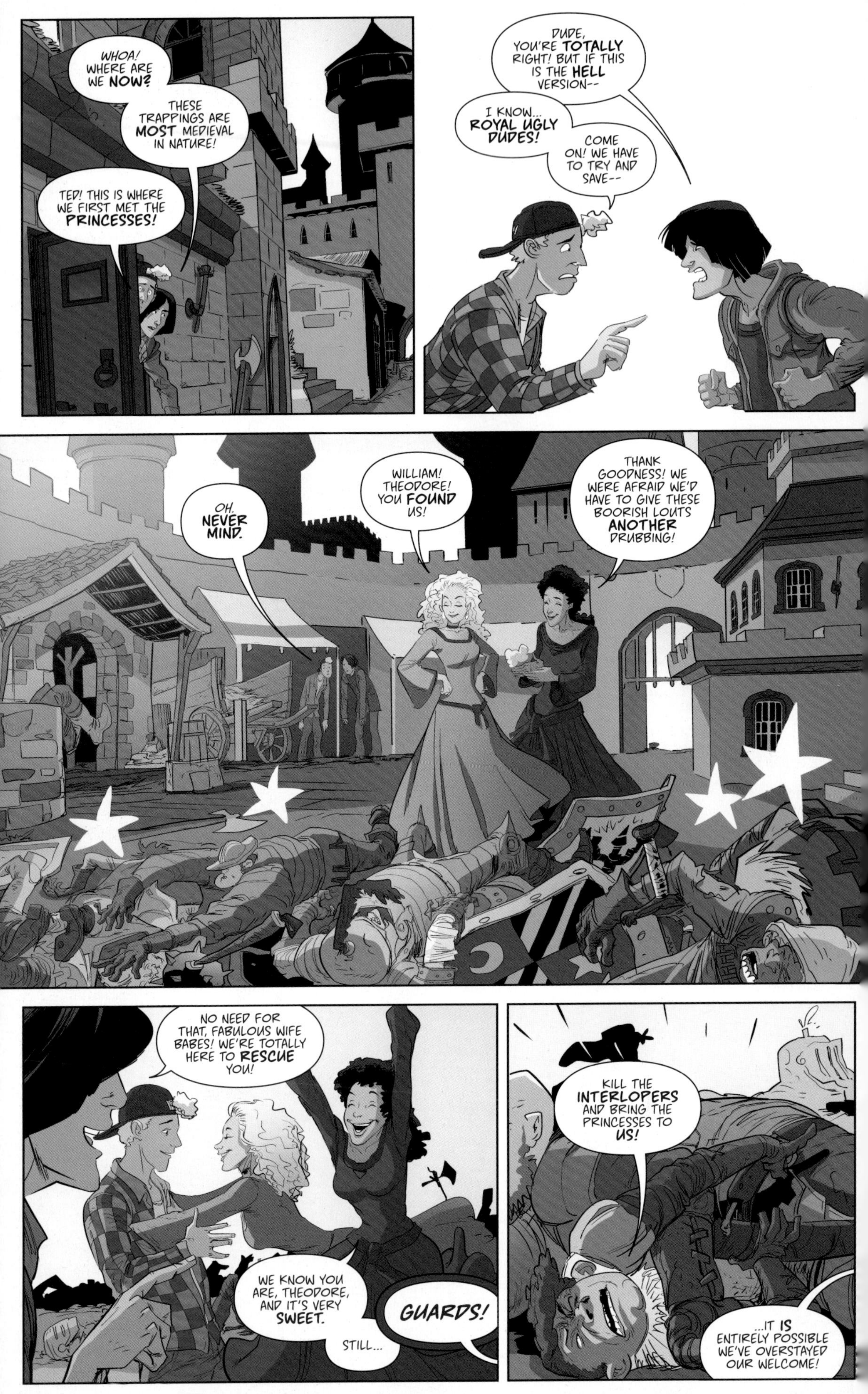
WHOA! WHERE ARE WE **NOW?**
THESE TRAPPINGS ARE **MOST** MEDIEVAL IN NATURE!
TED! THIS IS WHERE WE FIRST MET THE **PRINCESSES!**
DUDE, YOU'RE **TOTALLY** RIGHT! BUT IF THIS IS THE **HELL** VERSION--
I KNOW... **ROYAL UGLY DUDES!**
COME ON! WE HAVE TO TRY AND SAVE--
OH. **NEVER MIND.**
WILLIAM! THEODORE! YOU **FOUND** US!
THANK GOODNESS! WE WERE AFRAID WE'D HAVE TO GIVE THESE BOORISH LOUTS **ANOTHER** DRUBBING!
NO NEED FOR THAT, FABULOUS WIFE BABES! WE'RE TOTALLY HERE TO **RESCUE** YOU!
WE KNOW YOU ARE, THEODORE, AND IT'S VERY **SWEET.**
STILL...
GUARDS!
KILL THE **INTERLOPERS** AND BRING THE PRINCESSES TO **US!**
...IT **IS** ENTIRELY POSSIBLE WE'VE OVERSTAYED OUR WELCOME!

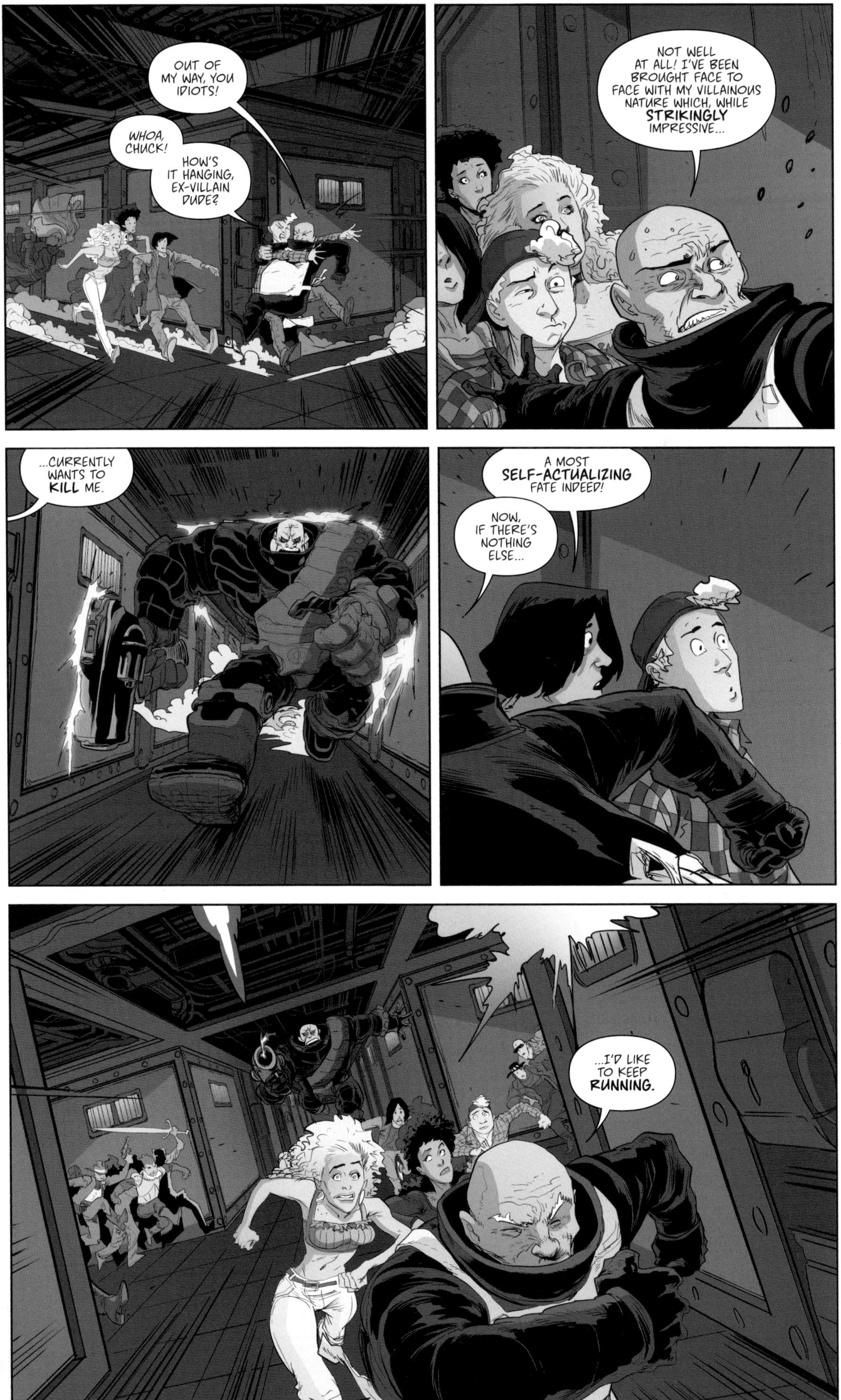
OUT OF MY WAY, YOU IDIOTS!
WHOA, CHUCK!
HOW'S IT HANGING, EX-VILLAIN DUDE?
NOT WELL AT ALL! I'VE BEEN BROUGHT FACE TO FACE WITH MY VILLAINOUS NATURE WHICH, WHILE STRIKINGLY IMPRESSIVE...
...CURRENTLY WANTS TO KILL ME.
A MOST SELF-ACTUALIZING FATE INDEED!
NOW, IF THERE'S NOTHING ELSE...
...I'D LIKE TO KEEP RUNNING.

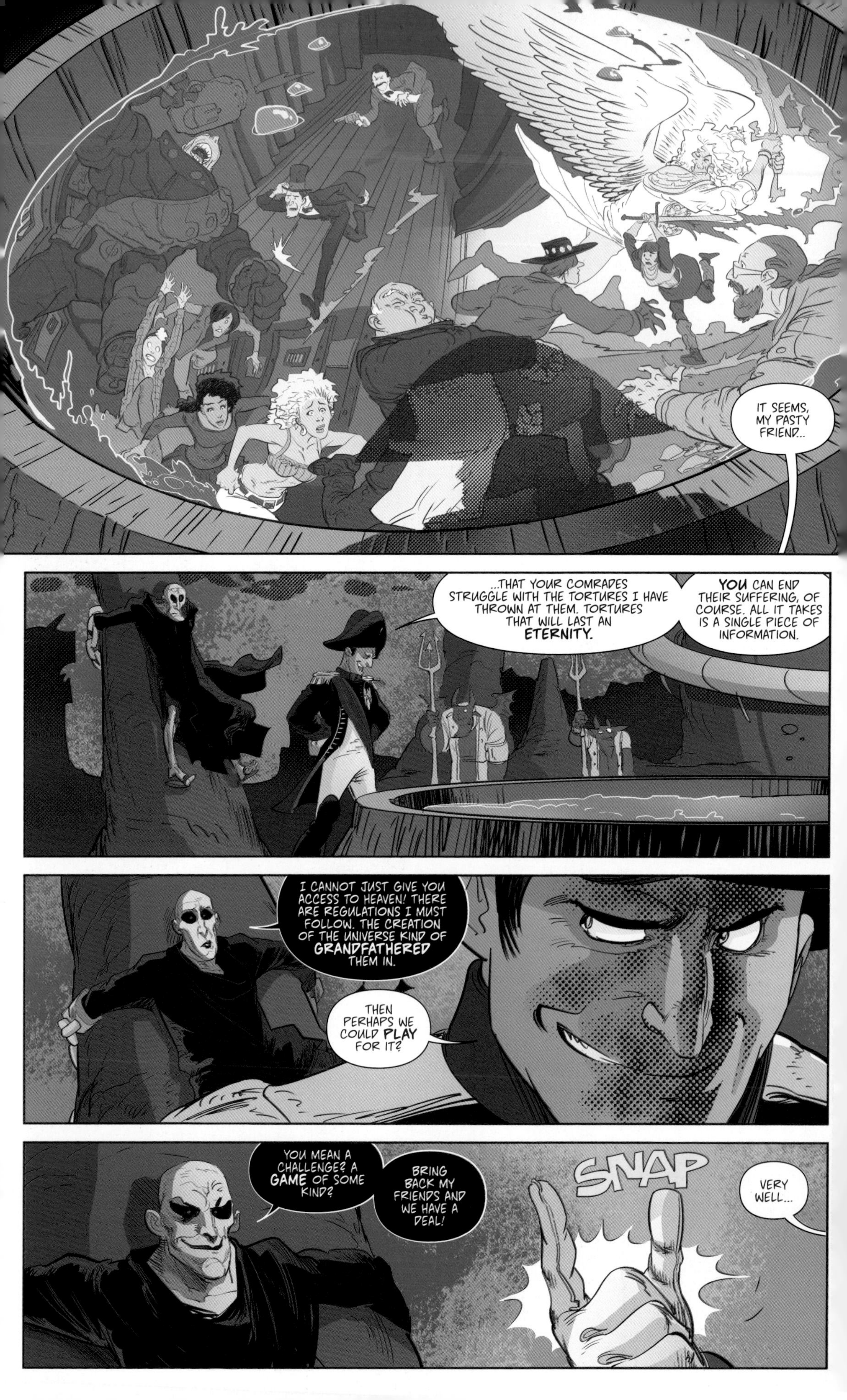
IT SEEMS, MY PASTY FRIEND...
...THAT YOUR COMRADES STRUGGLE WITH THE TORTURES I HAVE THROWN AT THEM. TORTURES THAT WILL LAST AN ETERNITY.
YOU CAN END THEIR SUFFERING, OF COURSE. ALL IT TAKES IS A SINGLE PIECE OF INFORMATION.
I CANNOT JUST GIVE YOU ACCESS TO HEAVEN! THERE ARE REGULATIONS I MUST FOLLOW. THE CREATION OF THE UNIVERSE KIND OF GRANDFATHERED THEM IN.
THEN PERHAPS WE COULD PLAY FOR IT?
YOU MEAN A CHALLENGE? A GAME OF SOME KIND?
BRING BACK MY FRIENDS AND WE HAVE A DEAL!
SNAP
VERY WELL...

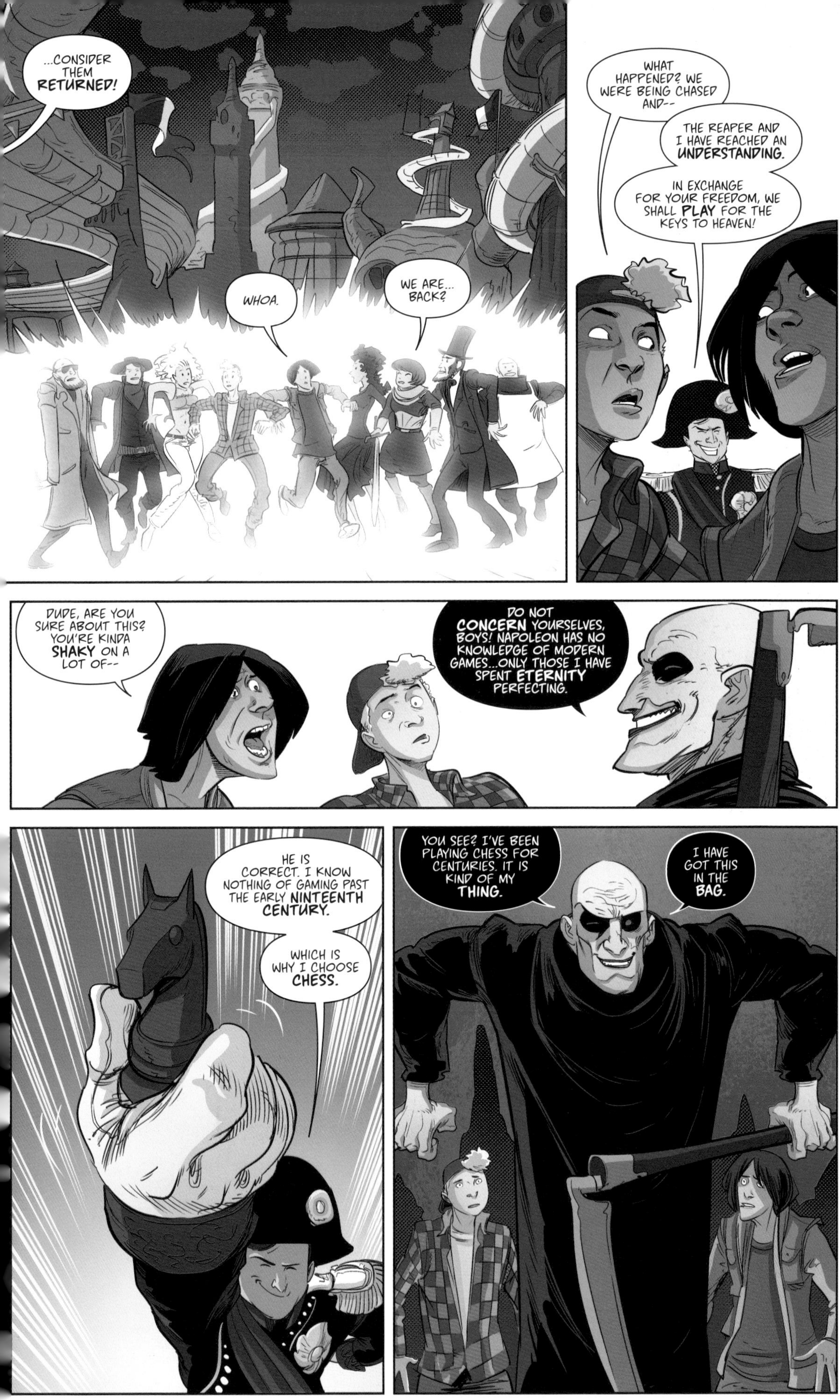
...CONSIDER THEM RETURNED!
WHOA.
WE ARE... BACK?
WHAT HAPPENED? WE WERE BEING CHASED AND--
THE REAPER AND I HAVE REACHED AN UNDERSTANDING.
IN EXCHANGE FOR YOUR FREEDOM, WE SHALL PLAY FOR THE KEYS TO HEAVEN!
DUDE, ARE YOU SURE ABOUT THIS? YOU'RE KINDA SHAKY ON A LOT OF--
DO NOT CONCERN YOURSELVES, BOYS! NAPOLEON HAS NO KNOWLEDGE OF MODERN GAMES...ONLY THOSE I HAVE SPENT ETERNITY PERFECTING.
HE IS CORRECT. I KNOW NOTHING OF GAMING PAST THE EARLY NINTEENTH CENTURY.
WHICH IS WHY I CHOOSE CHESS.
YOU SEE? I'VE BEEN PLAYING CHESS FOR CENTURIES. IT IS KIND OF MY THING.
I HAVE GOT THIS IN THE BAG.

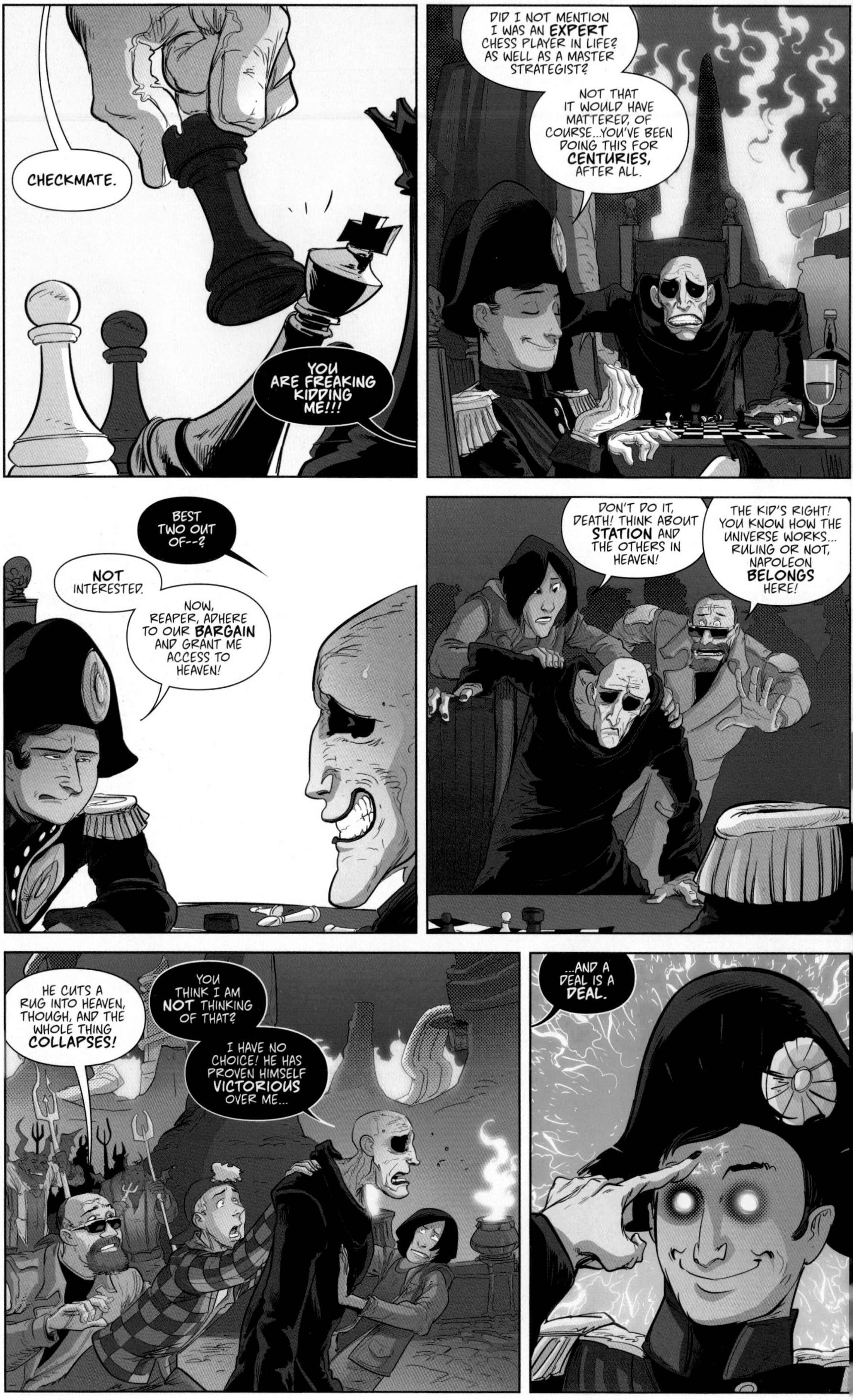
CHECKMATE.
YOU ARE FREAKING KIDDING ME!!!
DID I NOT MENTION I WAS AN EXPERT CHESS PLAYER IN LIFE? AS WELL AS A MASTER STRATEGIST?
NOT THAT IT WOULD HAVE MATTERED, OF COURSE...YOU'VE BEEN DOING THIS FOR CENTURIES, AFTER ALL.
BEST TWO OUT OF--?
NOT INTERESTED.
NOW, REAPER, ADHERE TO OUR BARGAIN AND GRANT ME ACCESS TO HEAVEN!
DON'T DO IT, DEATH! THINK ABOUT STATION AND THE OTHERS IN HEAVEN!
THE KID'S RIGHT! YOU KNOW HOW THE UNIVERSE WORKS... RULING OR NOT, NAPOLEON BELONGS HERE!
HE CUTS A RUG INTO HEAVEN, THOUGH, AND THE WHOLE THING COLLAPSES!
YOU THINK I AM NOT THINKING OF THAT?
I HAVE NO CHOICE! HE HAS PROVEN HIMSELF VICTORIOUS OVER ME...
...AND A DEAL IS A DEAL.

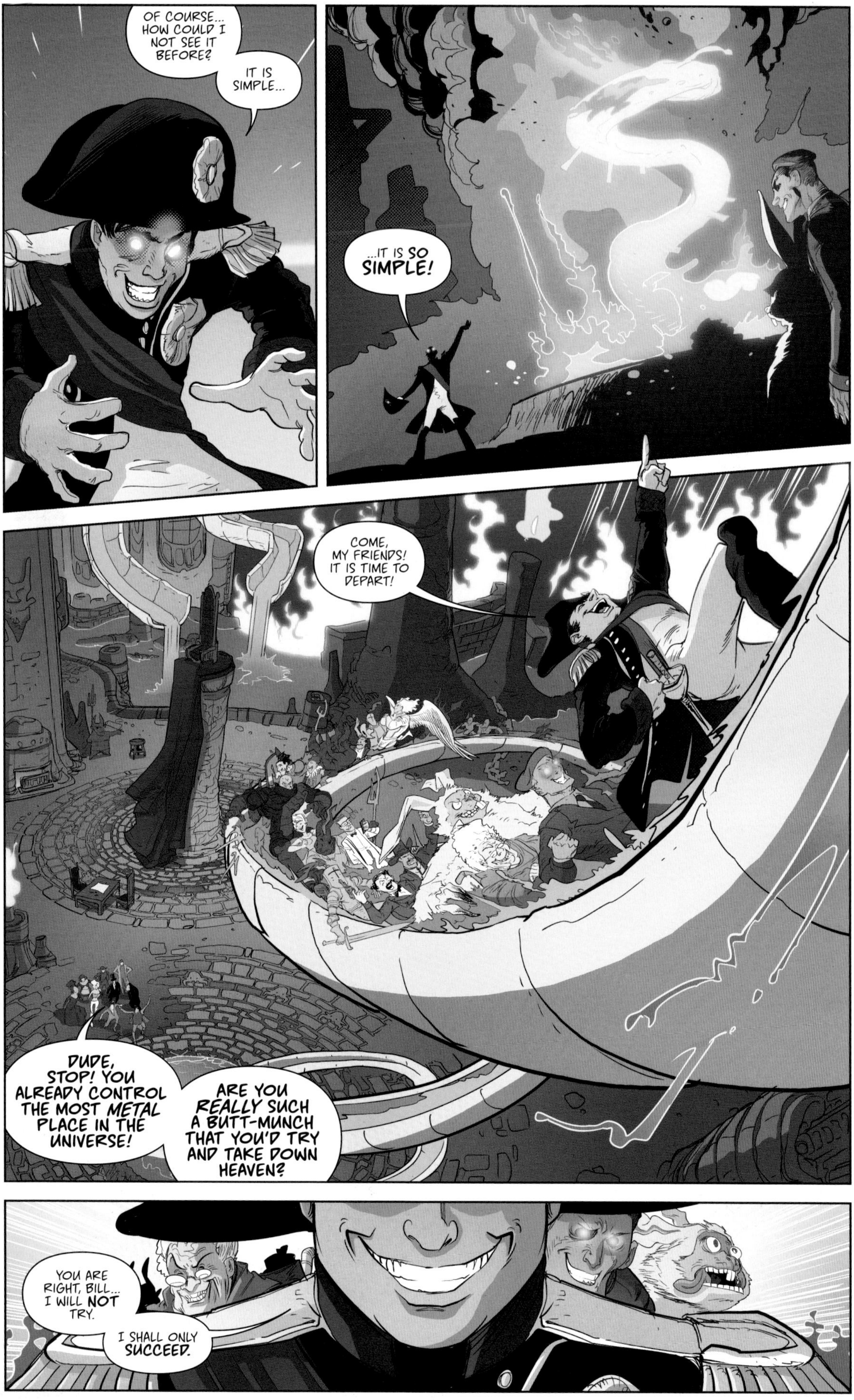
OF COURSE... HOW COULD I NOT SEE IT BEFORE?
IT IS SIMPLE...
...IT IS SO SIMPLE!
COME, MY FRIENDS! IT IS TIME TO DEPART!
DUDE, STOP! YOU ALREADY CONTROL THE MOST METAL PLACE IN THE UNIVERSE!
ARE YOU REALLY SUCH A BUTT-MUNCH THAT YOU'D TRY AND TAKE DOWN HEAVEN?
YOU ARE RIGHT, BILL... I WILL NOT TRY.
I SHALL ONLY SUCCEED.

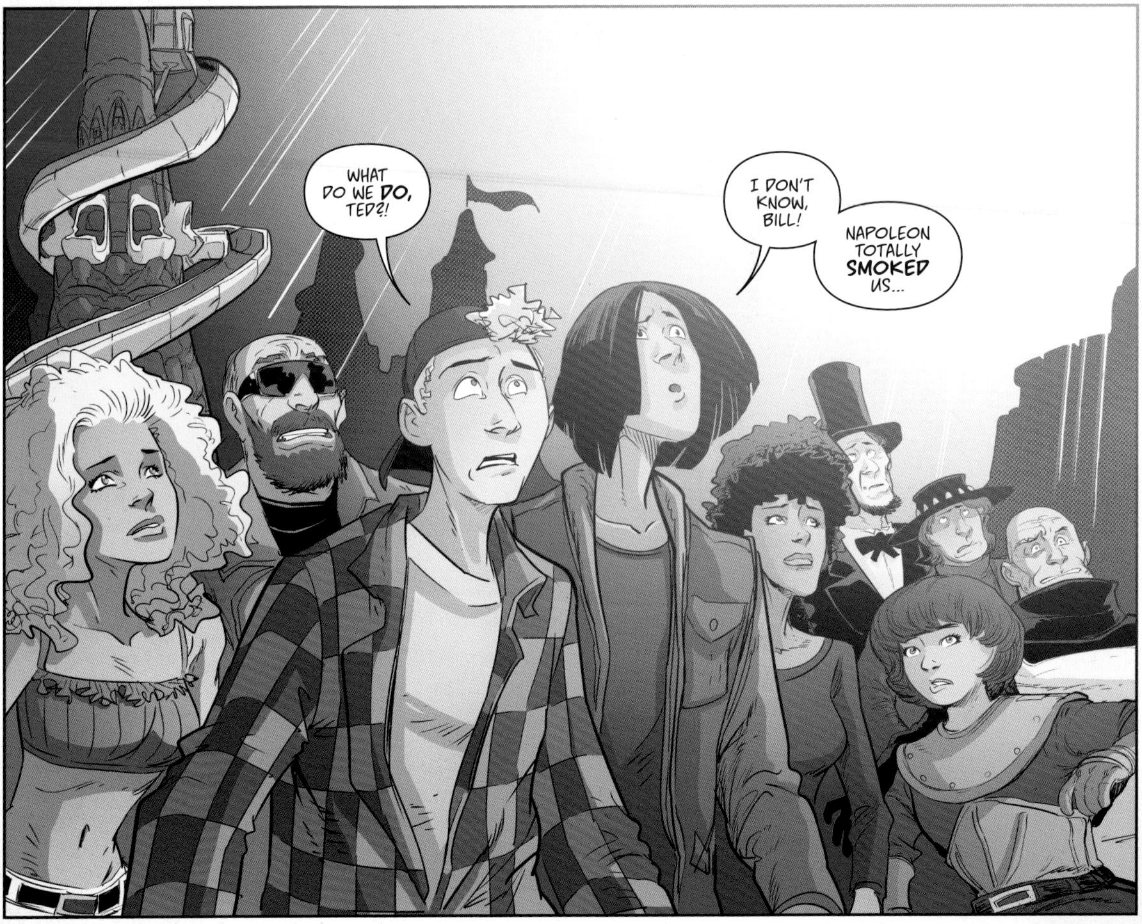
WHAT DO WE **DO,** TED?!
I DON'T KNOW, BILL!
NAPOLEON TOTALLY **SMOKED** US...

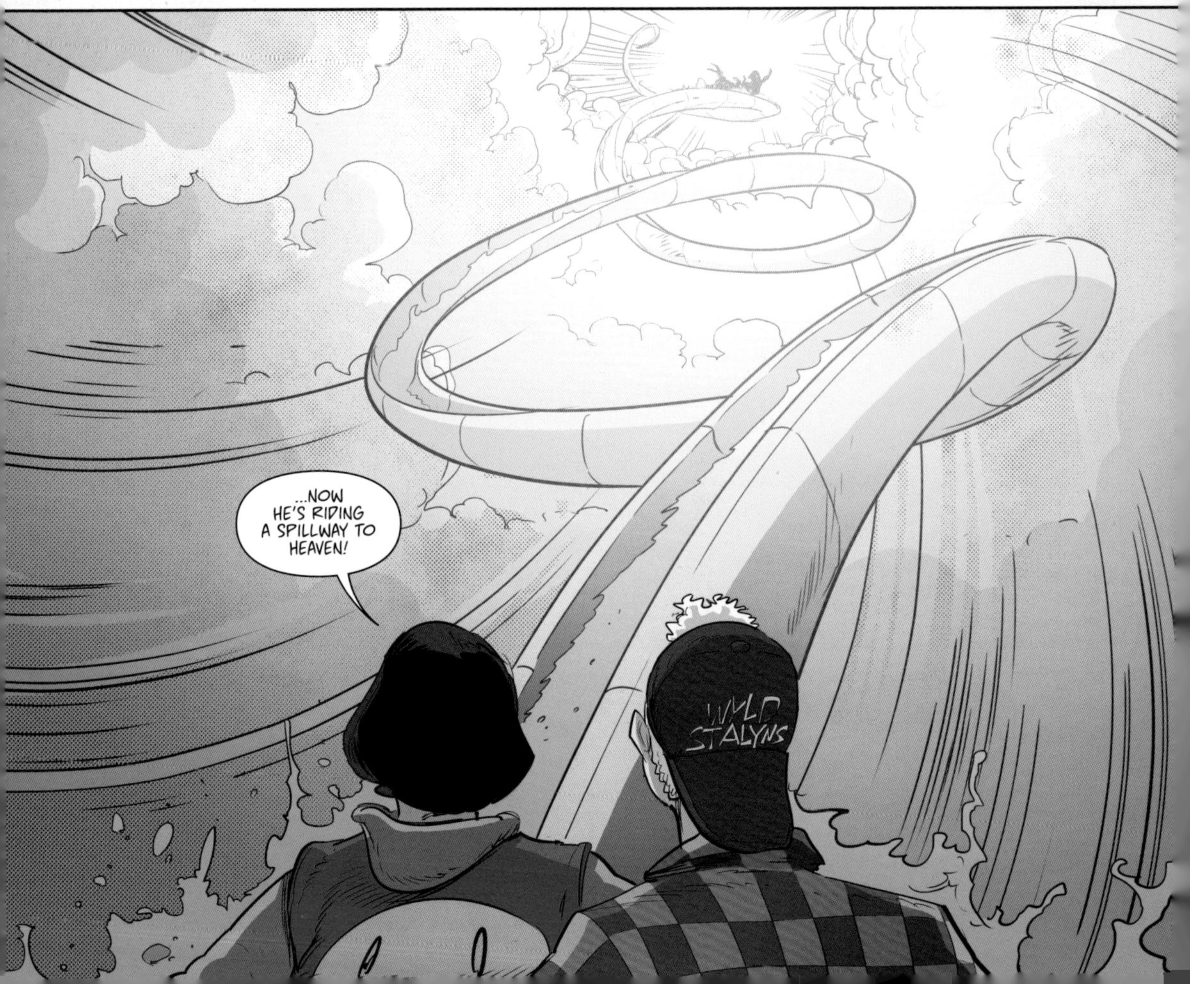
...NOW HE'S RIDING A SPILLWAY TO HEAVEN!
WYLD STALYNS

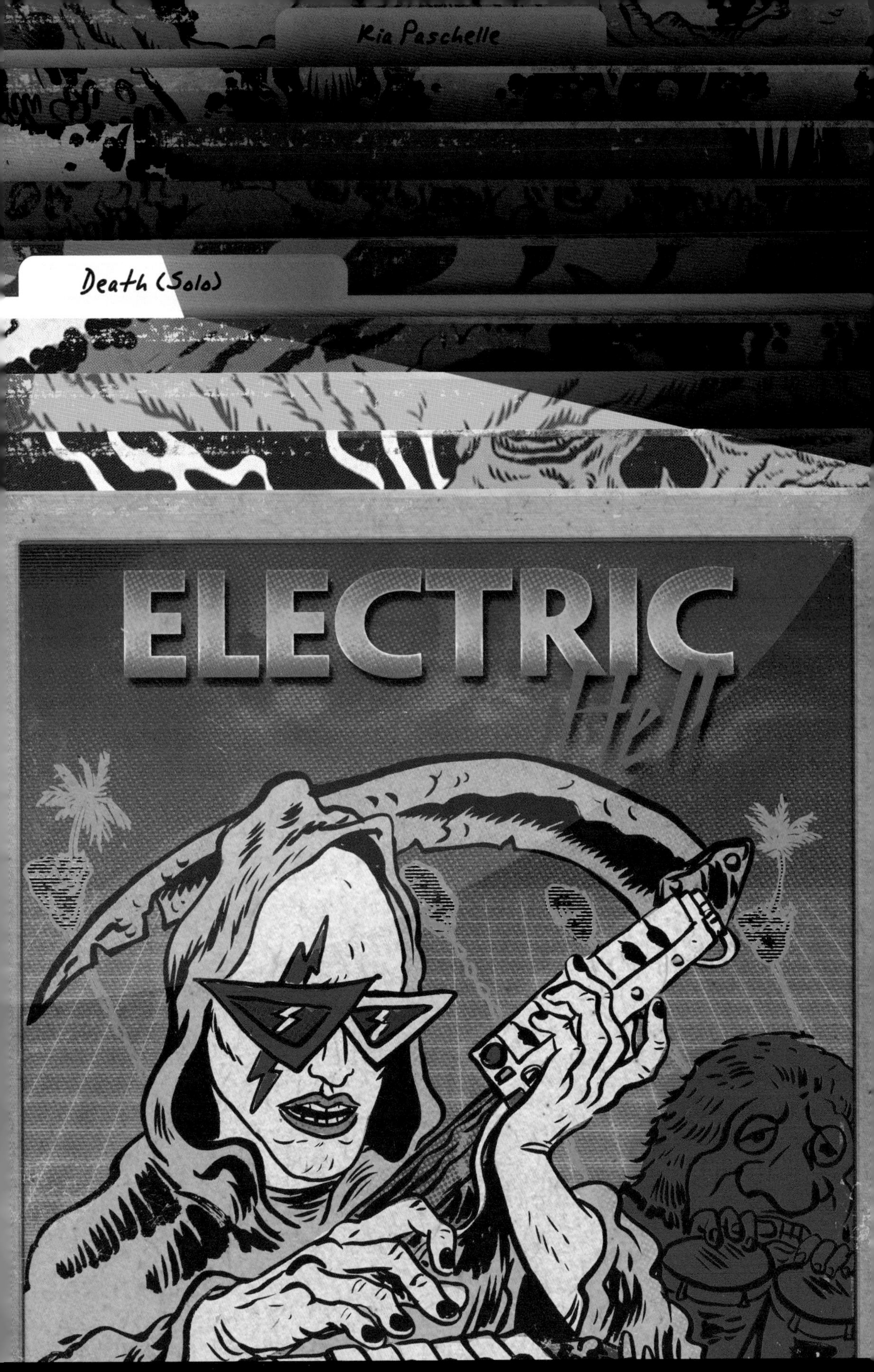
Kia Paschelle
Death (Solo)
ELECTRIC
Hell

ALEXIS ZIRITT ⚡ ISSUE TWO SUBSCRIPTION ALBUM COVER

CHAPTER THREE
PIT TO PARADISE

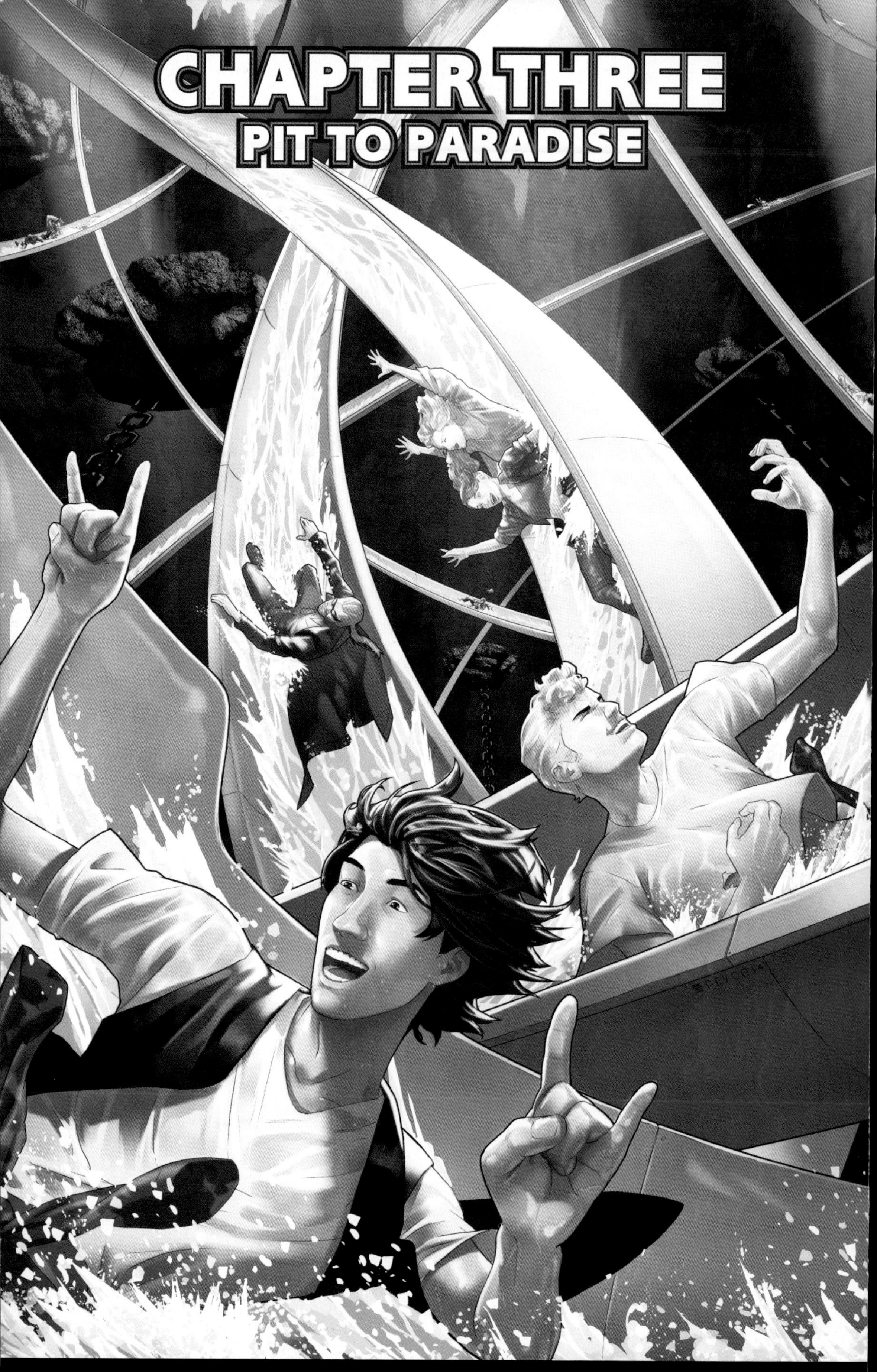

JAMAL CAMPBELL ⚡ ISSUE THREE MAIN COVER

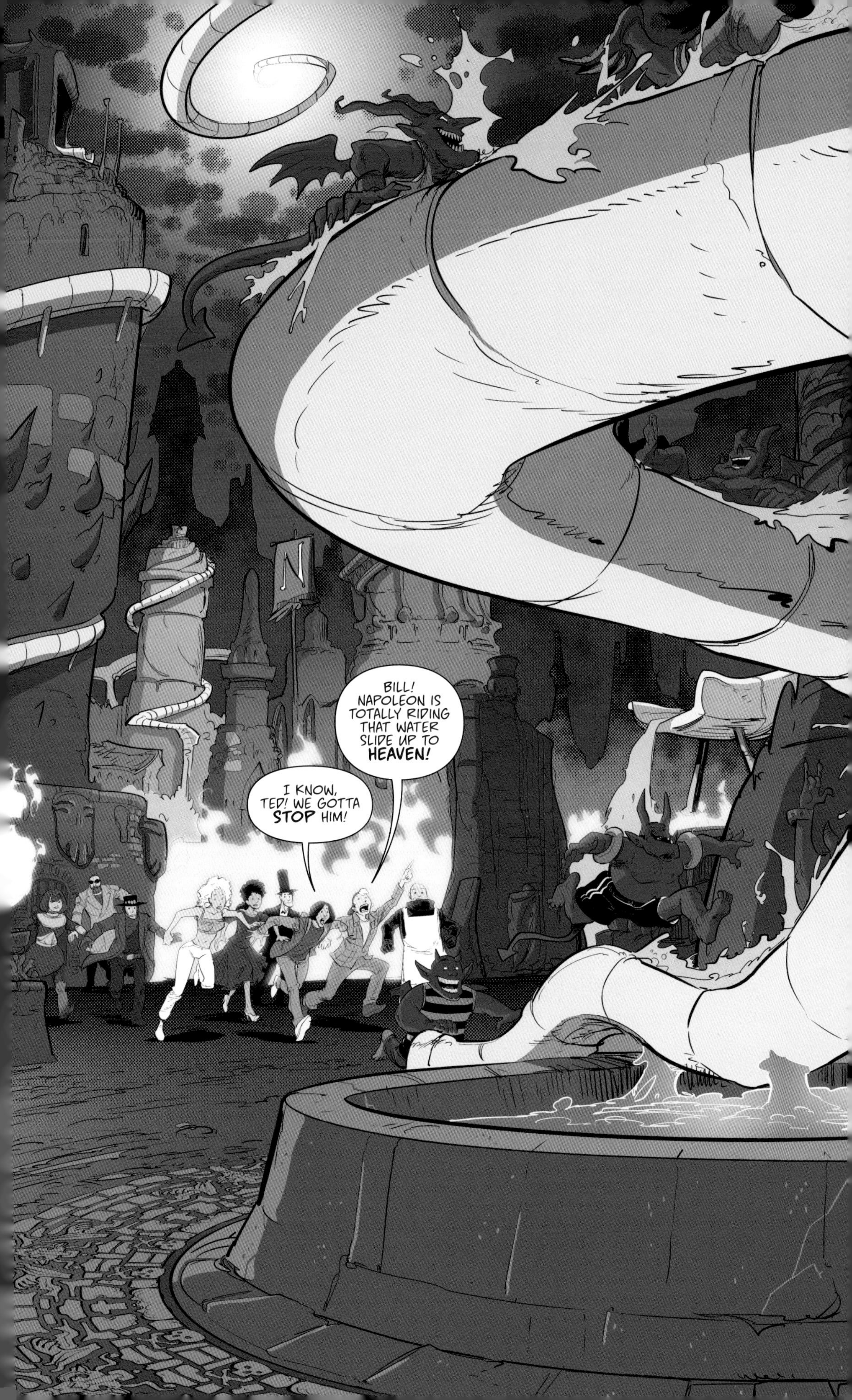
BILL! NAPOLEON IS TOTALLY RIDING THAT WATER SLIDE UP TO HEAVEN!
I KNOW, TED! WE GOTTA STOP HIM!

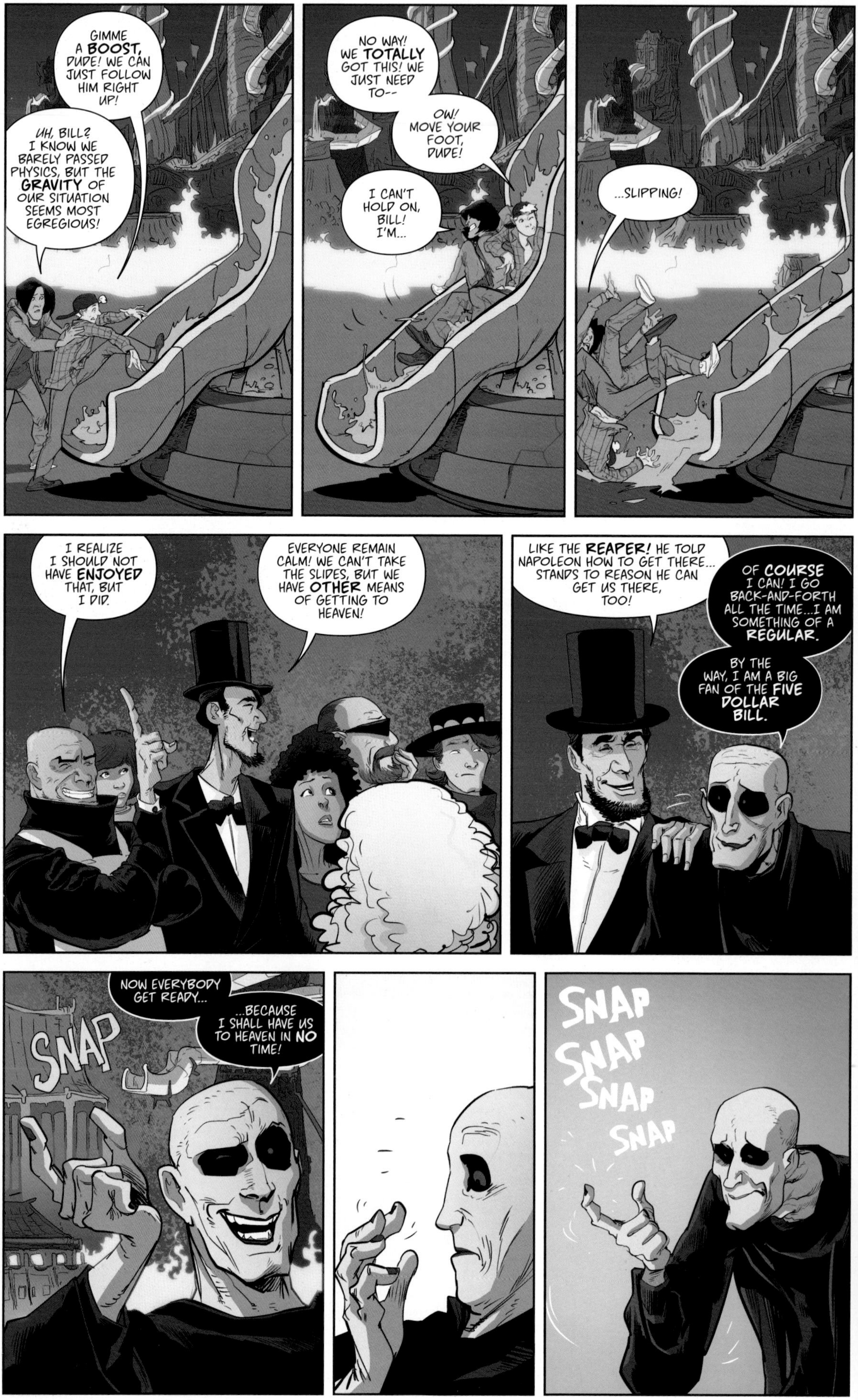
GIMME A BOOST, DUDE! WE CAN JUST FOLLOW HIM RIGHT UP!
UH, BILL? I KNOW WE BARELY PASSED PHYSICS, BUT THE GRAVITY OF OUR SITUATION SEEMS MOST EGREGIOUS!
NO WAY! WE TOTALLY GOT THIS! WE JUST NEED TO--
OW! MOVE YOUR FOOT, DUDE!
I CAN'T HOLD ON, BILL! I'M...
...SLIPPING!
I REALIZE I SHOULD NOT HAVE ENJOYED THAT, BUT I DID.
EVERYONE REMAIN CALM! WE CAN'T TAKE THE SLIDES, BUT WE HAVE OTHER MEANS OF GETTING TO HEAVEN!
LIKE THE REAPER! HE TOLD NAPOLEON HOW TO GET THERE... STANDS TO REASON HE CAN GET US THERE, TOO!
OF COURSE I CAN! I GO BACK-AND-FORTH ALL THE TIME...I AM SOMETHING OF A REGULAR.
BY THE WAY, I AM A BIG FAN OF THE FIVE DOLLAR BILL.
NOW EVERYBODY GET READY...
...BECAUSE I SHALL HAVE US TO HEAVEN IN NO TIME!
SNAP
SNAP
SNAP
SNAP
SNAP

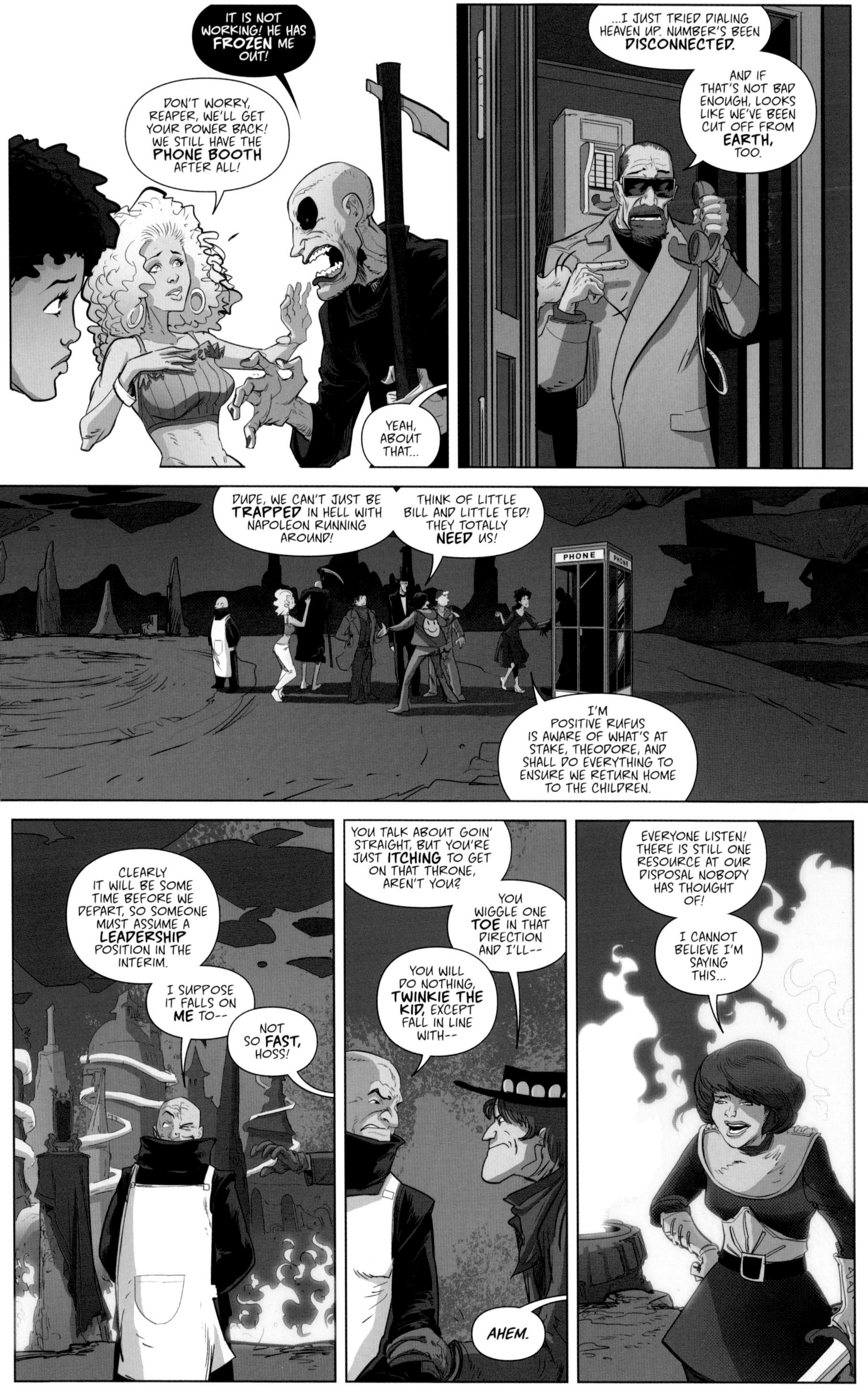
IT IS NOT WORKING! HE HAS FROZEN ME OUT!
DON'T WORRY, REAPER, WE'LL GET YOUR POWER BACK! WE STILL HAVE THE PHONE BOOTH AFTER ALL!
YEAH, ABOUT THAT...
...I JUST TRIED DIALING HEAVEN UP. NUMBER'S BEEN DISCONNECTED.
AND IF THAT'S NOT BAD ENOUGH, LOOKS LIKE WE'VE BEEN CUT OFF FROM EARTH, TOO.
DUDE, WE CAN'T JUST BE TRAPPED IN HELL WITH NAPOLEON RUNNING AROUND!
THINK OF LITTLE BILL AND LITTLE TED! THEY TOTALLY NEED US!
PHONE
PHONE
I'M POSITIVE RUFUS IS AWARE OF WHAT'S AT STAKE, THEODORE, AND SHALL DO EVERYTHING TO ENSURE WE RETURN HOME TO THE CHILDREN.
CLEARLY IT WILL BE SOME TIME BEFORE WE DEPART, SO SOMEONE MUST ASSUME A LEADERSHIP POSITION IN THE INTERIM.
I SUPPOSE IT FALLS ON ME TO--
NOT SO FAST, HOSS!
YOU TALK ABOUT GOIN' STRAIGHT, BUT YOU'RE JUST ITCHING TO GET ON THAT THRONE, AREN'T YOU?
YOU WIGGLE ONE TOE IN THAT DIRECTION AND I'LL--
YOU WILL DO NOTHING, TWINKIE THE KID, EXCEPT FALL IN LINE WITH--
AHEM.
EVERYONE LISTEN! THERE IS STILL ONE RESOURCE AT OUR DISPOSAL NOBODY HAS THOUGHT OF!
I CANNOT BELIEVE I'M SAYING THIS...

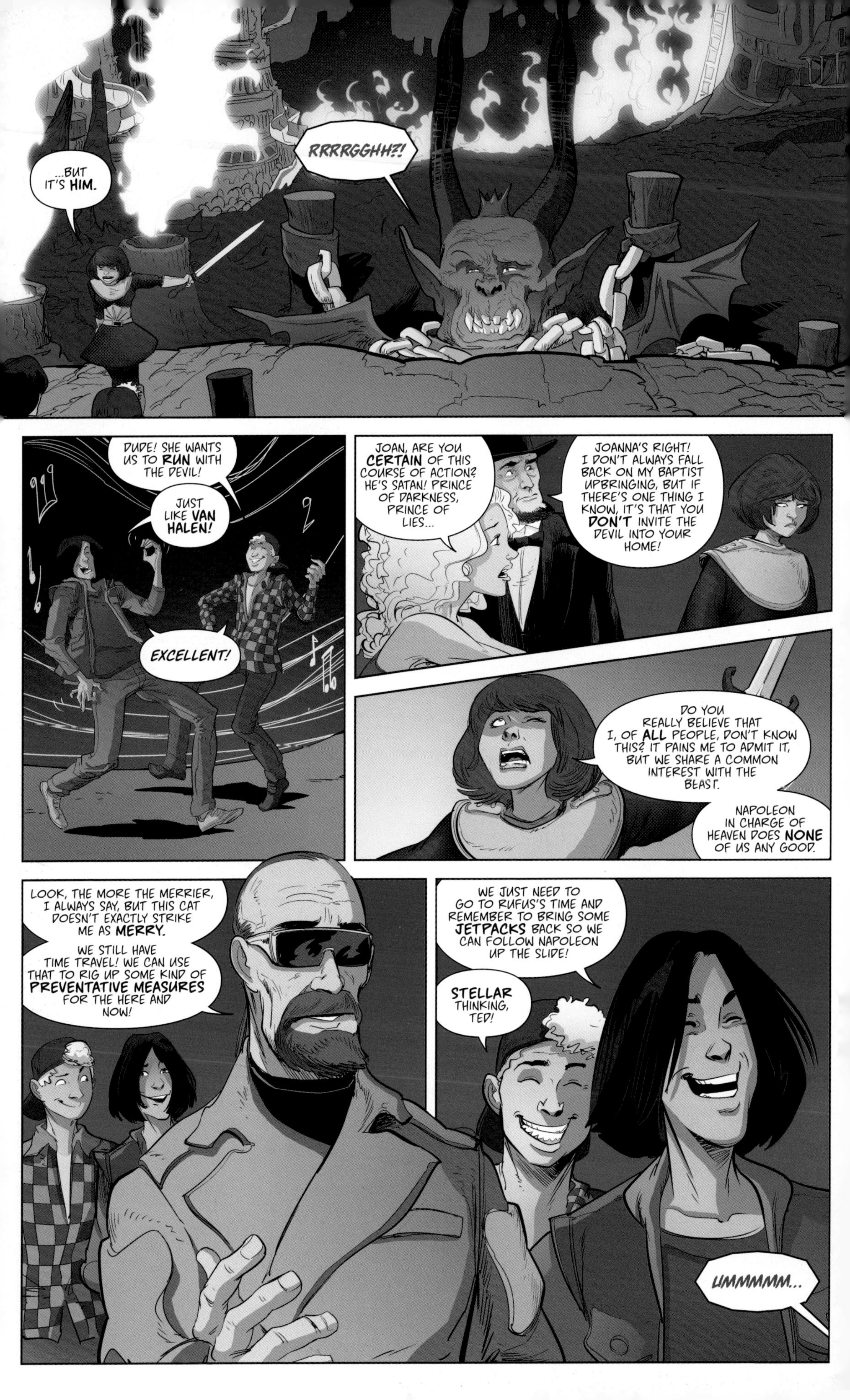
...BUT IT'S HIM.
RRRRGGHH?!
DUDE! SHE WANTS US TO RUN WITH THE DEVIL!
JUST LIKE VAN HALEN!
EXCELLENT!
JOAN, ARE YOU CERTAIN OF THIS COURSE OF ACTION? HE'S SATAN! PRINCE OF DARKNESS, PRINCE OF LIES...
JOANNA'S RIGHT! I DON'T ALWAYS FALL BACK ON MY BAPTIST UPBRINGING, BUT IF THERE'S ONE THING I KNOW, IT'S THAT YOU DON'T INVITE THE DEVIL INTO YOUR HOME!
DO YOU REALLY BELIEVE THAT I, OF ALL PEOPLE, DON'T KNOW THIS? IT PAINS ME TO ADMIT IT, BUT WE SHARE A COMMON INTEREST WITH THE BEAST.
NAPOLEON IN CHARGE OF HEAVEN DOES NONE OF US ANY GOOD.
LOOK, THE MORE THE MERRIER, I ALWAYS SAY, BUT THIS CAT DOESN'T EXACTLY STRIKE ME AS MERRY.
WE STILL HAVE TIME TRAVEL! WE CAN USE THAT TO RIG UP SOME KIND OF PREVENTATIVE MEASURES FOR THE HERE AND NOW!
WE JUST NEED TO GO TO RUFUS'S TIME AND REMEMBER TO BRING SOME JETPACKS BACK SO WE CAN FOLLOW NAPOLEON UP THE SLIDE!
STELLAR THINKING, TED!
UMMMMM...

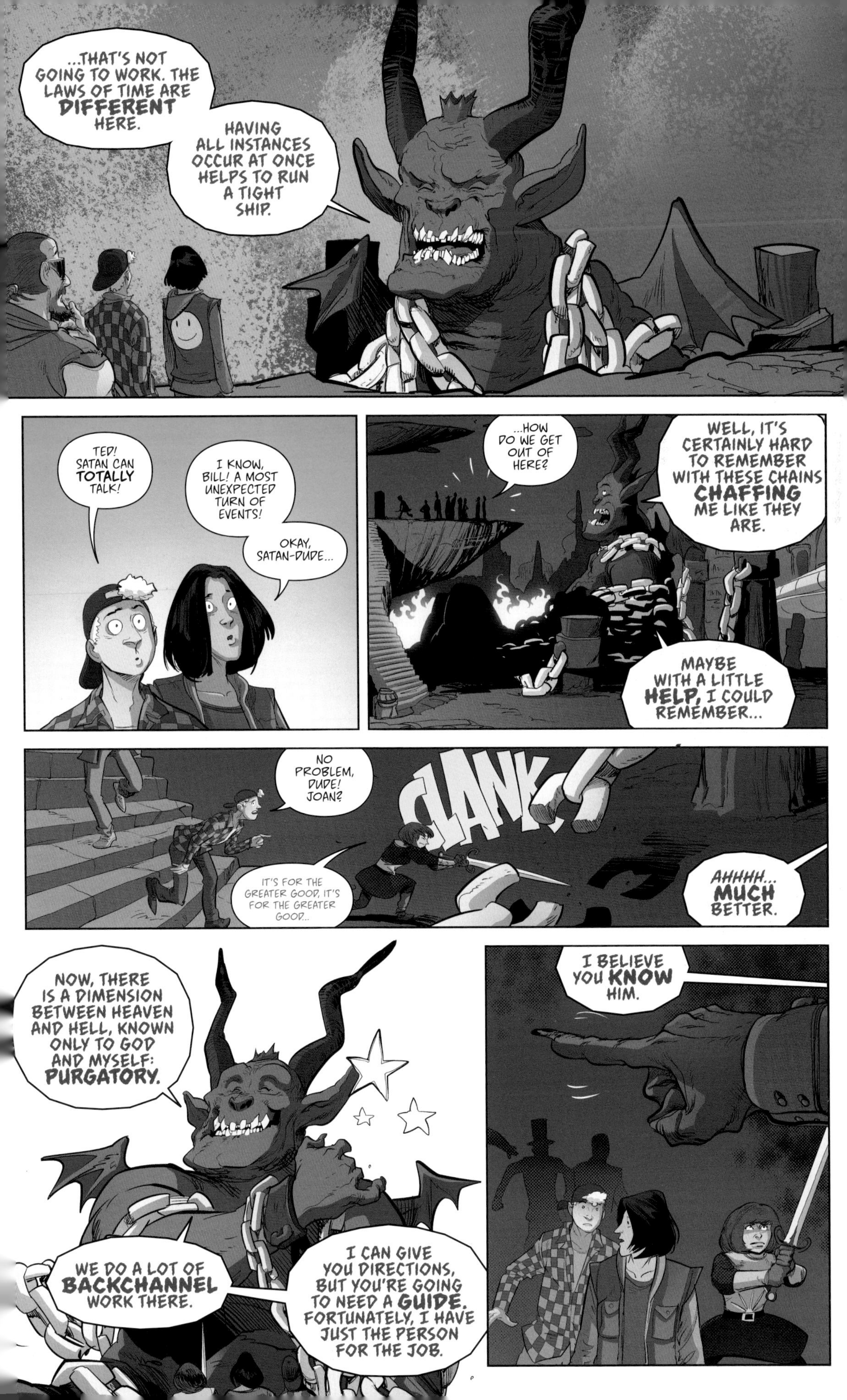
...THAT'S NOT GOING TO WORK. THE LAWS OF TIME ARE DIFFERENT HERE.
HAVING ALL INSTANCES OCCUR AT ONCE HELPS TO RUN A TIGHT SHIP.
TED! SATAN CAN TOTALLY TALK!
I KNOW, BILL! A MOST UNEXPECTED TURN OF EVENTS!
OKAY, SATAN-DUDE...
...HOW DO WE GET OUT OF HERE?
WELL, IT'S CERTAINLY HARD TO REMEMBER WITH THESE CHAINS CHAFFING ME LIKE THEY ARE.
MAYBE WITH A LITTLE HELP, I COULD REMEMBER...
NO PROBLEM, DUDE! JOAN?
CLANK
IT'S FOR THE GREATER GOOD, IT'S FOR THE GREATER GOOD...
AHHHH... MUCH BETTER.
NOW, THERE IS A DIMENSION BETWEEN HEAVEN AND HELL, KNOWN ONLY TO GOD AND MYSELF: PURGATORY.
WE DO A LOT OF BACKCHANNEL WORK THERE.
I CAN GIVE YOU DIRECTIONS, BUT YOU'RE GOING TO NEED A GUIDE. FORTUNATELY, I HAVE JUST THE PERSON FOR THE JOB.
I BELIEVE YOU KNOW HIM.

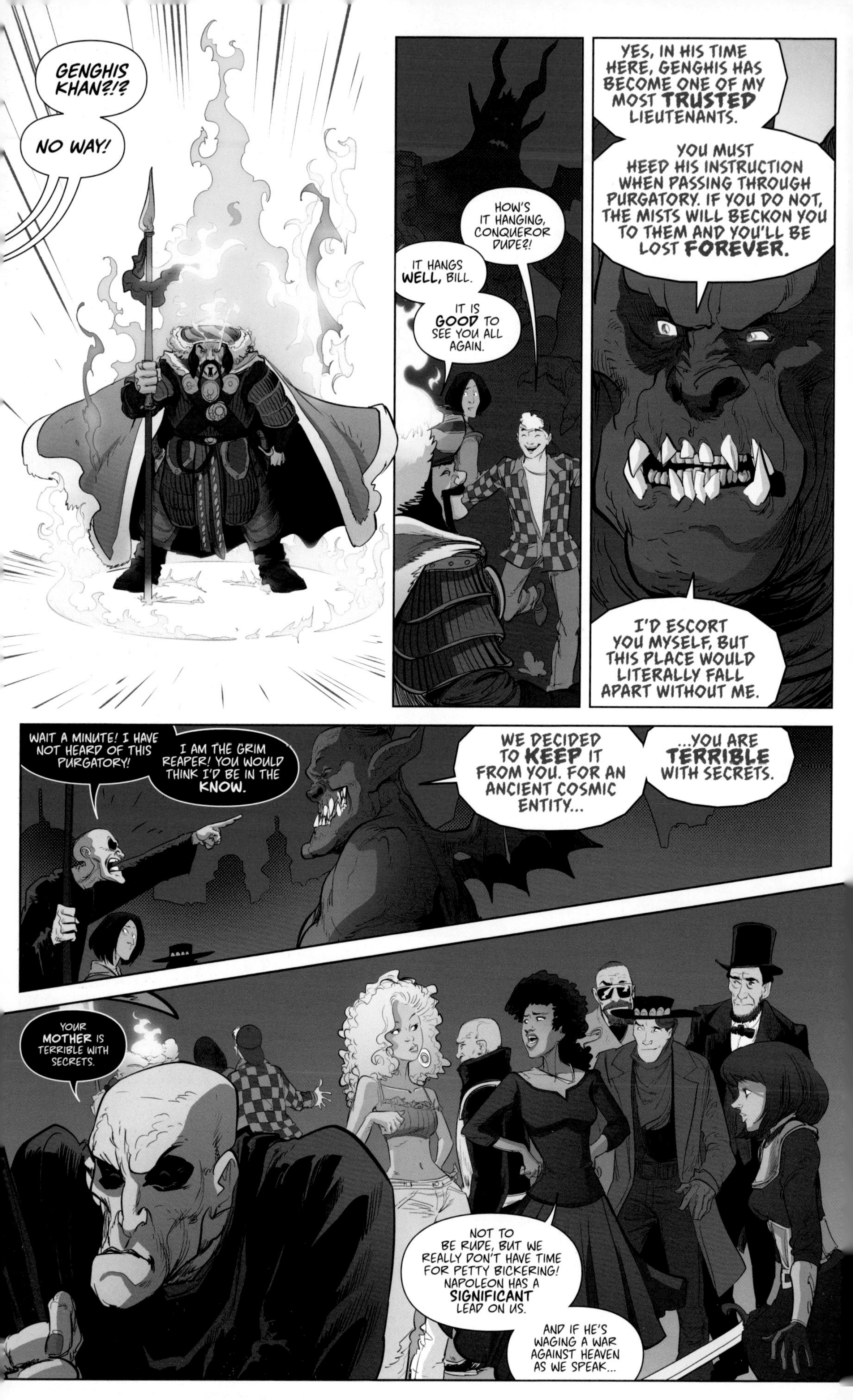
GENGHIS KHAN?!?
NO WAY!
HOW'S IT HANGING, CONQUEROR DUDE?!
IT HANGS WELL, BILL.
IT IS GOOD TO SEE YOU ALL AGAIN.
YES, IN HIS TIME HERE, GENGHIS HAS BECOME ONE OF MY MOST TRUSTED LIEUTENANTS.
YOU MUST HEED HIS INSTRUCTION WHEN PASSING THROUGH PURGATORY. IF YOU DO NOT, THE MISTS WILL BECKON YOU TO THEM AND YOU'LL BE LOST FOREVER.
I'D ESCORT YOU MYSELF, BUT THIS PLACE WOULD LITERALLY FALL APART WITHOUT ME.
WAIT A MINUTE! I HAVE NOT HEARD OF THIS PURGATORY!
I AM THE GRIM REAPER! YOU WOULD THINK I'D BE IN THE KNOW.
WE DECIDED TO KEEP IT FROM YOU. FOR AN ANCIENT COSMIC ENTITY...
...YOU ARE TERRIBLE WITH SECRETS.
YOUR MOTHER IS TERRIBLE WITH SECRETS.
NOT TO BE RUDE, BUT WE REALLY DON'T HAVE TIME FOR PETTY BICKERING! NAPOLEON HAS A SIGNIFICANT LEAD ON US.
AND IF HE'S WAGING A WAR AGAINST HEAVEN AS WE SPEAK...

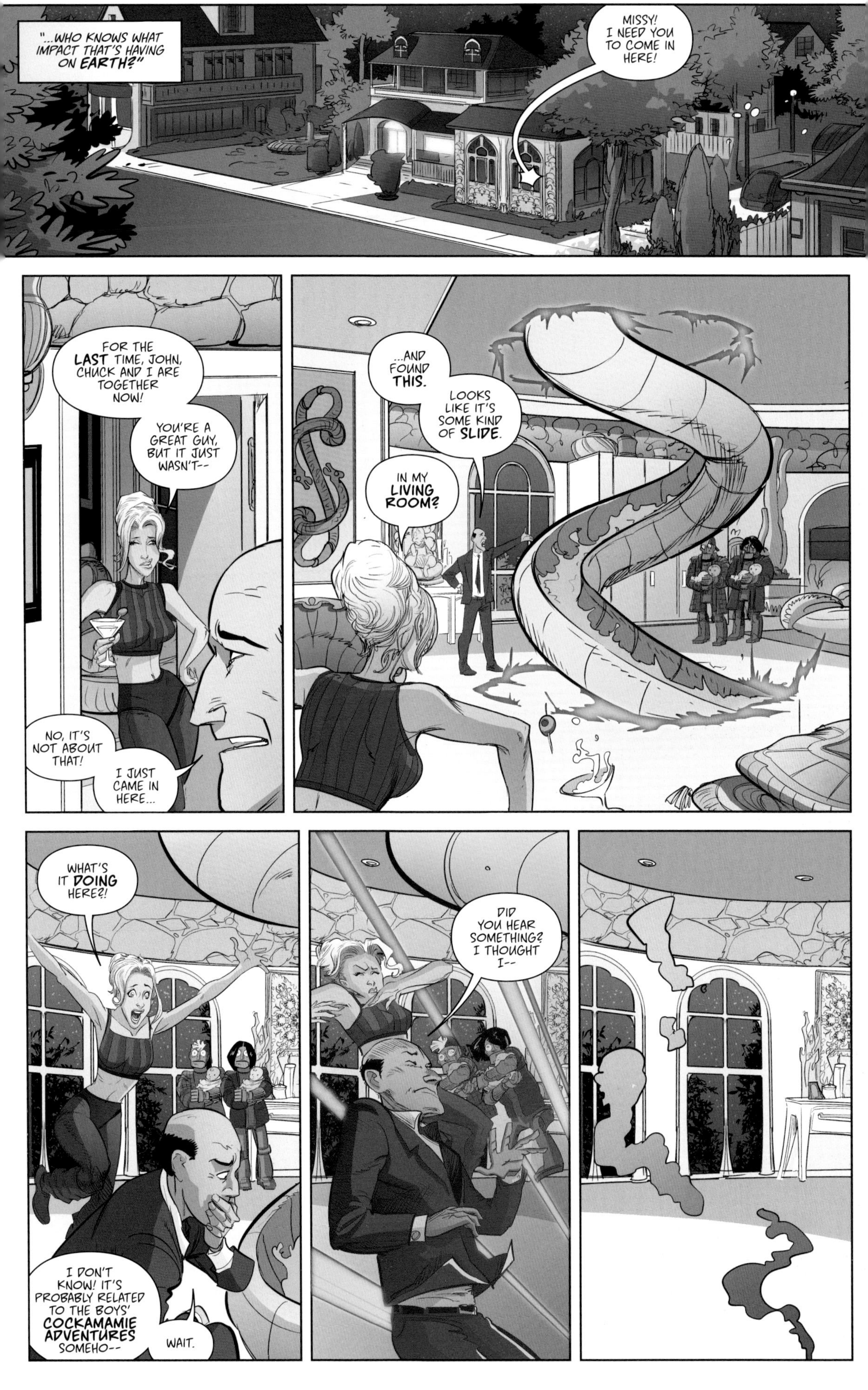
"...WHO KNOWS WHAT IMPACT THAT'S HAVING ON EARTH?"
MISSY! I NEED YOU TO COME IN HERE!
FOR THE LAST TIME, JOHN, CHUCK AND I ARE TOGETHER NOW!
YOU'RE A GREAT GUY, BUT IT JUST WASN'T--
NO, IT'S NOT ABOUT THAT!
I JUST CAME IN HERE...
...AND FOUND THIS.
LOOKS LIKE IT'S SOME KIND OF SLIDE.
IN MY LIVING ROOM?
WHAT'S IT DOING HERE?!
I DON'T KNOW! IT'S PROBABLY RELATED TO THE BOYS' COCKAMAMIE ADVENTURES SOMEHO--
WAIT.
DID YOU HEAR SOMETHING? I THOUGHT I--

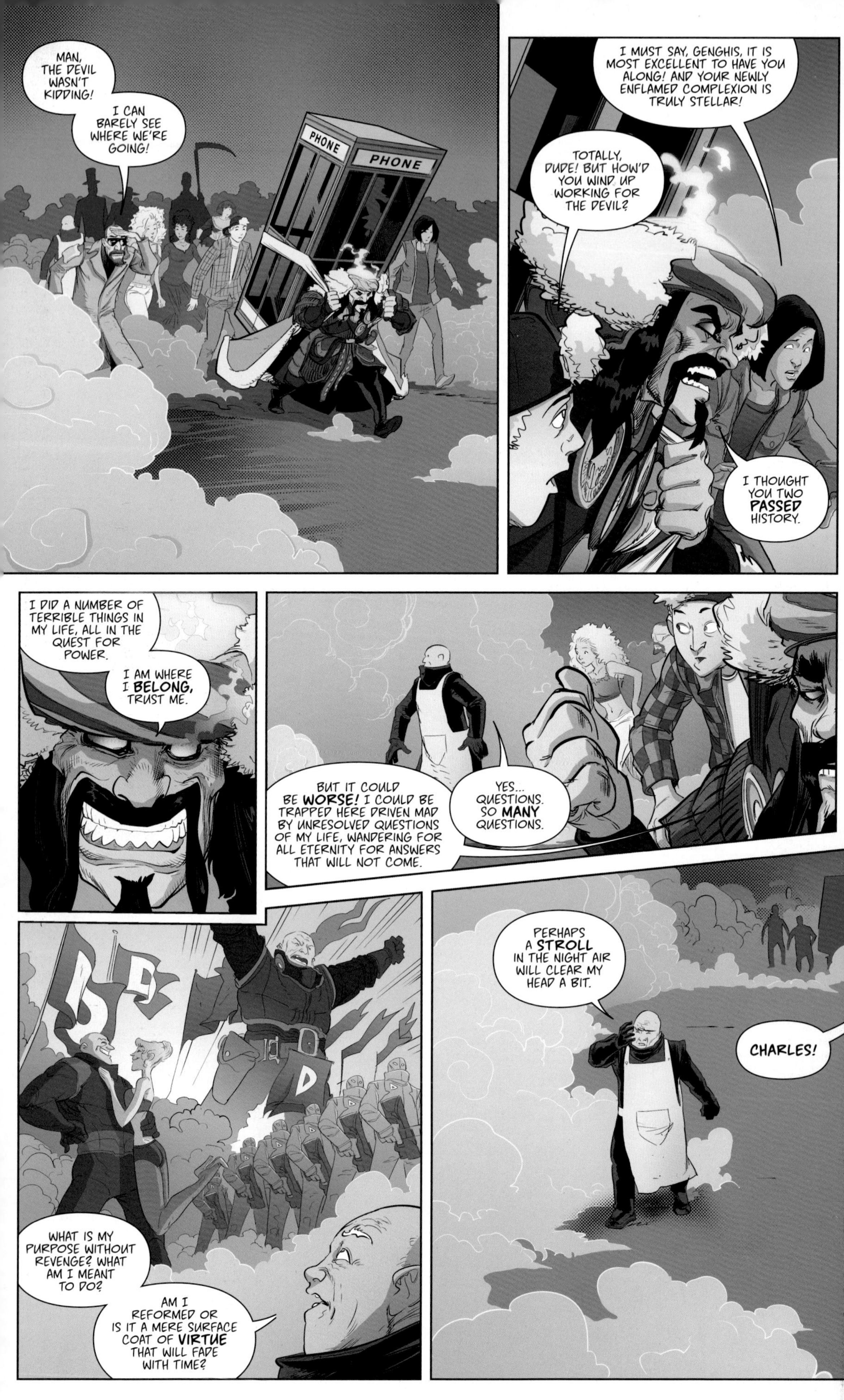
MAN, THE DEVIL WASN'T KIDDING!
I CAN BARELY SEE WHERE WE'RE GOING!
PHONE
PHONE
I MUST SAY, GENGHIS, IT IS MOST EXCELLENT TO HAVE YOU ALONG! AND YOUR NEWLY ENFLAMED COMPLEXION IS TRULY STELLAR!
TOTALLY, DUDE! BUT HOW'D YOU WIND UP WORKING FOR THE DEVIL?
I THOUGHT YOU TWO **PASSED** HISTORY.
I DID A NUMBER OF TERRIBLE THINGS IN MY LIFE, ALL IN THE QUEST FOR POWER.
I AM WHERE I **BELONG,** TRUST ME.
BUT IT COULD BE **WORSE!** I COULD BE TRAPPED HERE DRIVEN MAD BY UNRESOLVED QUESTIONS OF MY LIFE, WANDERING FOR ALL ETERNITY FOR ANSWERS THAT WILL NOT COME.
YES... QUESTIONS. SO **MANY** QUESTIONS.
WHAT IS MY PURPOSE WITHOUT REVENGE? WHAT AM I MEANT TO DO?
AM I REFORMED OR IS IT A MERE SURFACE COAT OF **VIRTUE** THAT WILL FADE WITH TIME?
PERHAPS A **STROLL** IN THE NIGHT AIR WILL CLEAR MY HEAD A BIT.
CHARLES!

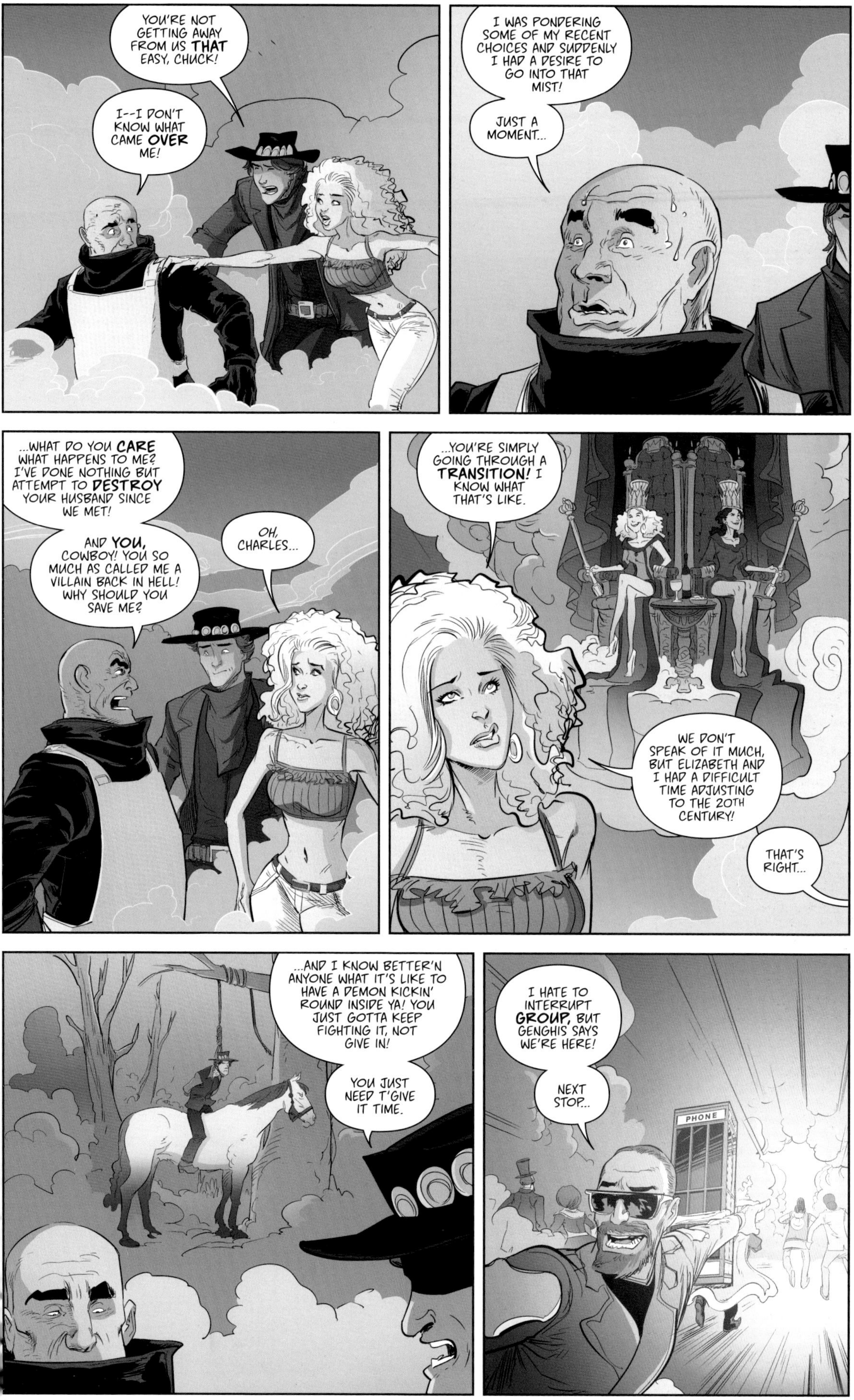
YOU'RE NOT GETTING AWAY FROM US THAT EASY, CHUCK!
I--I DON'T KNOW WHAT CAME OVER ME!
I WAS PONDERING SOME OF MY RECENT CHOICES AND SUDDENLY I HAD A DESIRE TO GO INTO THAT MIST!
JUST A MOMENT...
...WHAT DO YOU CARE WHAT HAPPENS TO ME? I'VE DONE NOTHING BUT ATTEMPT TO DESTROY YOUR HUSBAND SINCE WE MET!
AND YOU, COWBOY! YOU SO MUCH AS CALLED ME A VILLAIN BACK IN HELL! WHY SHOULD YOU SAVE ME?
OH, CHARLES...
...YOU'RE SIMPLY GOING THROUGH A TRANSITION! I KNOW WHAT THAT'S LIKE.
WE DON'T SPEAK OF IT MUCH, BUT ELIZABETH AND I HAD A DIFFICULT TIME ADJUSTING TO THE 20TH CENTURY!
THAT'S RIGHT...
...AND I KNOW BETTER'N ANYONE WHAT IT'S LIKE TO HAVE A DEMON KICKIN' ROUND INSIDE YA! YOU JUST GOTTA KEEP FIGHTING IT, NOT GIVE IN!
YOU JUST NEED T'GIVE IT TIME.
I HATE TO INTERRUPT GROUP, BUT GENGHIS SAYS WE'RE HERE!
NEXT STOP...
PHONE

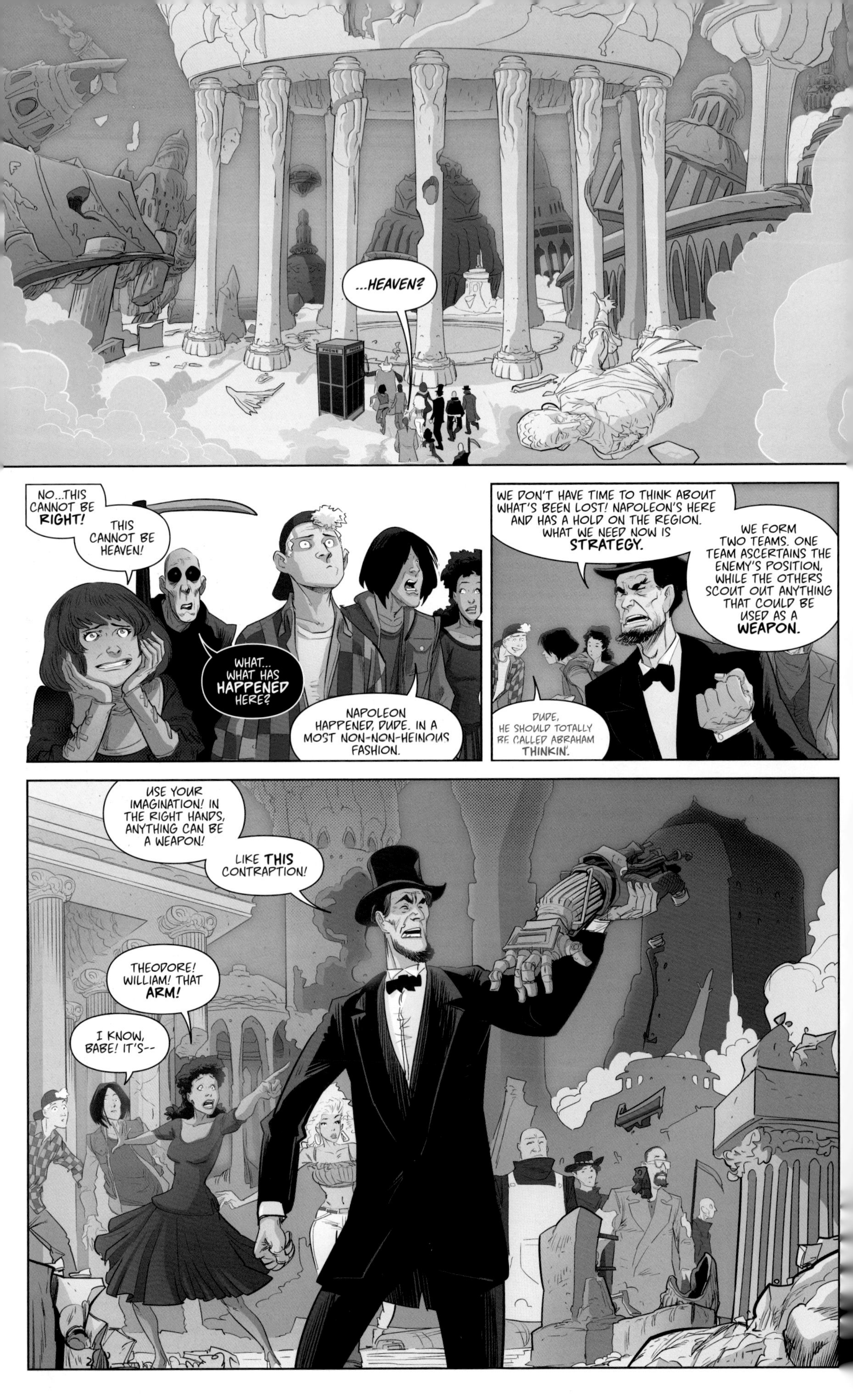
...HEAVEN?
PHONE
NO...THIS CANNOT BE RIGHT!
THIS CANNOT BE HEAVEN!
WHAT... WHAT HAS HAPPENED HERE?
NAPOLEON HAPPENED, DUDE. IN A MOST NON-NON-HEINOUS FASHION.
WE DON'T HAVE TIME TO THINK ABOUT WHAT'S BEEN LOST! NAPOLEON'S HERE AND HAS A HOLD ON THE REGION. WHAT WE NEED NOW IS STRATEGY.
WE FORM TWO TEAMS. ONE TEAM ASCERTAINS THE ENEMY'S POSITION, WHILE THE OTHERS SCOUT OUT ANYTHING THAT COULD BE USED AS A WEAPON.
DUDE, HE SHOULD TOTALLY BE CALLED ABRAHAM THINKIN'.
USE YOUR IMAGINATION! IN THE RIGHT HANDS, ANYTHING CAN BE A WEAPON!
LIKE THIS CONTRAPTION!
THEODORE! WILLIAM! THAT ARM!
I KNOW, BABE! IT'S--

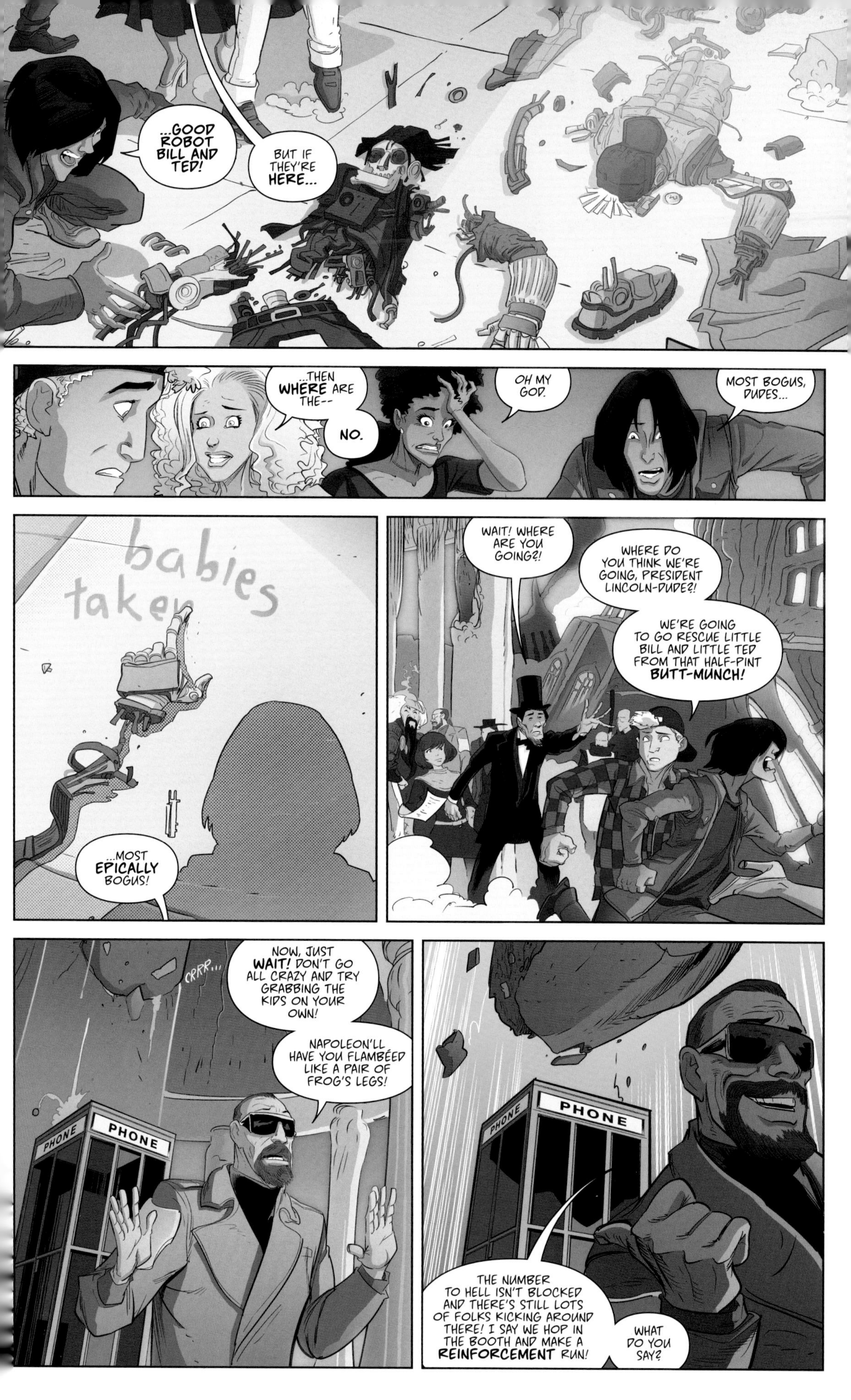
...GOOD ROBOT BILL AND TED!
BUT IF THEY'RE HERE...
...THEN WHERE ARE THE--
NO.
OH MY GOD.
MOST BOGUS, DUDES...
babies taken
...MOST EPICALLY BOGUS!
WAIT! WHERE ARE YOU GOING?!
WHERE DO YOU THINK WE'RE GOING, PRESIDENT LINCOLN-DUDE?!
WE'RE GOING TO GO RESCUE LITTLE BILL AND LITTLE TED FROM THAT HALF-PINT BUTT-MUNCH!
CRRR...
NOW, JUST WAIT! DON'T GO ALL CRAZY AND TRY GRABBING THE KIDS ON YOUR OWN!
NAPOLEON'LL HAVE YOU FLAMBÉED LIKE A PAIR OF FROG'S LEGS!
PHONE
PHONE
PHONE
PHONE
THE NUMBER TO HELL ISN'T BLOCKED AND THERE'S STILL LOTS OF FOLKS KICKING AROUND THERE! I SAY WE HOP IN THE BOOTH AND MAKE A REINFORCEMENT RUN!
WHAT DO YOU SAY?

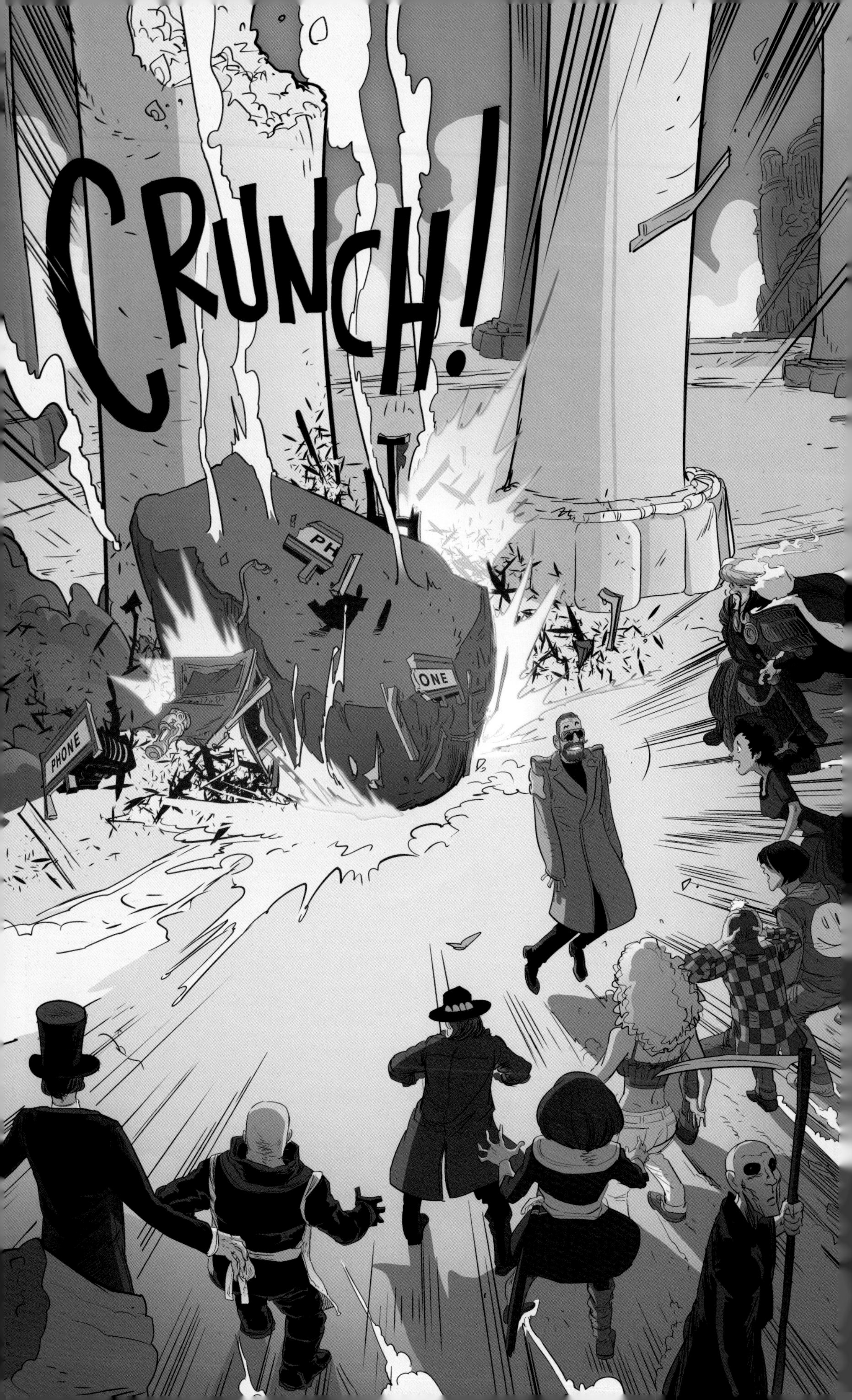
CRUNCH!
PH
ONE
PHONE

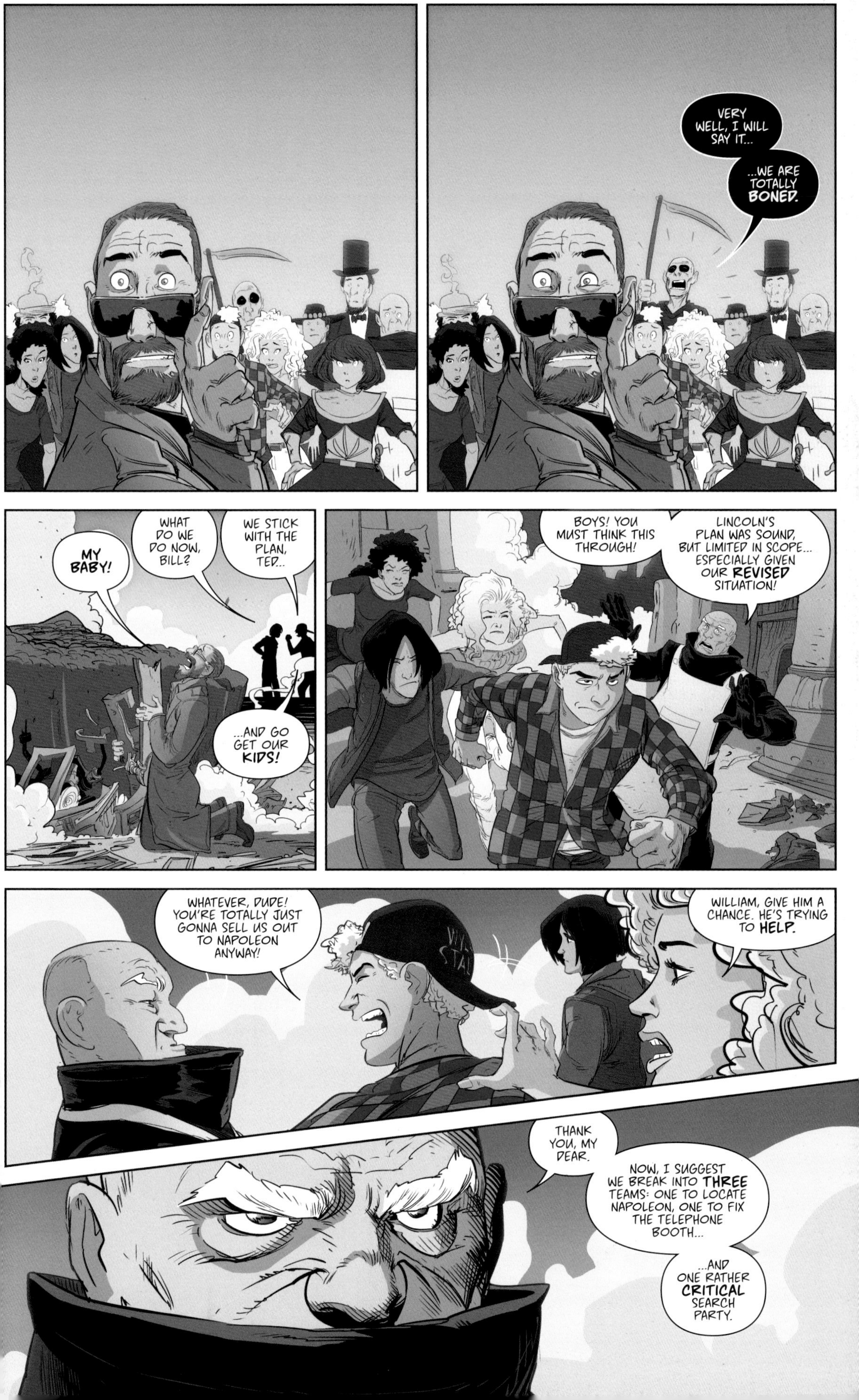
VERY WELL, I WILL SAY IT...
...WE ARE TOTALLY BONED.
MY BABY!
WHAT DO WE DO NOW, BILL?
WE STICK WITH THE PLAN, TED...
...AND GO GET OUR KIDS!
BOYS! YOU MUST THINK THIS THROUGH!
LINCOLN'S PLAN WAS SOUND, BUT LIMITED IN SCOPE... ESPECIALLY GIVEN OUR REVISED SITUATION!
WHATEVER, DUDE! YOU'RE TOTALLY JUST GONNA SELL US OUT TO NAPOLEON ANYWAY!
WILLIAM, GIVE HIM A CHANCE. HE'S TRYING TO HELP.
THANK YOU, MY DEAR.
NOW, I SUGGEST WE BREAK INTO THREE TEAMS: ONE TO LOCATE NAPOLEON, ONE TO FIX THE TELEPHONE BOOTH...
...AND ONE RATHER CRITICAL SEARCH PARTY.

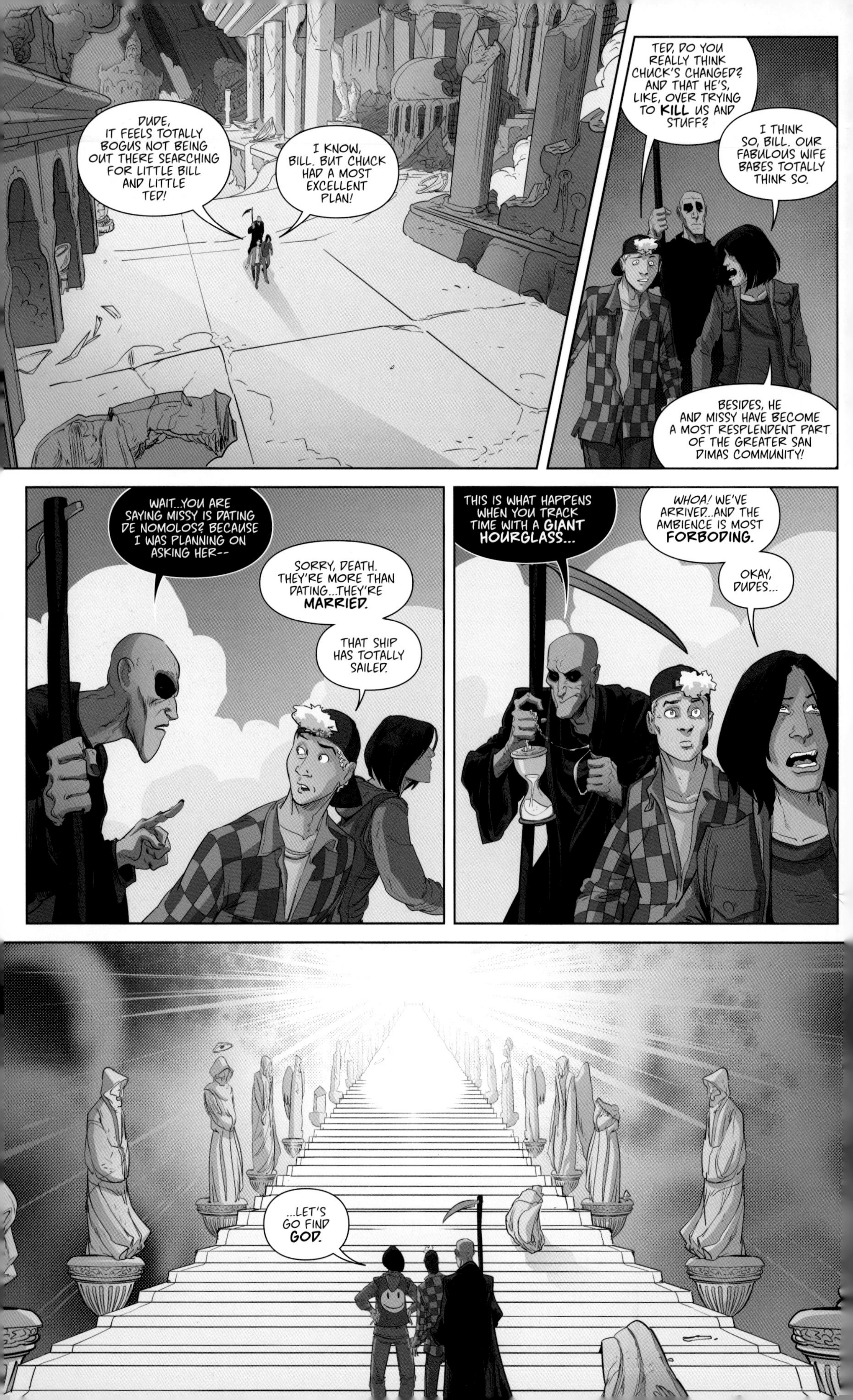
DUDE, IT FEELS TOTALLY BOGUS NOT BEING OUT THERE SEARCHING FOR LITTLE BILL AND LITTLE TED!
I KNOW, BILL. BUT CHUCK HAD A MOST EXCELLENT PLAN!
TED, DO YOU REALLY THINK CHUCK'S CHANGED? AND THAT HE'S, LIKE, OVER TRYING TO **KILL** US AND STUFF?
I THINK SO, BILL. OUR FABULOUS WIFE BABES TOTALLY THINK SO.
BESIDES, HE AND MISSY HAVE BECOME A MOST RESPLENDENT PART OF THE GREATER SAN DIMAS COMMUNITY!
WAIT...YOU ARE SAYING MISSY IS DATING DE NOMOLOS? BECAUSE I WAS PLANNING ON ASKING HER--
SORRY, DEATH. THEY'RE MORE THAN DATING...THEY'RE **MARRIED.**
THAT SHIP HAS TOTALLY SAILED.
THIS IS WHAT HAPPENS WHEN YOU TRACK TIME WITH A **GIANT HOURGLASS...**
WHOA! WE'VE ARRIVED...AND THE AMBIENCE IS MOST **FORBODING.**
OKAY, DUDES...
...LET'S GO FIND **GOD.**

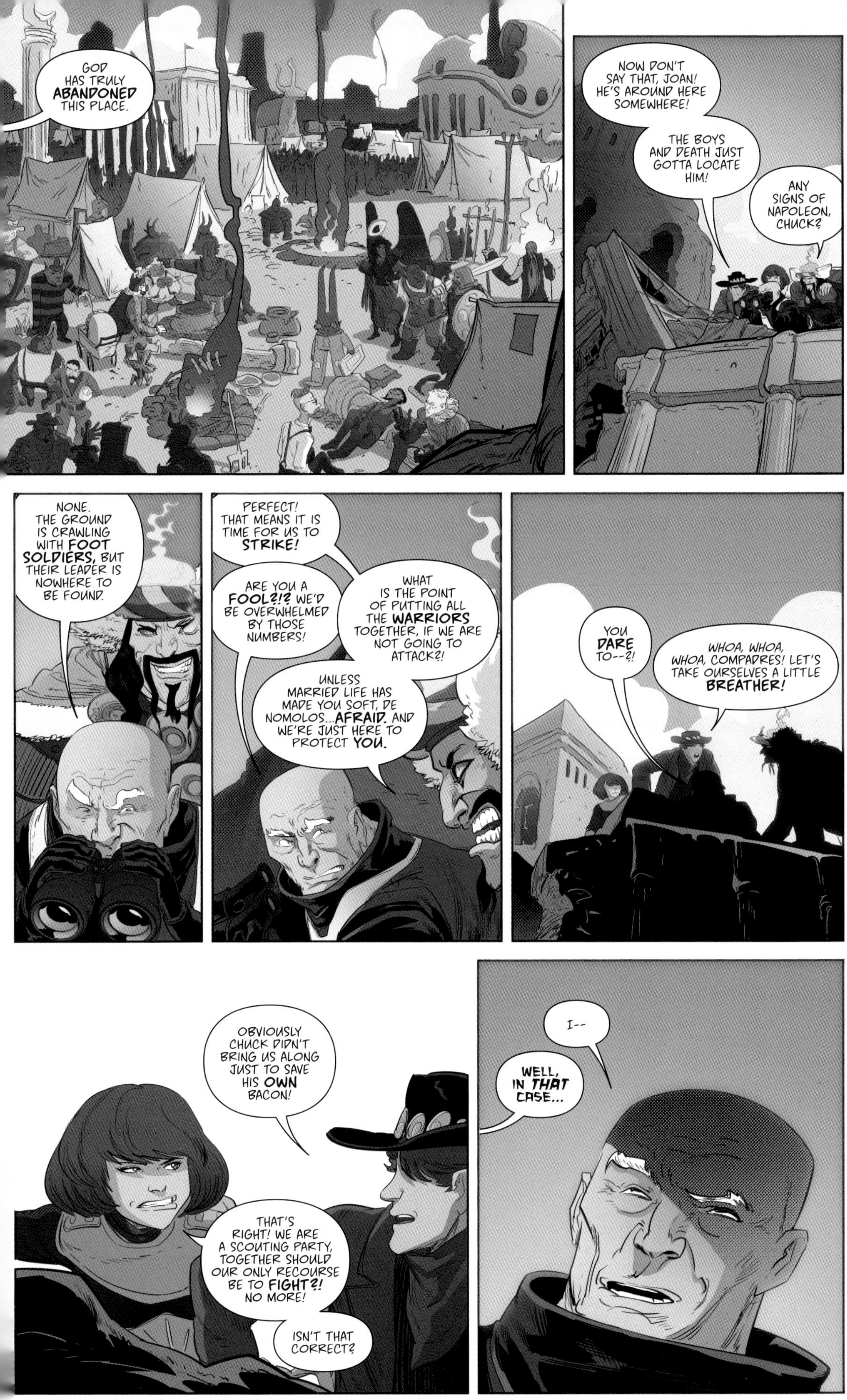
GOD HAS TRULY ABANDONED THIS PLACE.
NOW DON'T SAY THAT, JOAN! HE'S AROUND HERE SOMEWHERE!
THE BOYS AND DEATH JUST GOTTA LOCATE HIM!
ANY SIGNS OF NAPOLEON, CHUCK?
NONE. THE GROUND IS CRAWLING WITH FOOT SOLDIERS, BUT THEIR LEADER IS NOWHERE TO BE FOUND.
PERFECT! THAT MEANS IT IS TIME FOR US TO STRIKE!
ARE YOU A FOOL?!? WE'D BE OVERWHELMED BY THOSE NUMBERS!
WHAT IS THE POINT OF PUTTING ALL THE WARRIORS TOGETHER, IF WE ARE NOT GOING TO ATTACK?!
UNLESS MARRIED LIFE HAS MADE YOU SOFT, DE NOMOLOS...AFRAID. AND WE'RE JUST HERE TO PROTECT YOU.
YOU DARE TO--?!
WHOA, WHOA, WHOA, COMPADRES! LET'S TAKE OURSELVES A LITTLE BREATHER!
OBVIOUSLY CHUCK DIDN'T BRING US ALONG JUST TO SAVE HIS OWN BACON!
THAT'S RIGHT! WE ARE A SCOUTING PARTY, TOGETHER SHOULD OUR ONLY RECOURSE BE TO FIGHT?! NO MORE!
ISN'T THAT CORRECT?
I--
WELL, IN THAT CASE...

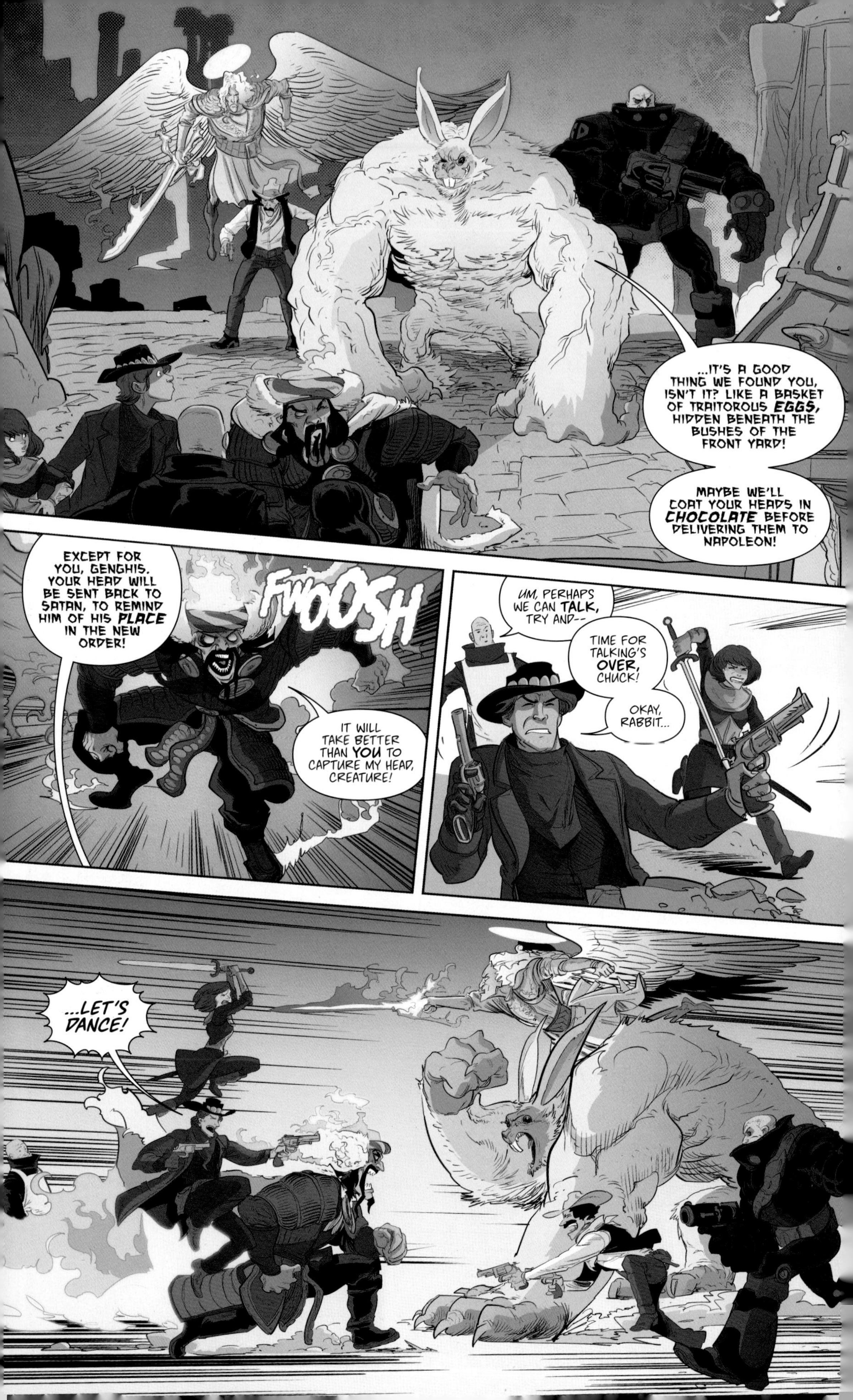

...IT'S A GOOD THING WE FOUND YOU, ISN'T IT? LIKE A BASKET OF TRAITOROUS EGGS, HIDDEN BENEATH THE BUSHES OF THE FRONT YARD!
MAYBE WE'LL COAT YOUR HEADS IN CHOCOLATE BEFORE DELIVERING THEM TO NAPOLEON!
EXCEPT FOR YOU, GENGHIS. YOUR HEAD WILL BE SENT BACK TO SATAN, TO REMIND HIM OF HIS PLACE IN THE NEW ORDER!
FWOOSH
IT WILL TAKE BETTER THAN YOU TO CAPTURE MY HEAD, CREATURE!
UM, PERHAPS WE CAN TALK, TRY AND--
TIME FOR TALKING'S OVER, CHUCK!
OKAY, RABBIT...
...LET'S DANCE!

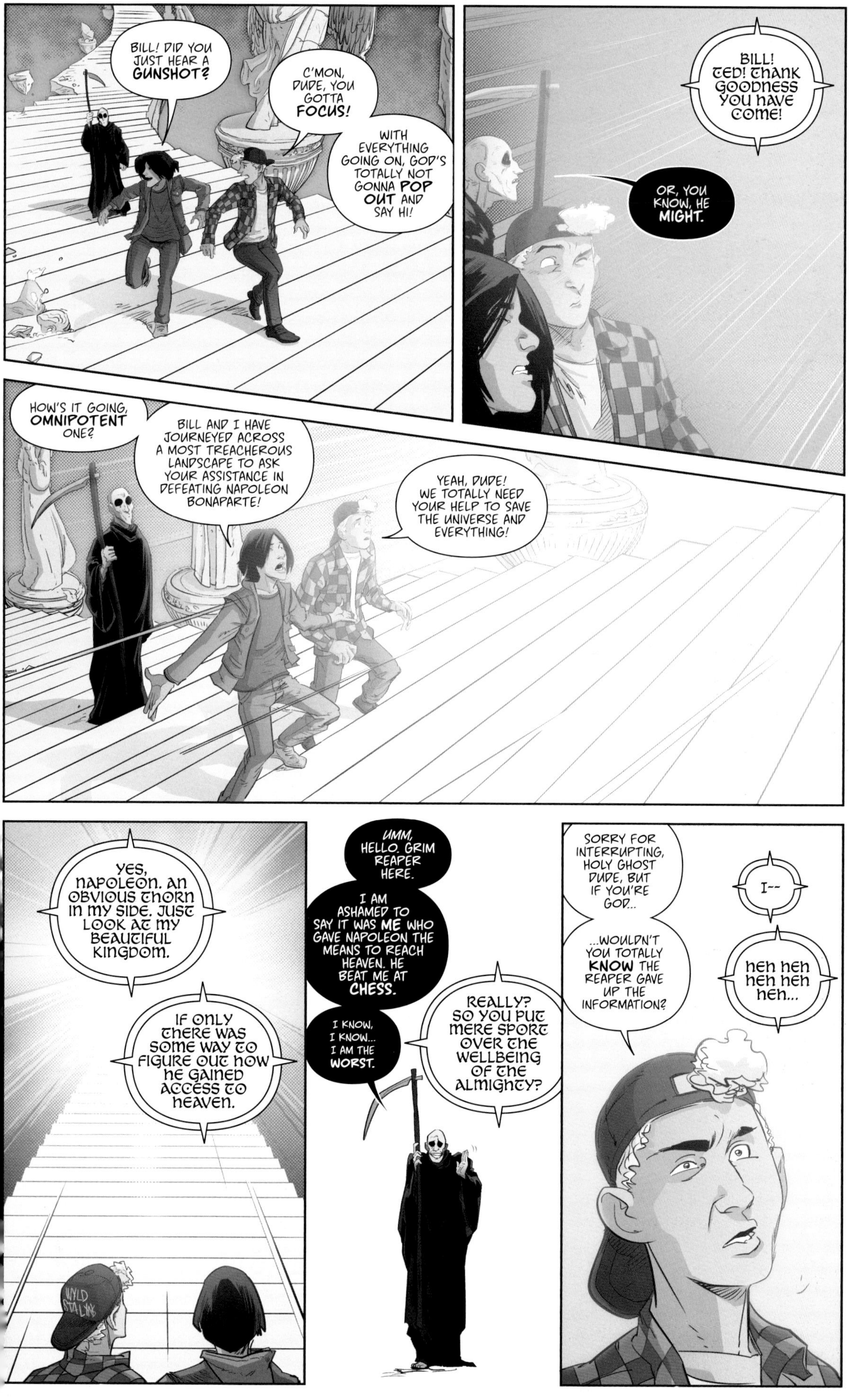
BILL! DID YOU JUST HEAR A GUNSHOT?
C'MON, DUDE, YOU GOTTA FOCUS!
WITH EVERYTHING GOING ON, GOD'S TOTALLY NOT GONNA POP OUT AND SAY HI!
BILL! TED! THANK GOODNESS YOU HAVE COME!
OR, YOU KNOW, HE MIGHT.
HOW'S IT GOING, OMNIPOTENT ONE?
BILL AND I HAVE JOURNEYED ACROSS A MOST TREACHEROUS LANDSCAPE TO ASK YOUR ASSISTANCE IN DEFEATING NAPOLEON BONAPARTE!
YEAH, DUDE! WE TOTALLY NEED YOUR HELP TO SAVE THE UNIVERSE AND EVERYTHING!
YES, NAPOLEON. AN OBVIOUS THORN IN MY SIDE. JUST LOOK AT MY BEAUTIFUL KINGDOM.
IF ONLY THERE WAS SOME WAY TO FIGURE OUT HOW HE GAINED ACCESS TO HEAVEN.
WYLD STALLYNS
UMM, HELLO. GRIM REAPER HERE.
I AM ASHAMED TO SAY IT WAS ME WHO GAVE NAPOLEON THE MEANS TO REACH HEAVEN. HE BEAT ME AT CHESS.
I KNOW, I KNOW... I AM THE WORST.
REALLY? SO YOU PUT MERE SPORT OVER THE WELLBEING OF THE ALMIGHTY?
SORRY FOR INTERRUPTING, HOLY GHOST DUDE, BUT IF YOU'RE GOD...
...WOULDN'T YOU TOTALLY KNOW THE REAPER GAVE UP THE INFORMATION?
I--
heh heh heh heh heh...

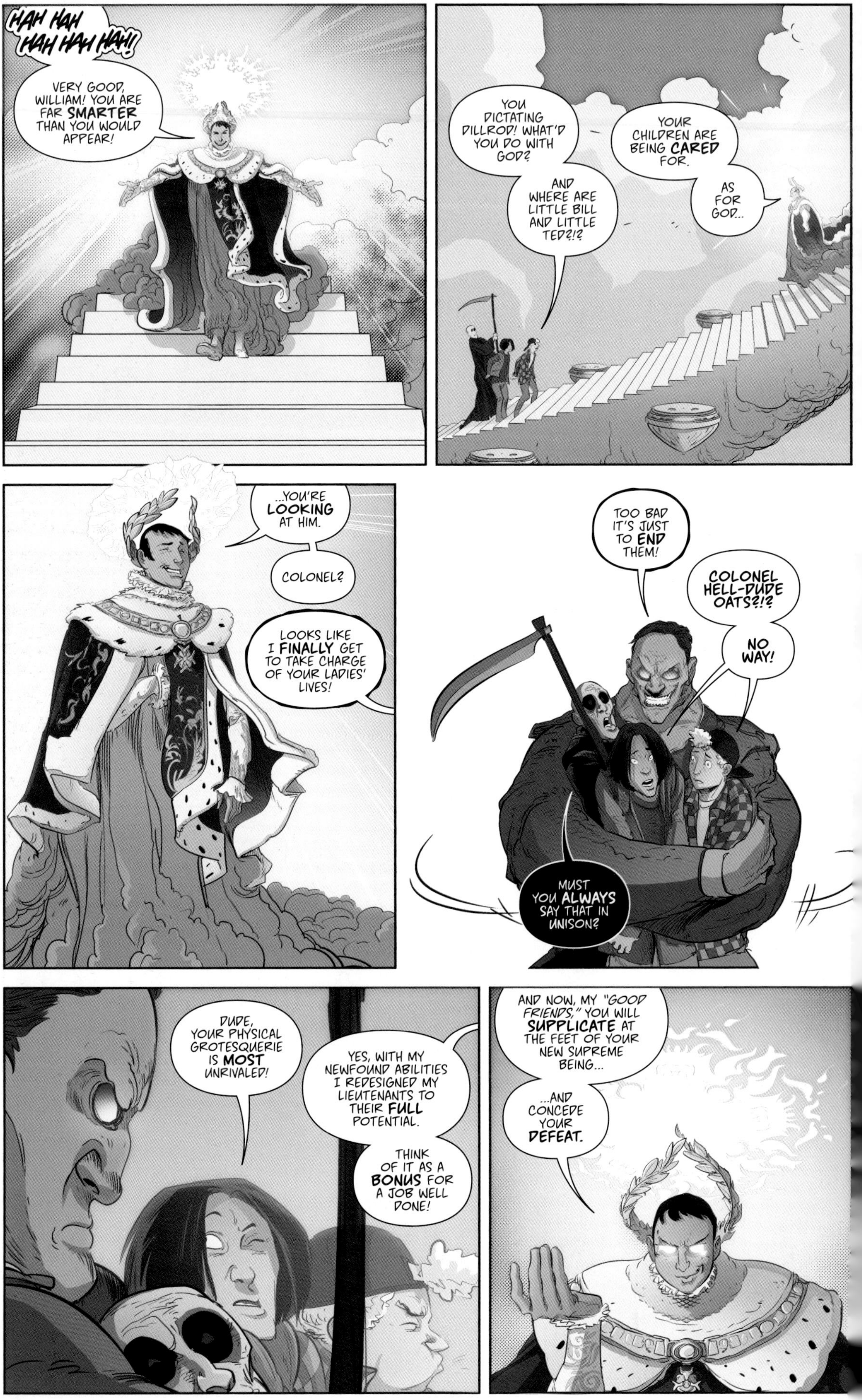
HAH HAH HAH HAH HAH!!
VERY GOOD, WILLIAM! YOU ARE FAR SMARTER THAN YOU WOULD APPEAR!
YOU DICTATING DILLROD! WHAT'D YOU DO WITH GOD?
AND WHERE ARE LITTLE BILL AND LITTLE TED?!?
YOUR CHILDREN ARE BEING CARED FOR.
AS FOR GOD...
...YOU'RE LOOKING AT HIM.
COLONEL?
LOOKS LIKE I FINALLY GET TO TAKE CHARGE OF YOUR LADIES' LIVES!
TOO BAD IT'S JUST TO END THEM!
COLONEL HELL-DUDE OATS?!?
NO WAY!
MUST YOU ALWAYS SAY THAT IN UNISON?
DUDE, YOUR PHYSICAL GROTESQUERIE IS MOST UNRIVALED!
YES, WITH MY NEWFOUND ABILITIES I REDESIGNED MY LIEUTENANTS TO THEIR FULL POTENTIAL.
THINK OF IT AS A BONUS FOR A JOB WELL DONE!
AND NOW, MY "GOOD FRIENDS," YOU WILL SUPPLICATE AT THE FEET OF YOUR NEW SUPREME BEING...
...AND CONCEDE YOUR DEFEAT.

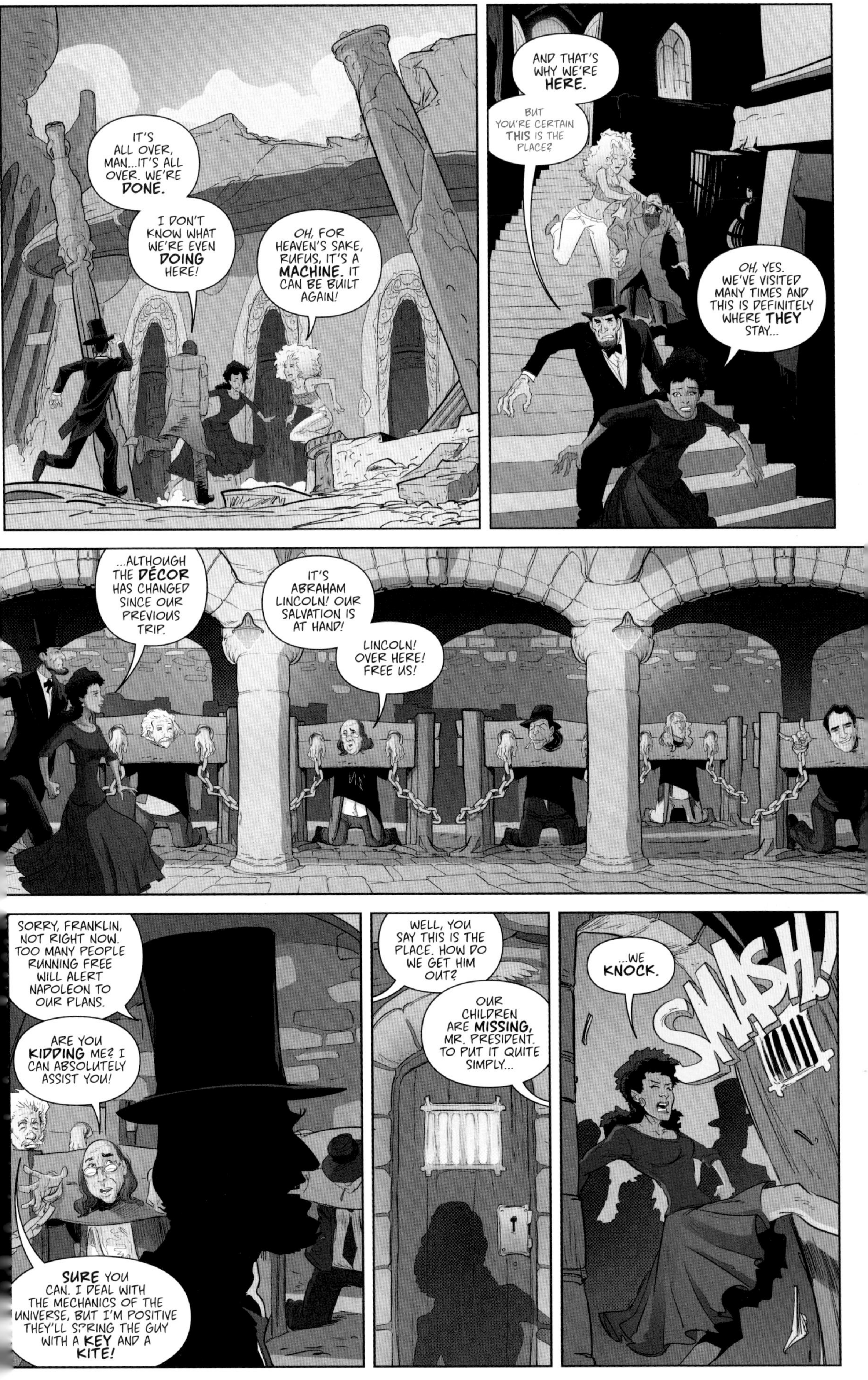
IT'S ALL OVER, MAN...IT'S ALL OVER. WE'RE DONE.
I DON'T KNOW WHAT WE'RE EVEN DOING HERE!
OH, FOR HEAVEN'S SAKE, RUFUS, IT'S A MACHINE. IT CAN BE BUILT AGAIN!
AND THAT'S WHY WE'RE HERE.
BUT YOU'RE CERTAIN THIS IS THE PLACE?
OH, YES. WE'VE VISITED MANY TIMES AND THIS IS DEFINITELY WHERE THEY STAY...
...ALTHOUGH THE DÉCOR HAS CHANGED SINCE OUR PREVIOUS TRIP.
IT'S ABRAHAM LINCOLN! OUR SALVATION IS AT HAND!
LINCOLN! OVER HERE! FREE US!
SORRY, FRANKLIN, NOT RIGHT NOW. TOO MANY PEOPLE RUNNING FREE WILL ALERT NAPOLEON TO OUR PLANS.
ARE YOU KIDDING ME? I CAN ABSOLUTELY ASSIST YOU!
SURE YOU CAN. I DEAL WITH THE MECHANICS OF THE UNIVERSE, BUT I'M POSITIVE THEY'LL SPRING THE GUY WITH A KEY AND A KITE!
WELL, YOU SAY THIS IS THE PLACE. HOW DO WE GET HIM OUT?
OUR CHILDREN ARE MISSING, MR. PRESIDENT. TO PUT IT QUITE SIMPLY...
...WE KNOCK.
SMASH!

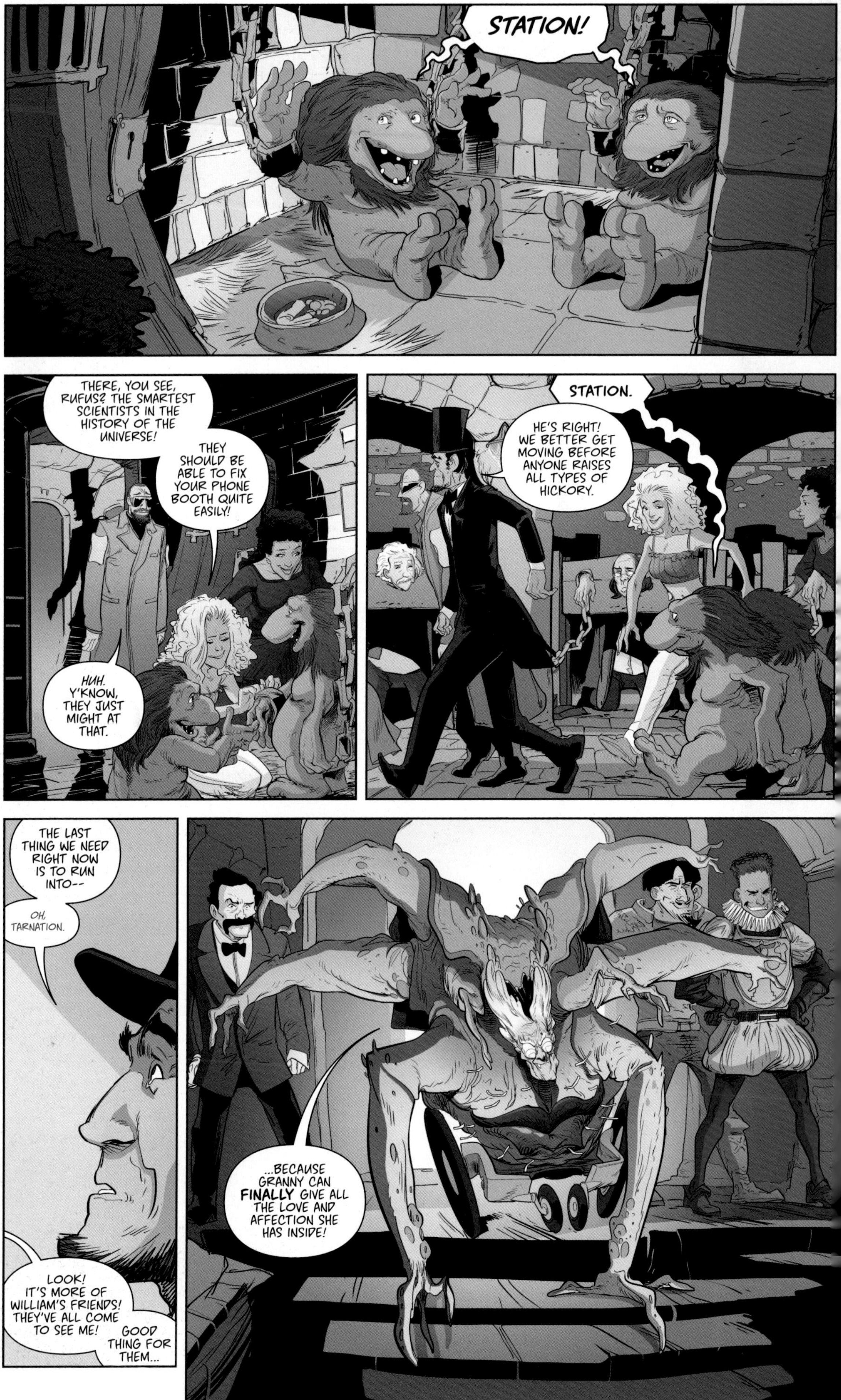
STATION!
THERE, YOU SEE, RUFUS? THE SMARTEST SCIENTISTS IN THE HISTORY OF THE UNIVERSE!
THEY SHOULD BE ABLE TO FIX YOUR PHONE BOOTH QUITE EASILY!
HUH. Y'KNOW, THEY JUST MIGHT AT THAT.
STATION.
HE'S RIGHT! WE BETTER GET MOVING BEFORE ANYONE RAISES ALL TYPES OF HICKORY.
THE LAST THING WE NEED RIGHT NOW IS TO RUN INTO--
OH, TARNATION.
LOOK! IT'S MORE OF WILLIAM'S FRIENDS! THEY'VE ALL COME TO SEE ME!
GOOD THING FOR THEM...
...BECAUSE GRANNY CAN FINALLY GIVE ALL THE LOVE AND AFFECTION SHE HAS INSIDE!

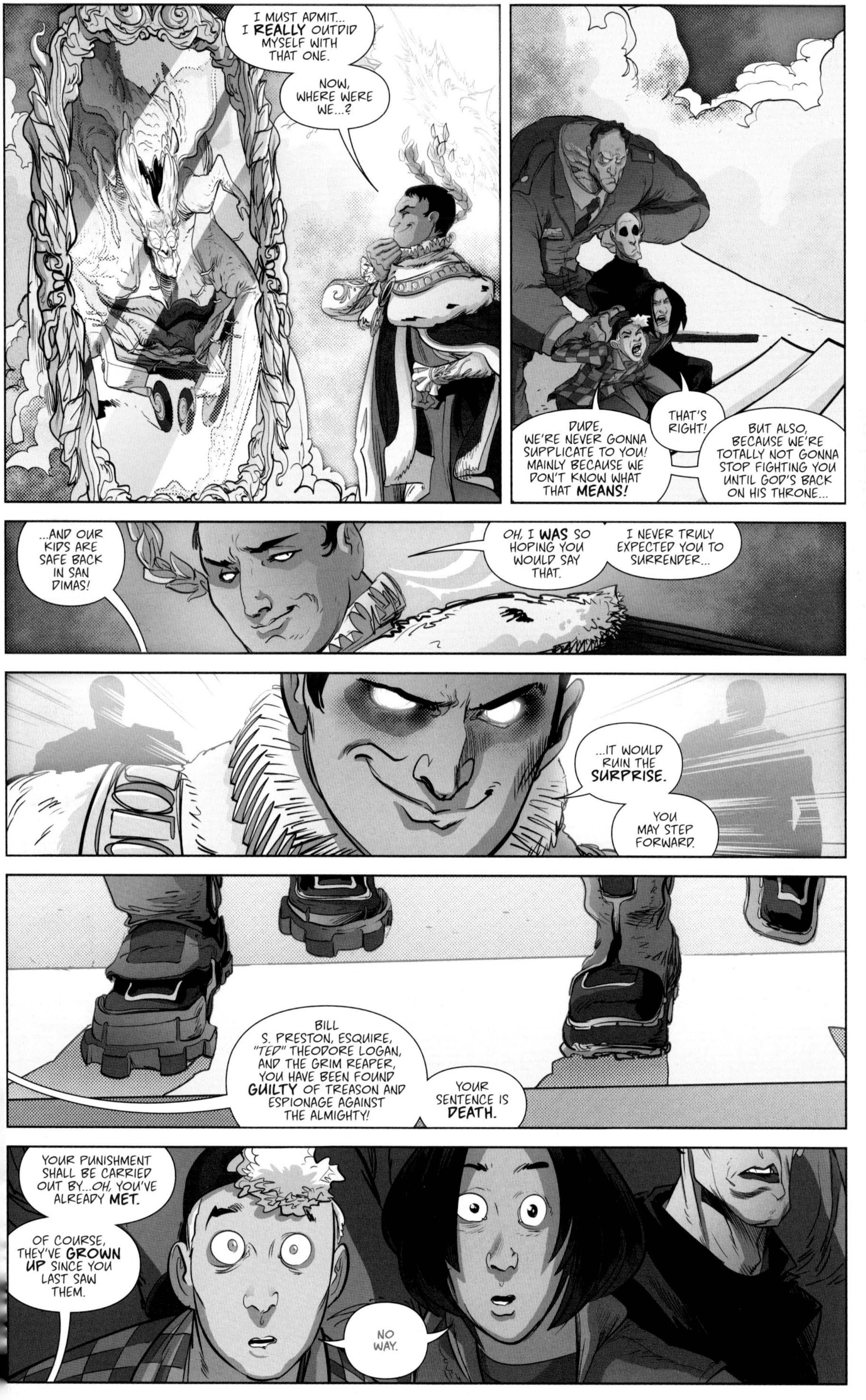
I MUST ADMIT... I **REALLY** OUTDID MYSELF WITH THAT ONE.
NOW, WHERE WERE WE...?
DUDE, WE'RE NEVER GONNA SUPPLICATE TO YOU! MAINLY BECAUSE WE DON'T KNOW WHAT THAT **MEANS!**
THAT'S RIGHT!
BUT ALSO, BECAUSE WE'RE TOTALLY NOT GONNA STOP FIGHTING YOU UNTIL GOD'S BACK ON HIS THRONE...
...AND OUR KIDS ARE SAFE BACK IN SAN DIMAS!
OH, I **WAS** SO HOPING YOU WOULD SAY THAT.
I NEVER TRULY EXPECTED YOU TO SURRENDER...
...IT WOULD RUIN THE **SURPRISE.**
YOU MAY STEP FORWARD.
BILL S. PRESTON, ESQUIRE, *"TED"* THEODORE LOGAN, AND THE GRIM REAPER, YOU HAVE BEEN FOUND **GUILTY** OF TREASON AND ESPIONAGE AGAINST THE ALMIGHTY!
YOUR SENTENCE IS **DEATH.**
YOUR PUNISHMENT SHALL BE CARRIED OUT BY...OH, YOU'VE ALREADY **MET.**
OF COURSE, THEY'VE **GROWN UP** SINCE YOU LAST SAW THEM.
NO WAY.

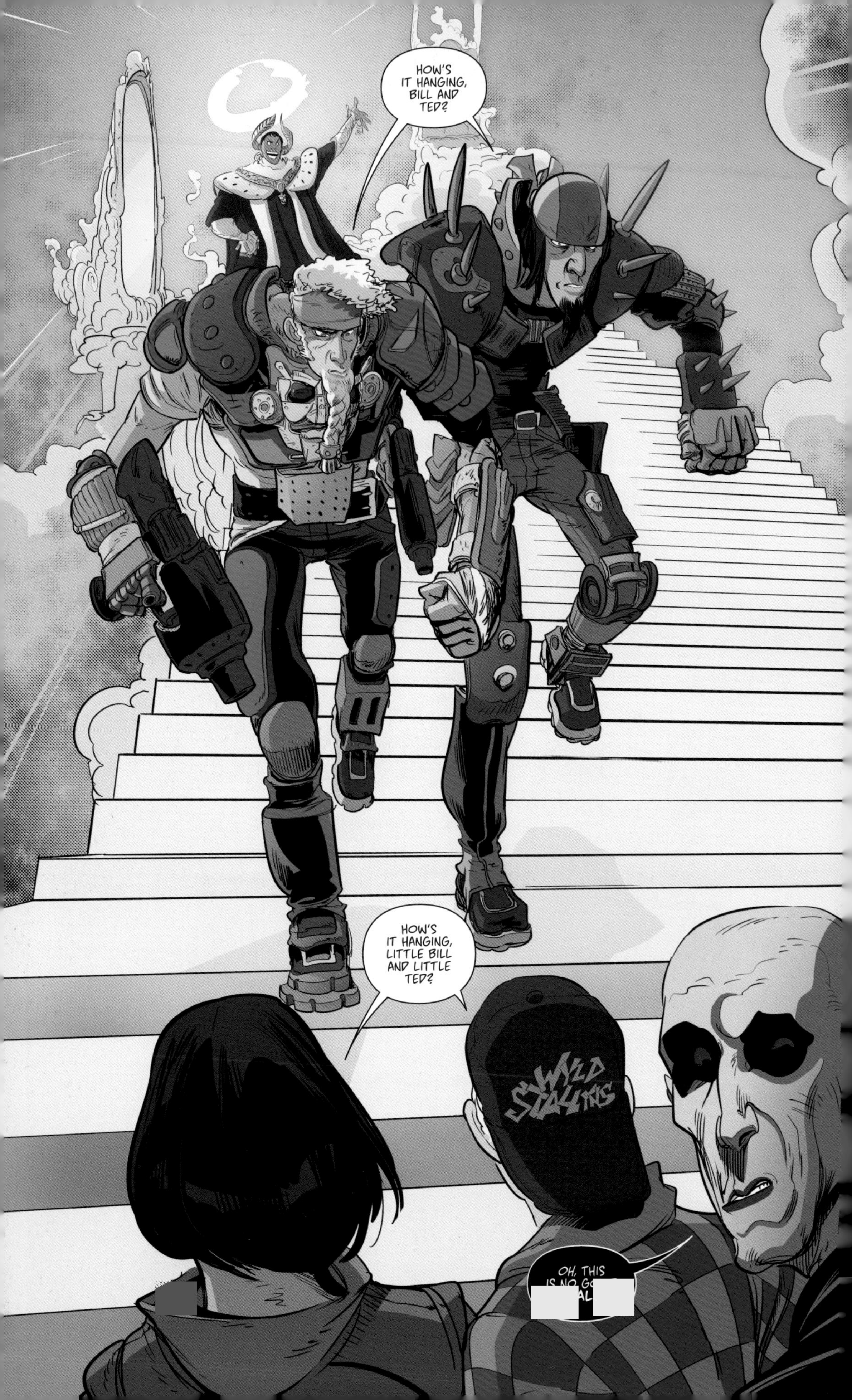
HOW'S IT HANGING, BILL AND TED?
HOW'S IT HANGING, LITTLE BILL AND LITTLE TED?
WYLD STALLYNS
OH, THIS IS NO

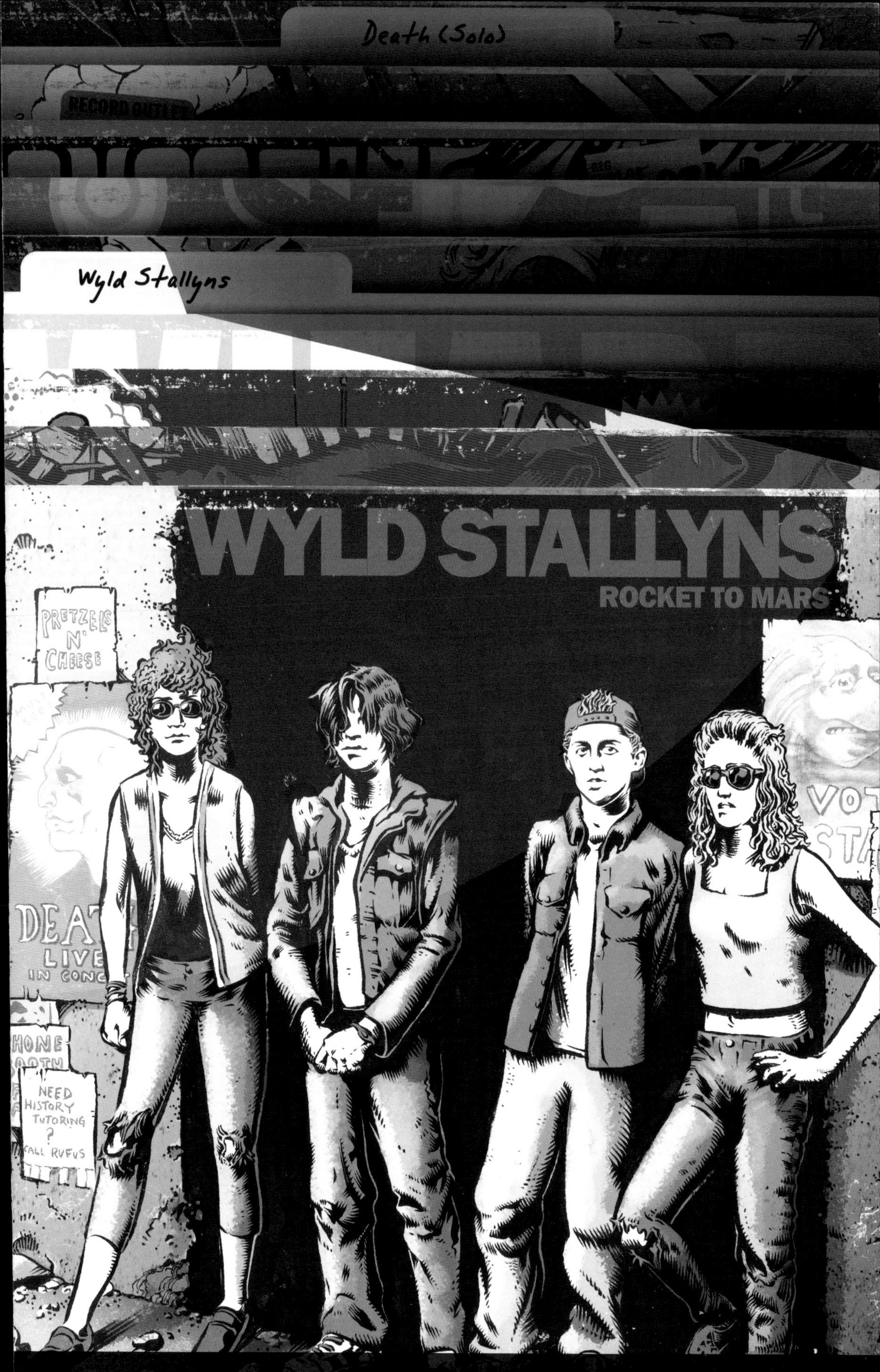

Death (Solo)
Wyld Stallyns
WYLD STALLYNS
ROCKET TO MARS
PRETZELS N' CHEESE
NEED HISTORY TUTORING ? CALL RUFUS

CONOR NOLAN ⚡ ISSUE THREE SUBSCRIPTION ALBUM COVER

CHAPTER FOUR
JUVENILE HELL

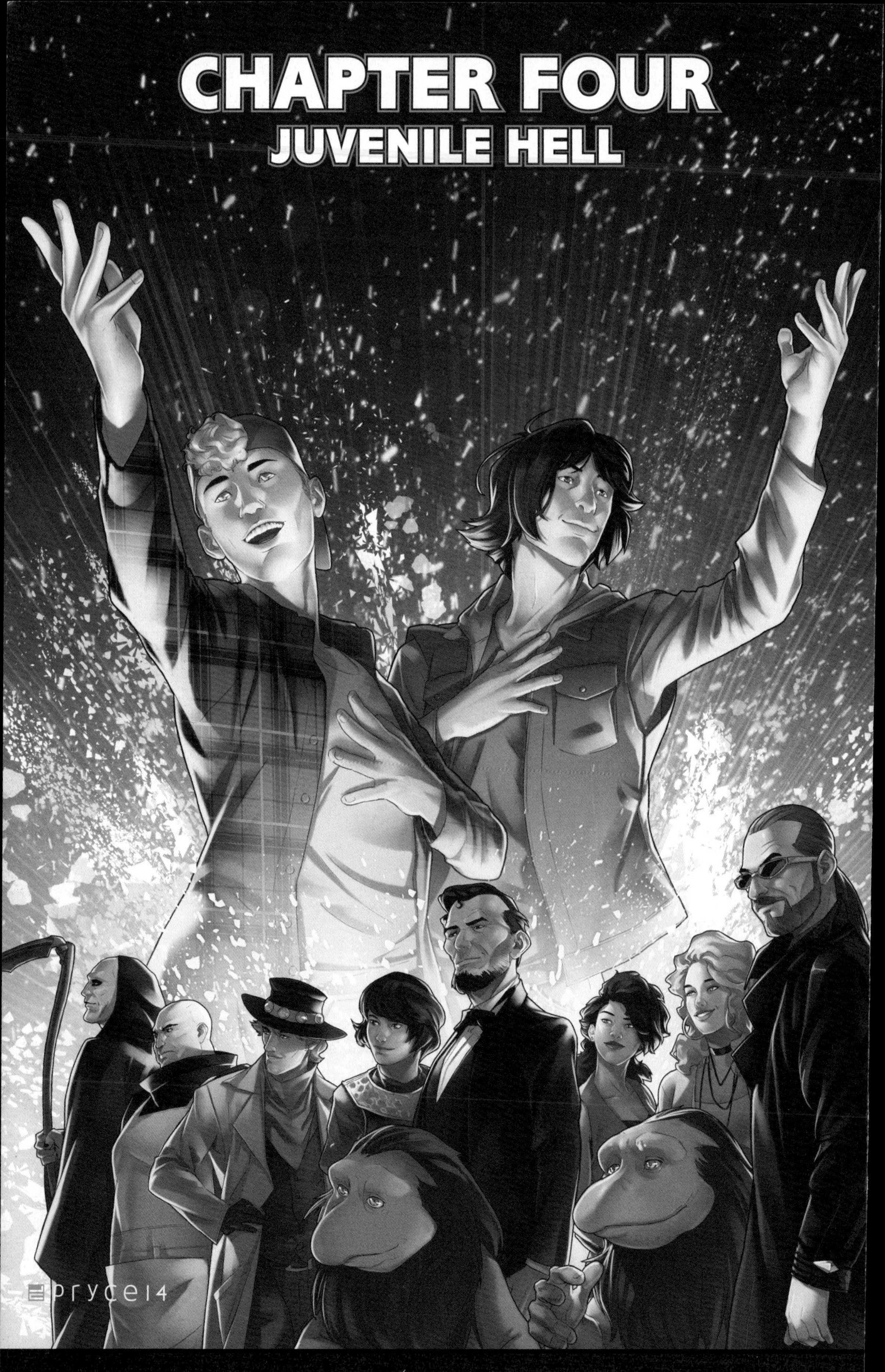
pryce14

JAMAL CAMPBELL ⚡ ISSUE FOUR MAIN COVER

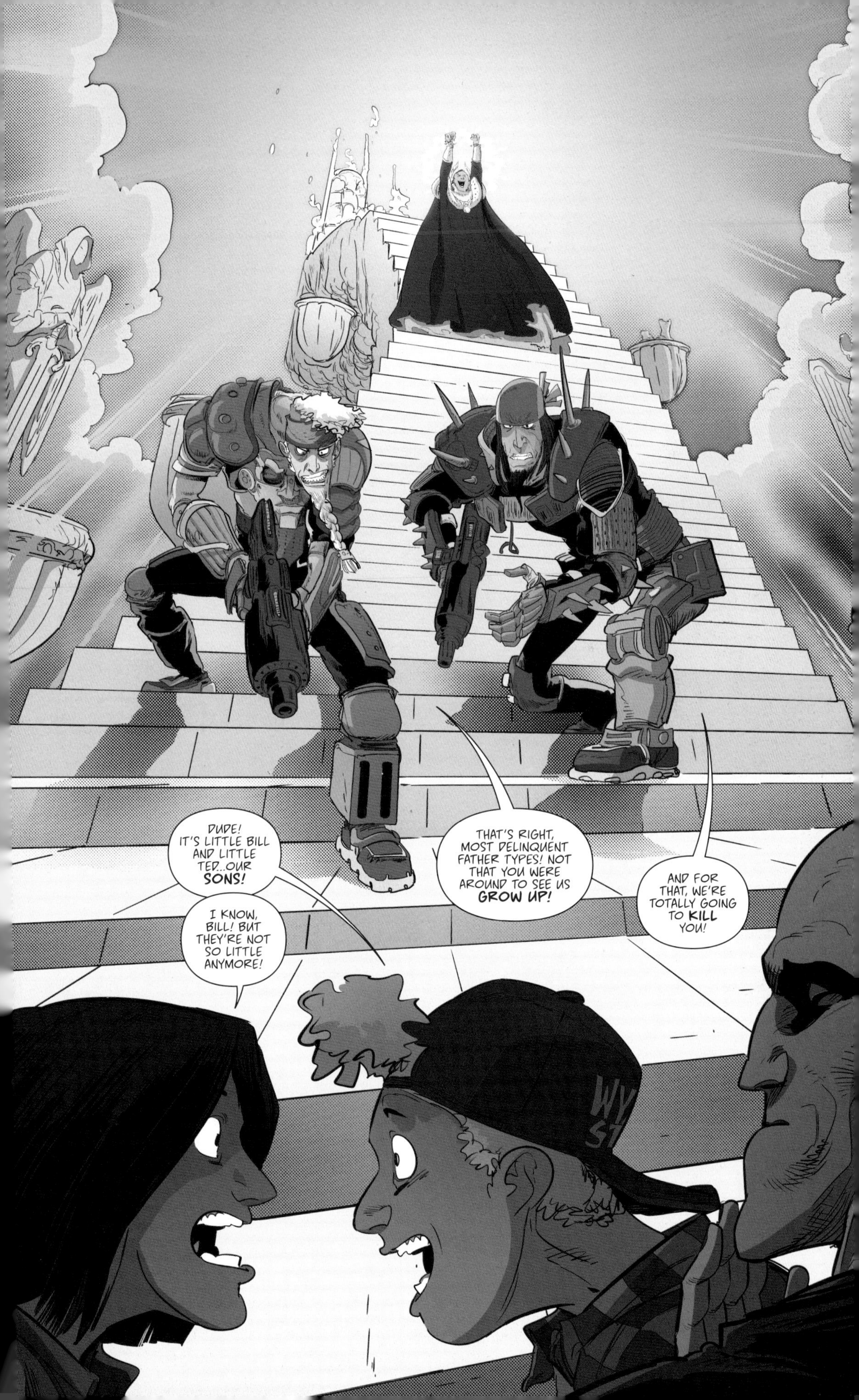
DUDE! IT'S LITTLE BILL AND LITTLE TED...OUR **SONS!**
I KNOW, BILL! BUT THEY'RE NOT SO LITTLE ANYMORE!
THAT'S RIGHT, MOST DELINQUENT FATHER TYPES! NOT THAT YOU WERE AROUND TO SEE US **GROW UP!**
AND FOR THAT, WE'RE TOTALLY GOING TO **KILL** YOU!

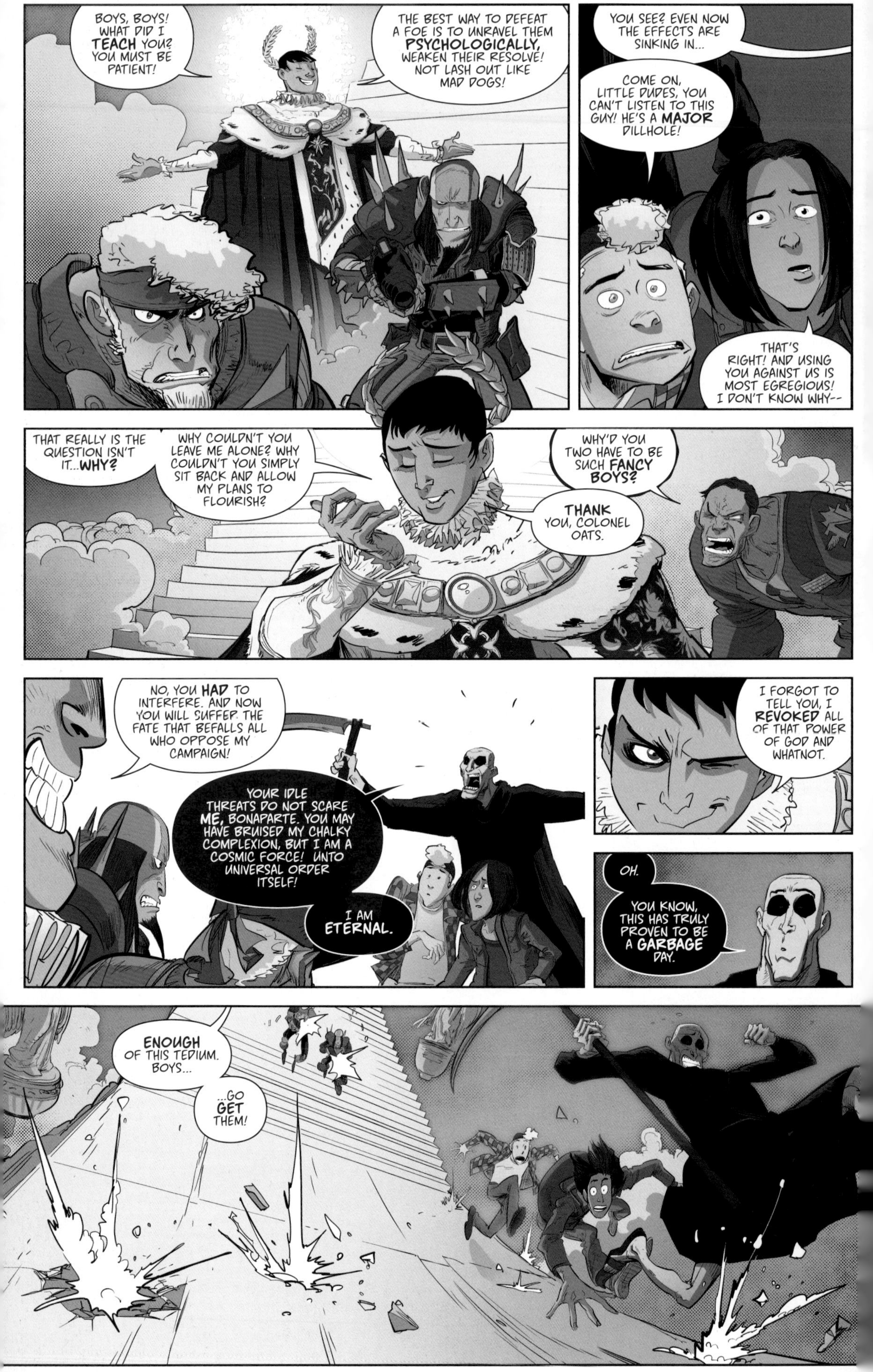
BOYS, BOYS! WHAT DID I TEACH YOU? YOU MUST BE PATIENT!
THE BEST WAY TO DEFEAT A FOE IS TO UNRAVEL THEM PSYCHOLOGICALLY, WEAKEN THEIR RESOLVE! NOT LASH OUT LIKE MAD DOGS!
YOU SEE? EVEN NOW THE EFFECTS ARE SINKING IN...
COME ON, LITTLE DUDES, YOU CAN'T LISTEN TO THIS GUY! HE'S A MAJOR DILLHOLE!
THAT'S RIGHT! AND USING YOU AGAINST US IS MOST EGREGIOUS! I DON'T KNOW WHY--
THAT REALLY IS THE QUESTION ISN'T IT...WHY?
WHY COULDN'T YOU LEAVE ME ALONE? WHY COULDN'T YOU SIMPLY SIT BACK AND ALLOW MY PLANS TO FLOURISH?
WHY'D YOU TWO HAVE TO BE SUCH FANCY BOYS?
THANK YOU, COLONEL OATS.
NO, YOU HAD TO INTERFERE. AND NOW YOU WILL SUFFER THE FATE THAT BEFALLS ALL WHO OPPOSE MY CAMPAIGN!
YOUR IDLE THREATS DO NOT SCARE ME, BONAPARTE. YOU MAY HAVE BRUISED MY CHALKY COMPLEXION, BUT I AM A COSMIC FORCE! UNTO UNIVERSAL ORDER ITSELF!
I AM ETERNAL.
I FORGOT TO TELL YOU, I REVOKED ALL OF THAT POWER OF GOD AND WHATNOT.
OH.
YOU KNOW, THIS HAS TRULY PROVEN TO BE A GARBAGE DAY.
ENOUGH OF THIS TEDIUM. BOYS...
...GO GET THEM!

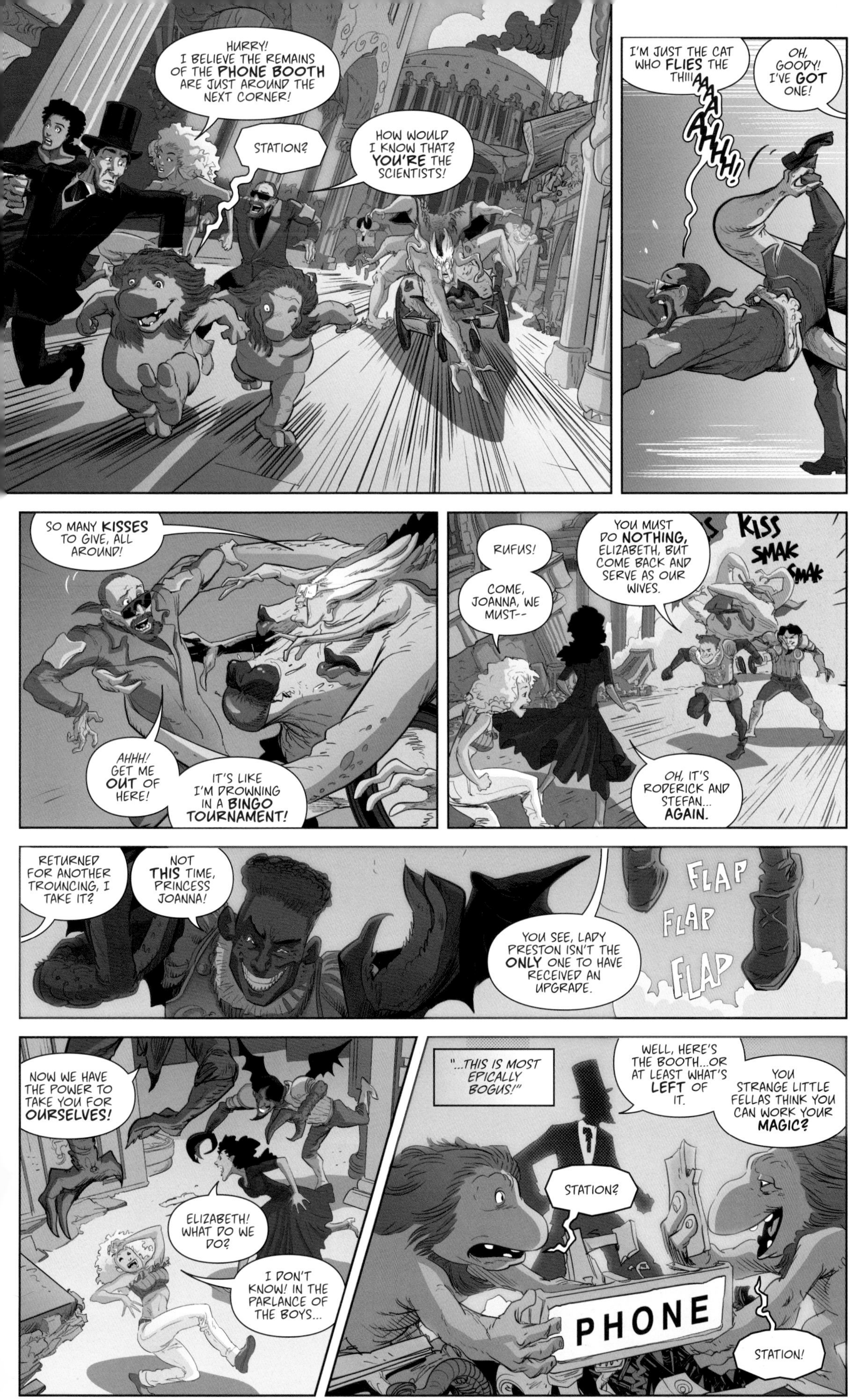
HURRY! I BELIEVE THE REMAINS OF THE PHONE BOOTH ARE JUST AROUND THE NEXT CORNER!
STATION?
HOW WOULD I KNOW THAT? YOU'RE THE SCIENTISTS!
I'M JUST THE CAT WHO FLIES THE THIIIAAAAAHHH!!
OH, GOODY! I'VE GOT ONE!
SO MANY KISSES TO GIVE, ALL AROUND!
AHHH! GET ME OUT OF HERE!
IT'S LIKE I'M DROWNING IN A BINGO TOURNAMENT!
KISS
SMAK
SMAK
RUFUS!
COME, JOANNA, WE MUST--
YOU MUST DO NOTHING, ELIZABETH, BUT COME BACK AND SERVE AS OUR WIVES.
OH, IT'S RODERICK AND STEFAN... AGAIN.
RETURNED FOR ANOTHER TROUNCING, I TAKE IT?
NOT THIS TIME, PRINCESS JOANNA!
YOU SEE, LADY PRESTON ISN'T THE ONLY ONE TO HAVE RECEIVED AN UPGRADE.
FLAP
FLAP
FLAP
NOW WE HAVE THE POWER TO TAKE YOU FOR OURSELVES!
ELIZABETH! WHAT DO WE DO?
I DON'T KNOW! IN THE PARLANCE OF THE BOYS...
"...THIS IS MOST EPICALLY BOGUS!"
WELL, HERE'S THE BOOTH...OR AT LEAST WHAT'S LEFT OF IT.
YOU STRANGE LITTLE FELLAS THINK YOU CAN WORK YOUR MAGIC?
STATION?
PHONE
STATION!

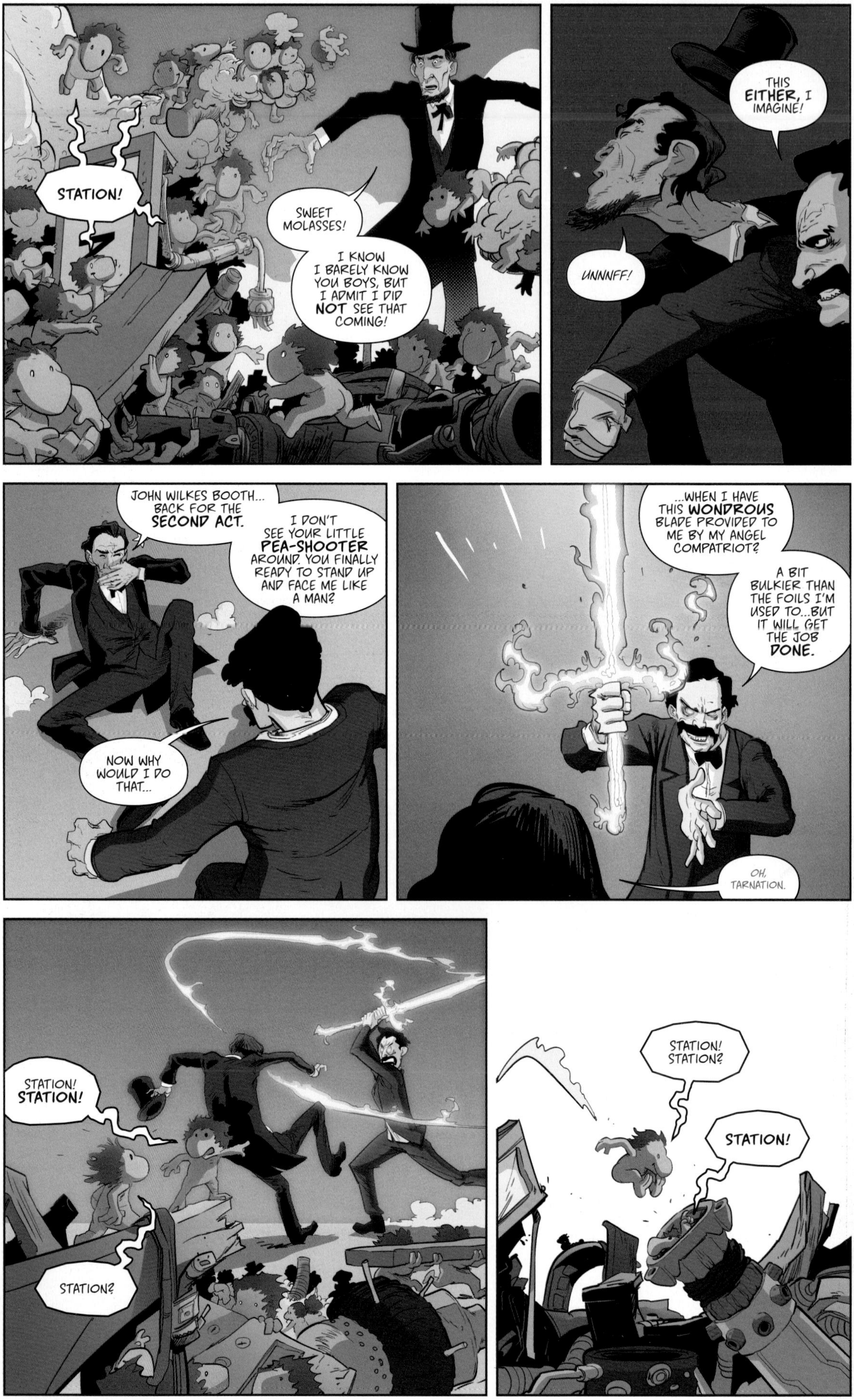
STATION!
SWEET MOLASSES!
I KNOW I BARELY KNOW YOU BOYS, BUT I ADMIT I DID NOT SEE THAT COMING!
THIS EITHER, I IMAGINE!
UNNNFF!
JOHN WILKES BOOTH... BACK FOR THE SECOND ACT.
I DON'T SEE YOUR LITTLE PEA-SHOOTER AROUND. YOU FINALLY READY TO STAND UP AND FACE ME LIKE A MAN?
NOW WHY WOULD I DO THAT...
...WHEN I HAVE THIS WONDROUS BLADE PROVIDED TO ME BY MY ANGEL COMPATRIOT?
A BIT BULKIER THAN THE FOILS I'M USED TO...BUT IT WILL GET THE JOB DONE.
OH, TARNATION.
STATION! STATION!
STATION?
STATION! STATION?
STATION!

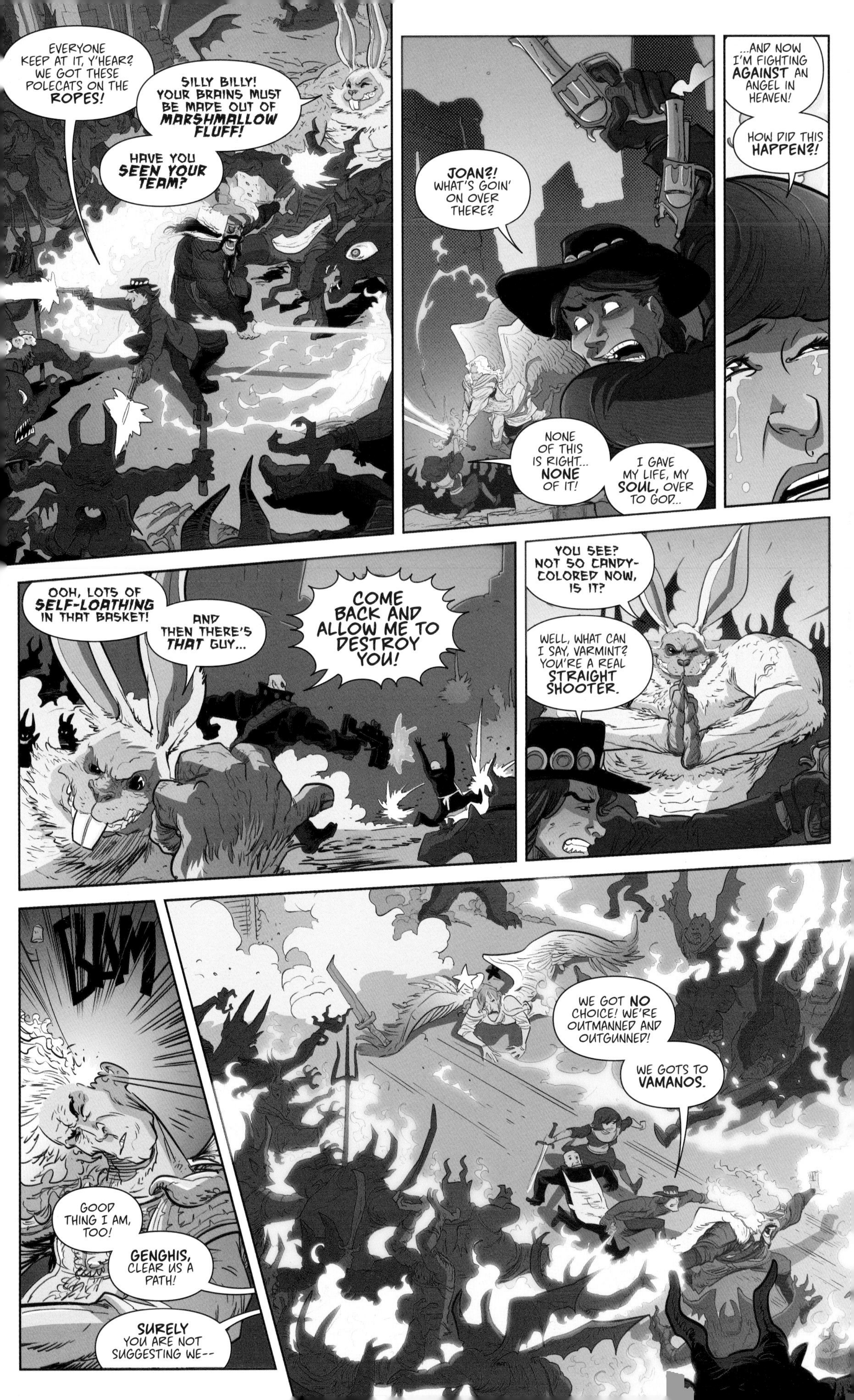
EVERYONE KEEP AT IT, Y'HEAR? WE GOT THESE POLECATS ON THE ROPES!
SILLY BILLY! YOUR BRAINS MUST BE MADE OUT OF MARSHMALLOW FLUFF!
HAVE YOU SEEN YOUR TEAM?
JOAN?! WHAT'S GOIN' ON OVER THERE?
NONE OF THIS IS RIGHT... NONE OF IT!
I GAVE MY LIFE, MY SOUL, OVER TO GOD...
...AND NOW I'M FIGHTING AGAINST AN ANGEL IN HEAVEN!
HOW DID THIS HAPPEN?!
OOH, LOTS OF SELF-LOATHING IN THAT BASKET!
AND THEN THERE'S THAT GUY...
COME BACK AND ALLOW ME TO DESTROY YOU!
YOU SEE? NOT SO CANDY-COLORED NOW, IS IT?
WELL, WHAT CAN I SAY, VARMINT? YOU'RE A REAL STRAIGHT SHOOTER.
BLAM
GOOD THING I AM, TOO!
GENGHIS, CLEAR US A PATH!
SURELY YOU ARE NOT SUGGESTING WE--
WE GOT NO CHOICE! WE'RE OUTMANNED AND OUTGUNNED!
WE GOTS TO VAMANOS.

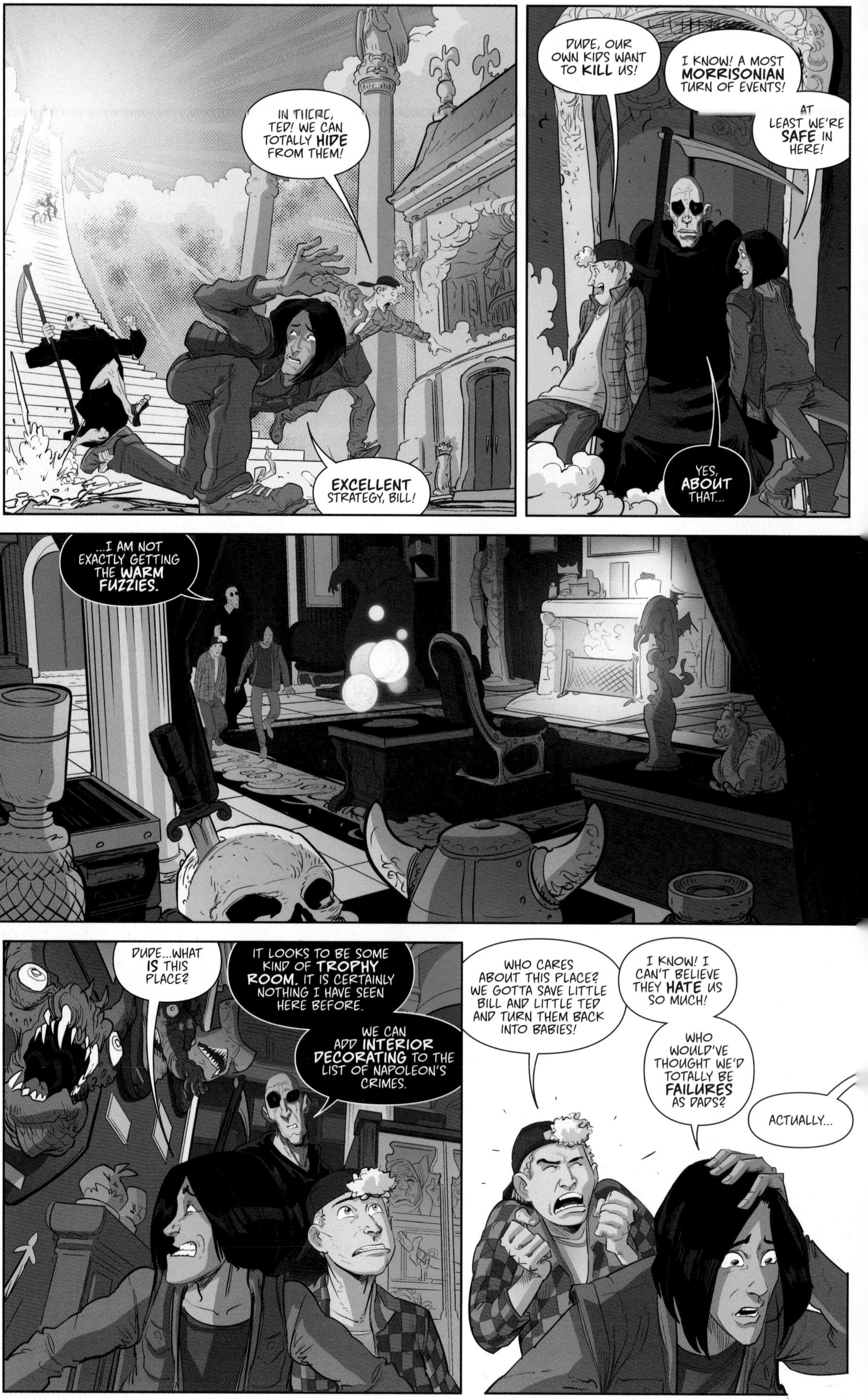
IN THERE, TED! WE CAN TOTALLY HIDE FROM THEM!
EXCELLENT STRATEGY, BILL!
DUDE, OUR OWN KIDS WANT TO KILL US!
I KNOW! A MOST MORRISONIAN TURN OF EVENTS!
AT LEAST WE'RE SAFE IN HERE!
YES, ABOUT THAT...
...I AM NOT EXACTLY GETTING THE WARM FUZZIES.
DUDE...WHAT IS THIS PLACE?
IT LOOKS TO BE SOME KIND OF TROPHY ROOM. IT IS CERTAINLY NOTHING I HAVE SEEN HERE BEFORE.
WE CAN ADD INTERIOR DECORATING TO THE LIST OF NAPOLEON'S CRIMES.
WHO CARES ABOUT THIS PLACE? WE GOTTA SAVE LITTLE BILL AND LITTLE TED AND TURN THEM BACK INTO BABIES!
I KNOW! I CAN'T BELIEVE THEY HATE US SO MUCH!
WHO WOULD'VE THOUGHT WE'D TOTALLY BE FAILURES AS DADS?
ACTUALLY...

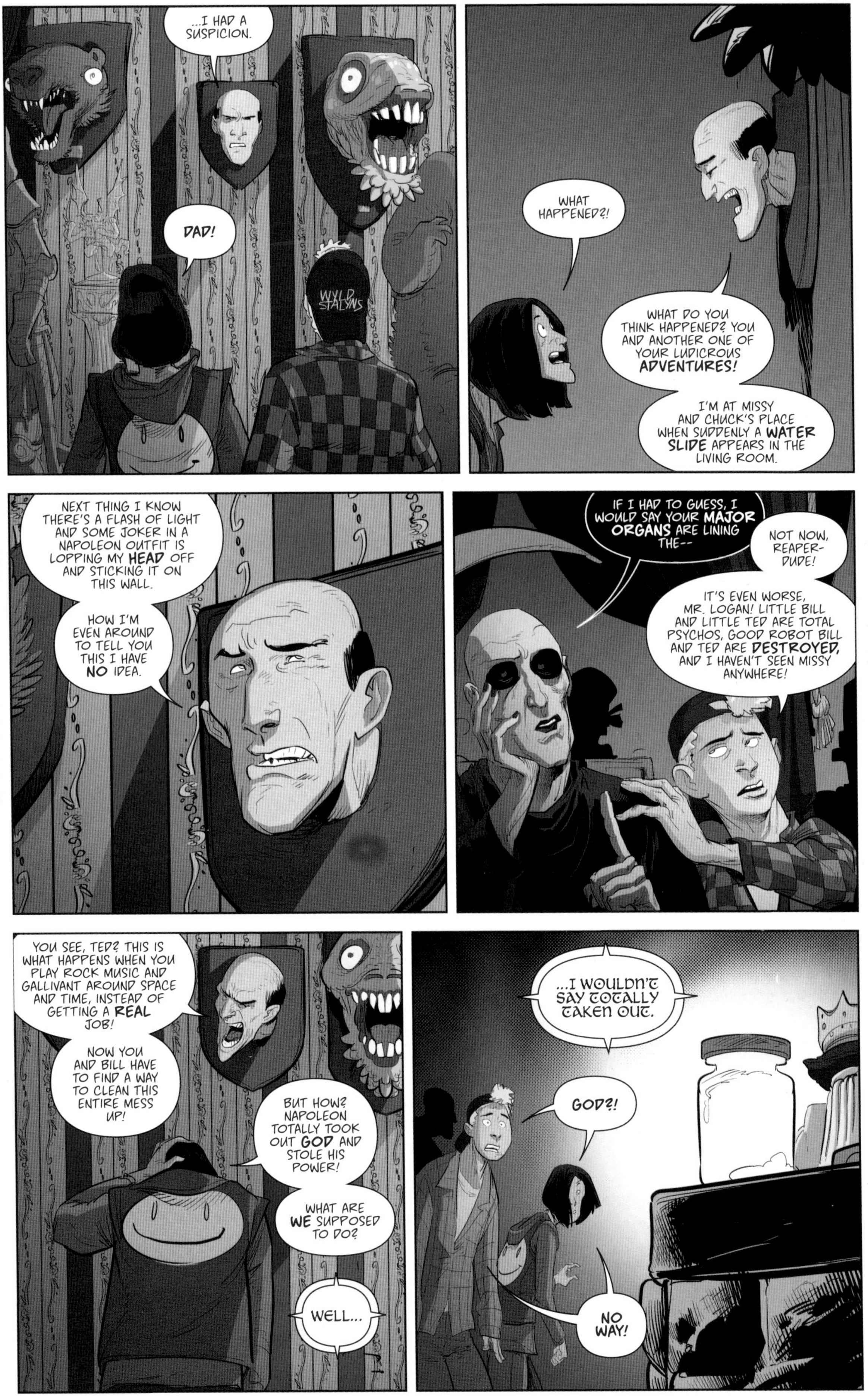
...I HAD A SUSPICION.
DAD!
WYLD STALYNS
WHAT HAPPENED?!
WHAT DO YOU THINK HAPPENED? YOU AND ANOTHER ONE OF YOUR LUDICROUS ADVENTURES!
I'M AT MISSY AND CHUCK'S PLACE WHEN SUDDENLY A WATER SLIDE APPEARS IN THE LIVING ROOM.
NEXT THING I KNOW THERE'S A FLASH OF LIGHT AND SOME JOKER IN A NAPOLEON OUTFIT IS LOPPING MY HEAD OFF AND STICKING IT ON THIS WALL.
HOW I'M EVEN AROUND TO TELL YOU THIS I HAVE NO IDEA.
IF I HAD TO GUESS, I WOULD SAY YOUR MAJOR ORGANS ARE LINING THE--
NOT NOW, REAPER-DUDE!
IT'S EVEN WORSE, MR. LOGAN! LITTLE BILL AND LITTLE TED ARE TOTAL PSYCHOS, GOOD ROBOT BILL AND TED ARE DESTROYED, AND I HAVEN'T SEEN MISSY ANYWHERE!
YOU SEE, TED? THIS IS WHAT HAPPENS WHEN YOU PLAY ROCK MUSIC AND GALLIVANT AROUND SPACE AND TIME, INSTEAD OF GETTING A REAL JOB!
NOW YOU AND BILL HAVE TO FIND A WAY TO CLEAN THIS ENTIRE MESS UP!
BUT HOW? NAPOLEON TOTALLY TOOK OUT GOD AND STOLE HIS POWER!
WHAT ARE WE SUPPOSED TO DO?
WELL...
...I WOULDN'T SAY TOTALLY TAKEN OUT.
GOD?!
NO WAY!

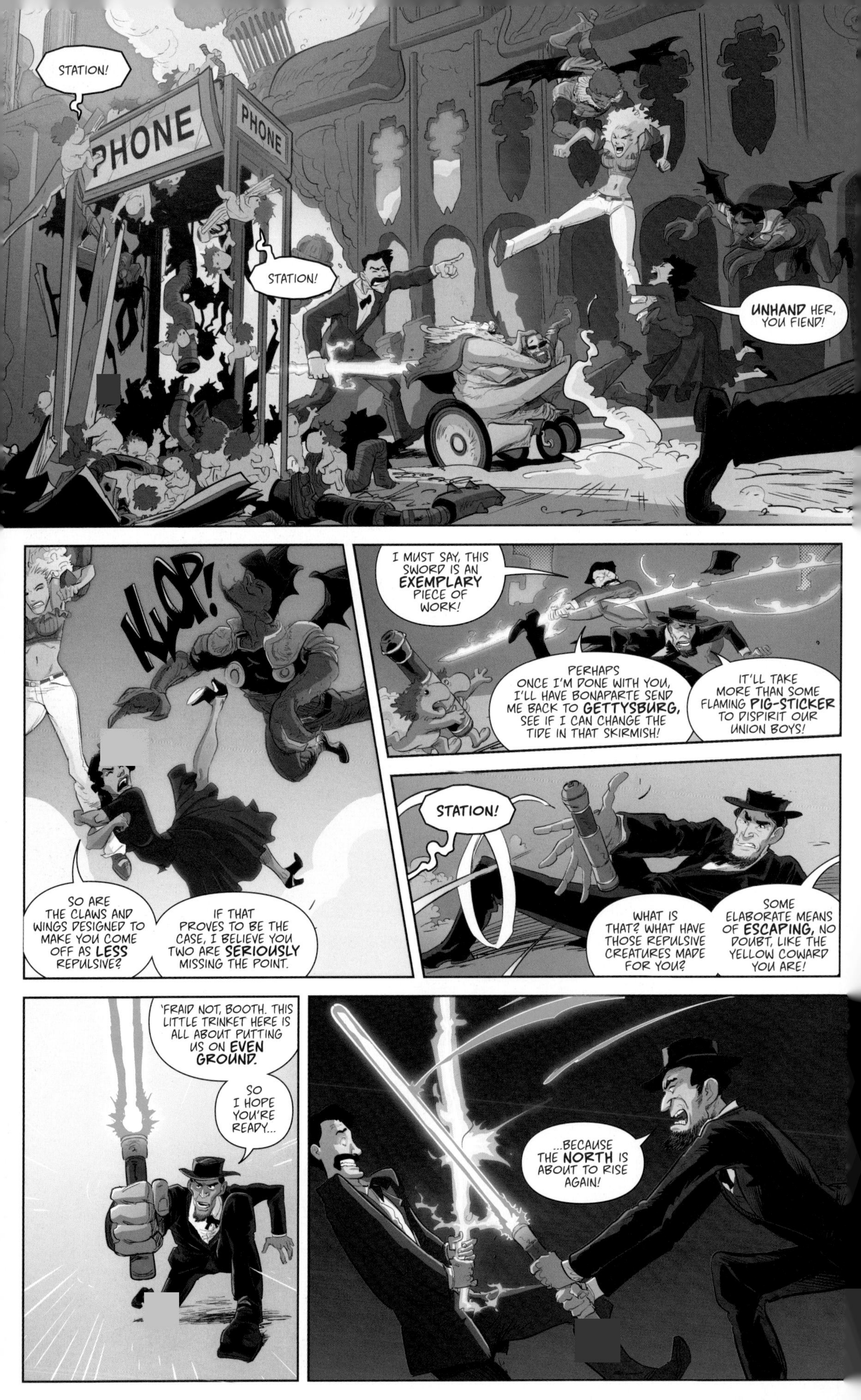
STATION!
PHONE
PHONE
STATION!
UNHAND HER, YOU FIEND!
KLOP!
SO ARE THE CLAWS AND WINGS DESIGNED TO MAKE YOU COME OFF AS LESS REPULSIVE?
IF THAT PROVES TO BE THE CASE, I BELIEVE YOU TWO ARE SERIOUSLY MISSING THE POINT.
I MUST SAY, THIS SWORD IS AN EXEMPLARY PIECE OF WORK!
PERHAPS ONCE I'M DONE WITH YOU, I'LL HAVE BONAPARTE SEND ME BACK TO GETTYSBURG, SEE IF I CAN CHANGE THE TIDE IN THAT SKIRMISH!
IT'LL TAKE MORE THAN SOME FLAMING PIG-STICKER TO DISPIRIT OUR UNION BOYS!
STATION!
WHAT IS THAT? WHAT HAVE THOSE REPULSIVE CREATURES MADE FOR YOU?
SOME ELABORATE MEANS OF ESCAPING, NO DOUBT, LIKE THE YELLOW COWARD YOU ARE!
'FRAID NOT, BOOTH. THIS LITTLE TRINKET HERE IS ALL ABOUT PUTTING US ON EVEN GROUND.
SO I HOPE YOU'RE READY...
...BECAUSE THE NORTH IS ABOUT TO RISE AGAIN!

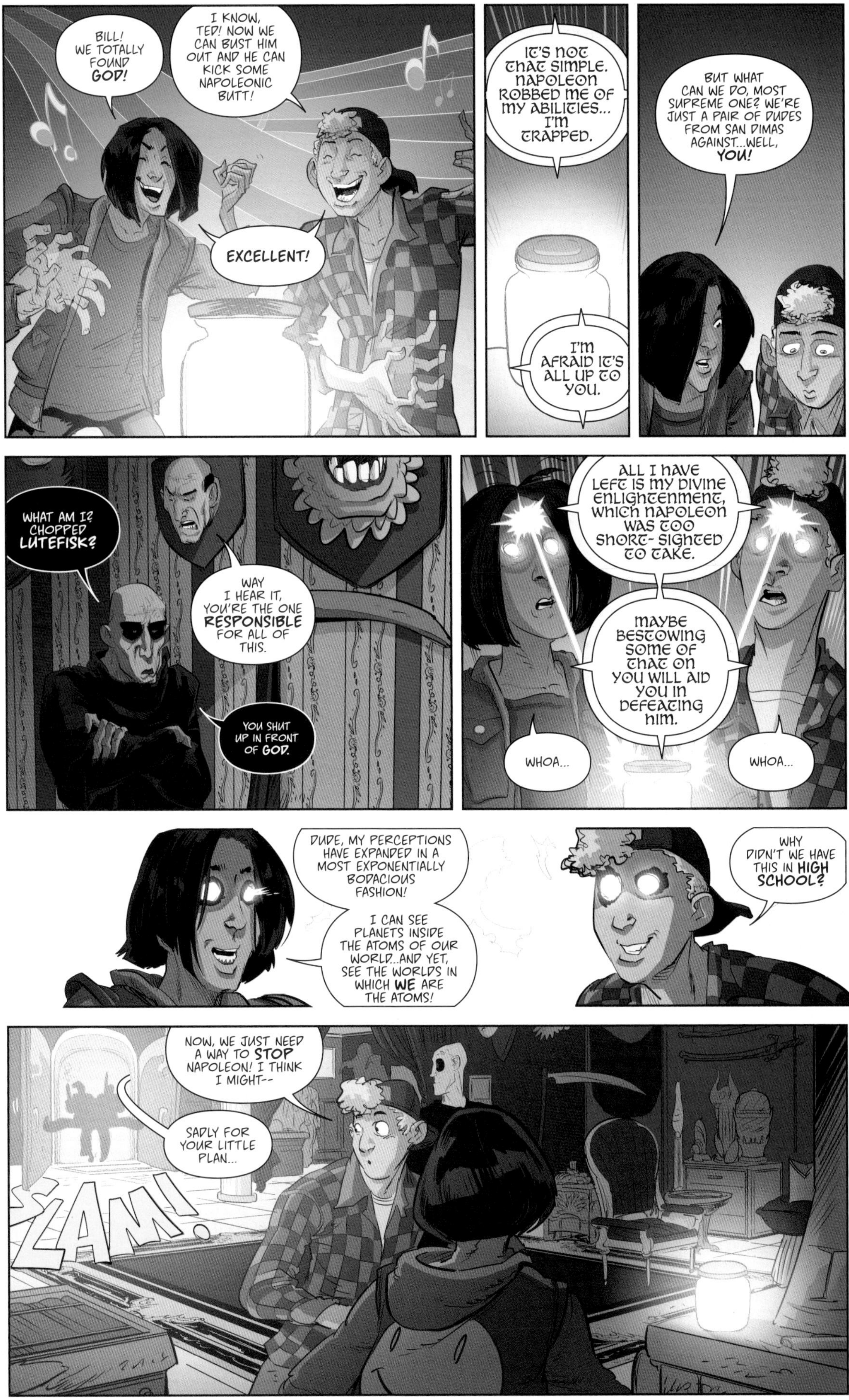
BILL! WE TOTALLY FOUND GOD!
I KNOW, TED! NOW WE CAN BUST HIM OUT AND HE CAN KICK SOME NAPOLEONIC BUTT!
EXCELLENT!
IT'S NOT THAT SIMPLE. NAPOLEON ROBBED ME OF MY ABILITIES... I'M TRAPPED.
I'M AFRAID IT'S ALL UP TO YOU.
BUT WHAT CAN WE DO, MOST SUPREME ONE? WE'RE JUST A PAIR OF DUDES FROM SAN DIMAS AGAINST...WELL, YOU!
WHAT AM I? CHOPPED LUTEFISK?
WAY I HEAR IT, YOU'RE THE ONE RESPONSIBLE FOR ALL OF THIS.
YOU SHUT UP IN FRONT OF GOD.
ALL I HAVE LEFT IS MY DIVINE ENLIGHTENMENT, WHICH NAPOLEON WAS TOO SHORT- SIGHTED TO TAKE.
MAYBE BESTOWING SOME OF THAT ON YOU WILL AID YOU IN DEFEATING HIM.
WHOA...
WHOA...
DUDE, MY PERCEPTIONS HAVE EXPANDED IN A MOST EXPONENTIALLY BODACIOUS FASHION!
I CAN SEE PLANETS INSIDE THE ATOMS OF OUR WORLD...AND YET, SEE THE WORLDS IN WHICH WE ARE THE ATOMS!
WHY DIDN'T WE HAVE THIS IN HIGH SCHOOL?
NOW, WE JUST NEED A WAY TO STOP NAPOLEON! I THINK I MIGHT--
SADLY FOR YOUR LITTLE PLAN...
SLAM!

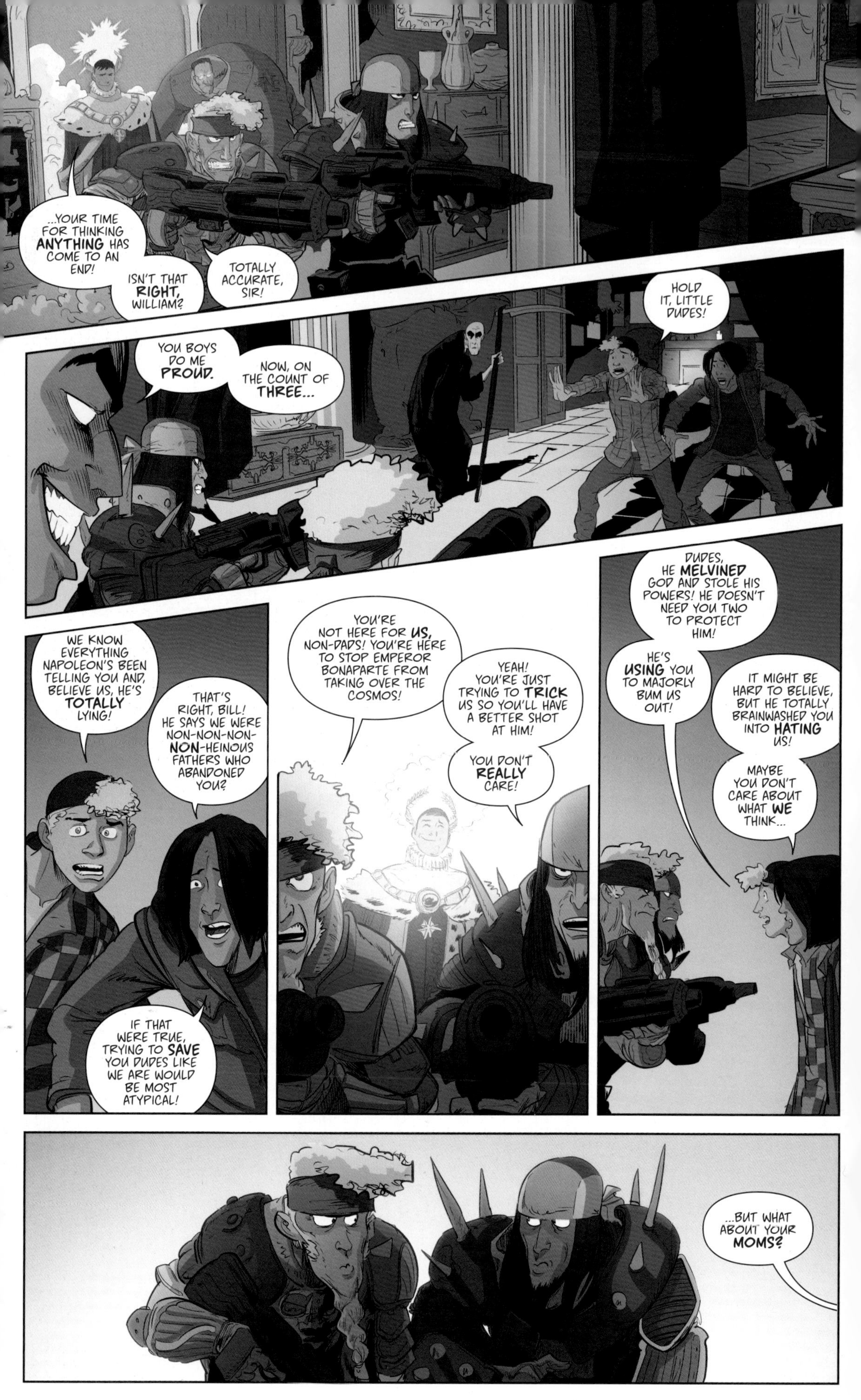
...YOUR TIME FOR THINKING ANYTHING HAS COME TO AN END!
ISN'T THAT RIGHT, WILLIAM?
TOTALLY ACCURATE, SIR!
HOLD IT, LITTLE DUDES!
YOU BOYS DO ME PROUD.
NOW, ON THE COUNT OF THREE...
WE KNOW EVERYTHING NAPOLEON'S BEEN TELLING YOU AND, BELIEVE US, HE'S TOTALLY LYING!
THAT'S RIGHT, BILL! HE SAYS WE WERE NON-NON-NON-NON-HEINOUS FATHERS WHO ABANDONED YOU?
IF THAT WERE TRUE, TRYING TO SAVE YOU DUDES LIKE WE ARE WOULD BE MOST ATYPICAL!
YOU'RE NOT HERE FOR US, NON-DADS! YOU'RE HERE TO STOP EMPEROR BONAPARTE FROM TAKING OVER THE COSMOS!
YEAH! YOU'RE JUST TRYING TO TRICK US SO YOU'LL HAVE A BETTER SHOT AT HIM!
YOU DON'T REALLY CARE!
DUDES, HE MELVINED GOD AND STOLE HIS POWERS! HE DOESN'T NEED YOU TWO TO PROTECT HIM!
HE'S USING YOU TO MAJORLY BUM US OUT!
IT MIGHT BE HARD TO BELIEVE, BUT HE TOTALLY BRAINWASHED YOU INTO HATING US!
MAYBE YOU DON'T CARE ABOUT WHAT WE THINK...
...BUT WHAT ABOUT YOUR MOMS?

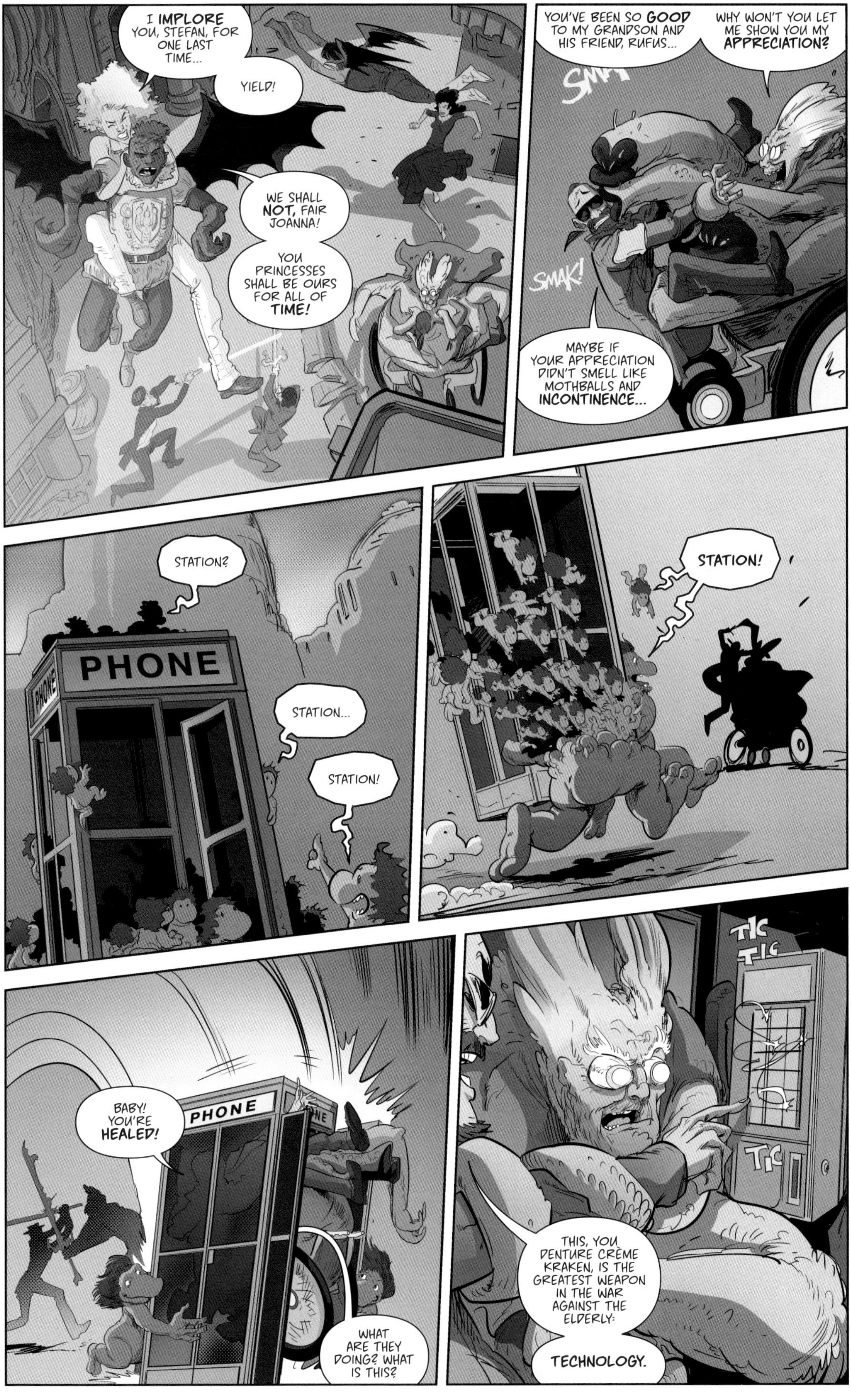

I IMPLORE YOU, STEFAN, FOR ONE LAST TIME...
YIELD!
WE SHALL NOT, FAIR JOANNA!
YOU PRINCESSES SHALL BE OURS FOR ALL OF TIME!
YOU'VE BEEN SO GOOD TO MY GRANDSON AND HIS FRIEND, RUFUS...
WHY WON'T YOU LET ME SHOW YOU MY APPRECIATION?
SMAK!
MAYBE IF YOUR APPRECIATION DIDN'T SMELL LIKE MOTHBALLS AND INCONTINENCE...
STATION?
PHONE
STATION...
STATION!
STATION!
BABY! YOU'RE HEALED!
PHONE
WHAT ARE THEY DOING? WHAT IS THIS?
TIC
TIC
TIC
THIS, YOU DENTURE CRÈME KRAKEN, IS THE GREATEST WEAPON IN THE WAR AGAINST THE ELDERLY:
TECHNOLOGY.

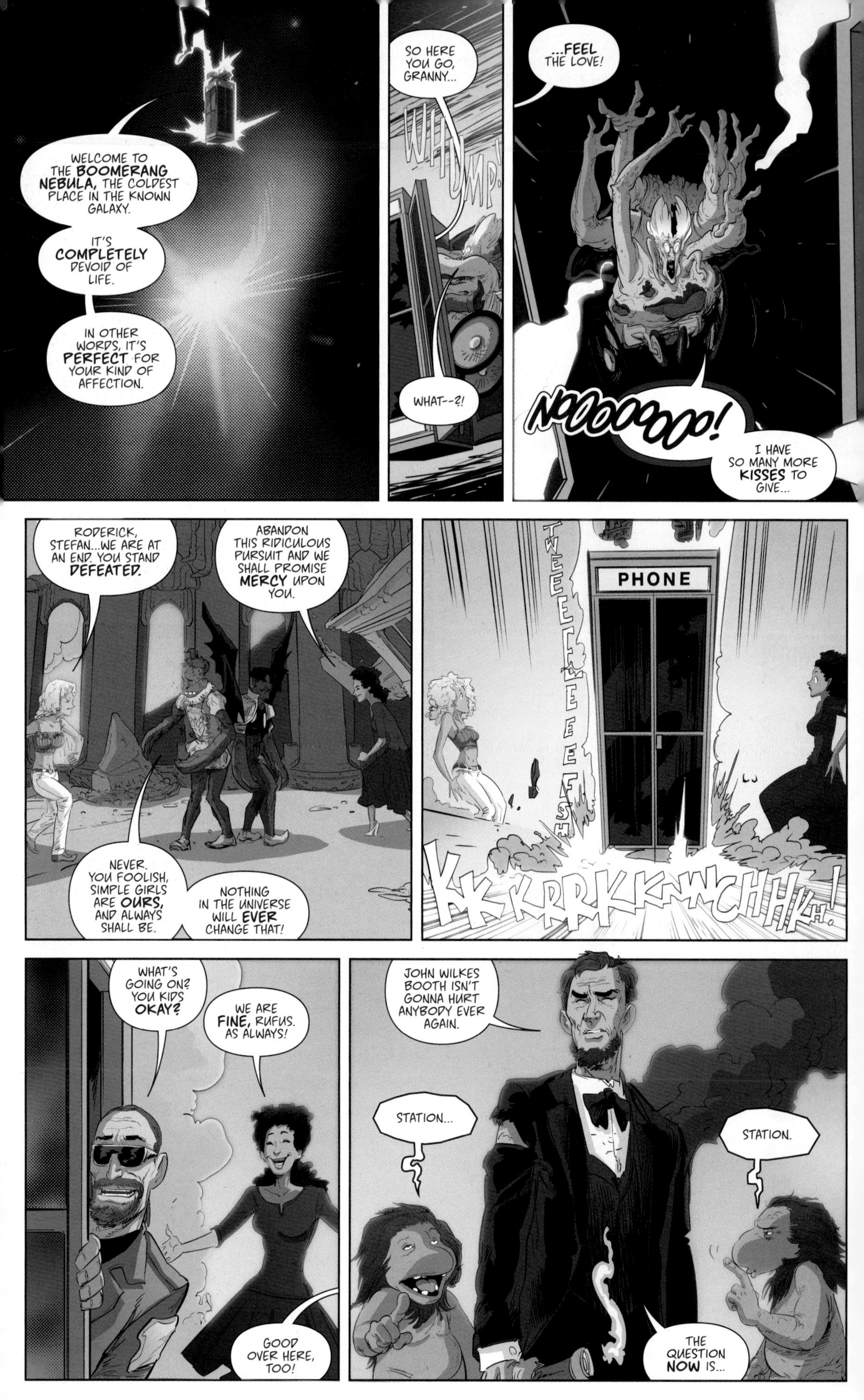
WELCOME TO THE BOOMERANG NEBULA, THE COLDEST PLACE IN THE KNOWN GALAXY.
IT'S COMPLETELY DEVOID OF LIFE.
IN OTHER WORDS, IT'S PERFECT FOR YOUR KIND OF AFFECTION.
SO HERE YOU GO, GRANNY...
WHUMP!
WHAT--?!
...FEEL THE LOVE!
NOOOOOOOO!
I HAVE SO MANY MORE KISSES TO GIVE...
RODERICK, STEFAN...WE ARE AT AN END. YOU STAND DEFEATED.
ABANDON THIS RIDICULOUS PURSUIT AND WE SHALL PROMISE MERCY UPON YOU.
NEVER. YOU FOOLISH, SIMPLE GIRLS ARE OURS, AND ALWAYS SHALL BE.
NOTHING IN THE UNIVERSE WILL EVER CHANGE THAT!
PHONE
TWEEEEEEEEEEFSH
KKKRRKKKWWCHHHKH!
WHAT'S GOING ON? YOU KIDS OKAY?
WE ARE FINE, RUFUS. AS ALWAYS!
GOOD OVER HERE, TOO!
JOHN WILKES BOOTH ISN'T GONNA HURT ANYBODY EVER AGAIN.
STATION...
STATION.
THE QUESTION NOW IS...

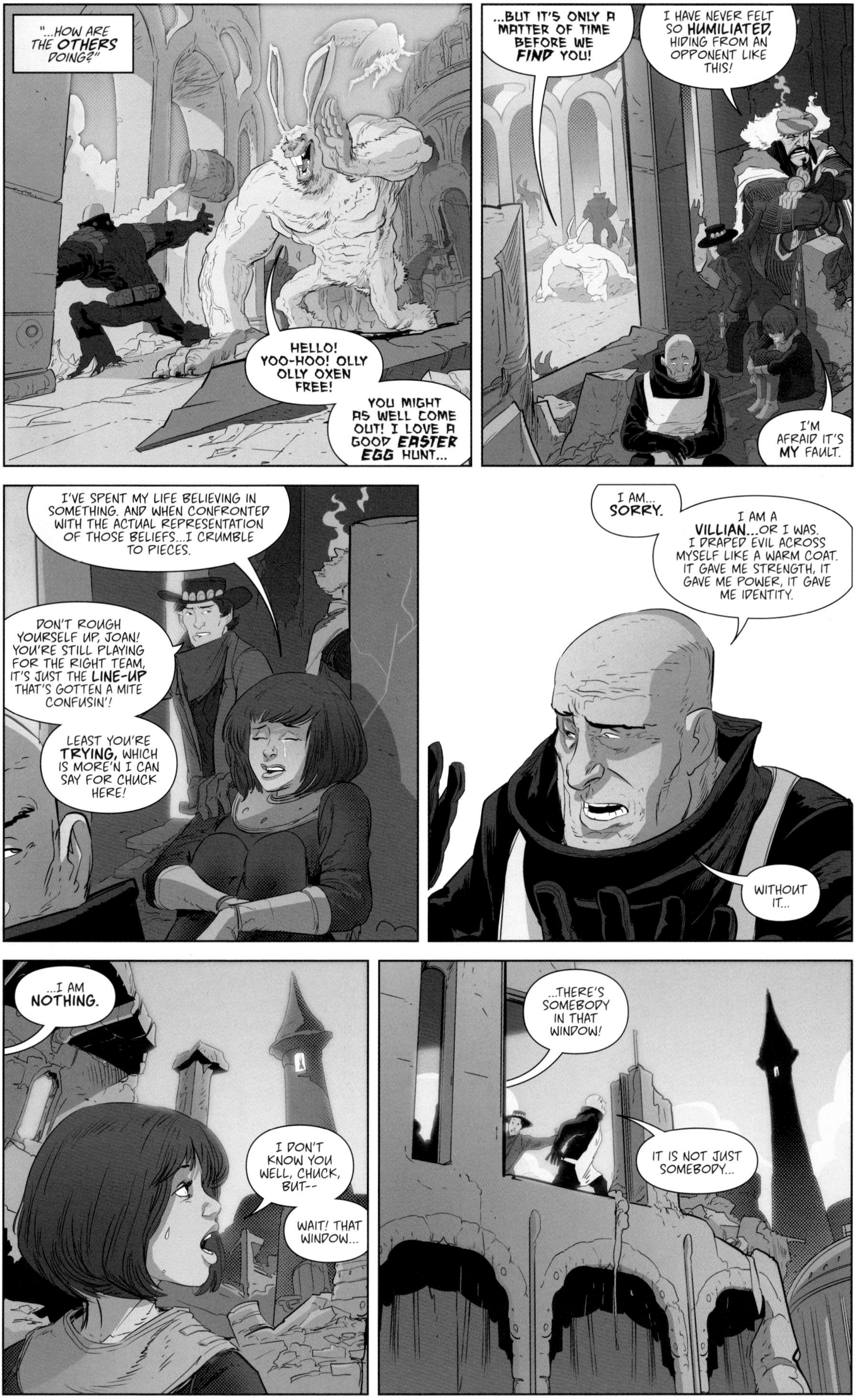
"...HOW ARE THE OTHERS DOING?"
HELLO! YOO-HOO! OLLY OLLY OXEN FREE!
YOU MIGHT AS WELL COME OUT! I LOVE A GOOD EASTER EGG HUNT...
...BUT IT'S ONLY A MATTER OF TIME BEFORE WE FIND YOU!
I HAVE NEVER FELT SO HUMILIATED, HIDING FROM AN OPPONENT LIKE THIS!
I'M AFRAID IT'S MY FAULT.
I'VE SPENT MY LIFE BELIEVING IN SOMETHING. AND WHEN CONFRONTED WITH THE ACTUAL REPRESENTATION OF THOSE BELIEFS...I CRUMBLE TO PIECES.
DON'T ROUGH YOURSELF UP, JOAN! YOU'RE STILL PLAYING FOR THE RIGHT TEAM, IT'S JUST THE LINE-UP THAT'S GOTTEN A MITE CONFUSIN'!
LEAST YOU'RE TRYING, WHICH IS MORE'N I CAN SAY FOR CHUCK HERE!
I AM... SORRY.
I AM A VILLIAN...OR I WAS. I DRAPED EVIL ACROSS MYSELF LIKE A WARM COAT. IT GAVE ME STRENGTH, IT GAVE ME POWER, IT GAVE ME IDENTITY.
WITHOUT IT...
...I AM NOTHING.
I DON'T KNOW YOU WELL, CHUCK, BUT--
WAIT! THAT WINDOW...
...THERE'S SOMEBODY IN THAT WINDOW!
IT IS NOT JUST SOMEBODY...

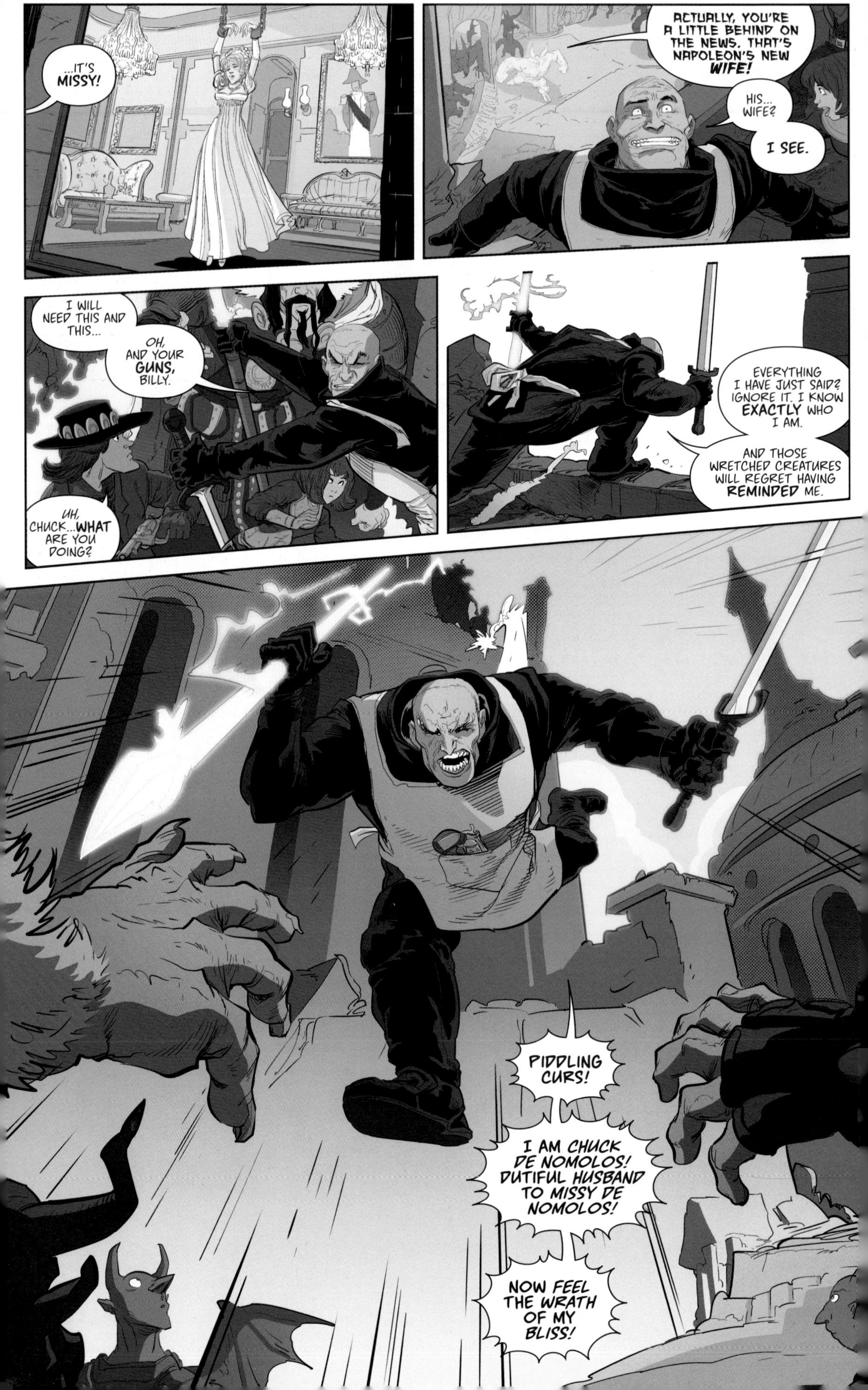
...IT'S MISSY!
ACTUALLY, YOU'RE A LITTLE BEHIND ON THE NEWS. THAT'S NAPOLEON'S NEW WIFE!
HIS... WIFE?
I SEE.
I WILL NEED THIS AND THIS...
OH, AND YOUR GUNS, BILLY.
UH, CHUCK...WHAT ARE YOU DOING?
EVERYTHING I HAVE JUST SAID? IGNORE IT. I KNOW EXACTLY WHO I AM.
AND THOSE WRETCHED CREATURES WILL REGRET HAVING REMINDED ME.
PIDDLING CURS!
I AM CHUCK DE NOMOLOS! DUTIFUL HUSBAND TO MISSY DE NOMOLOS!
NOW FEEL THE WRATH OF MY BLISS!

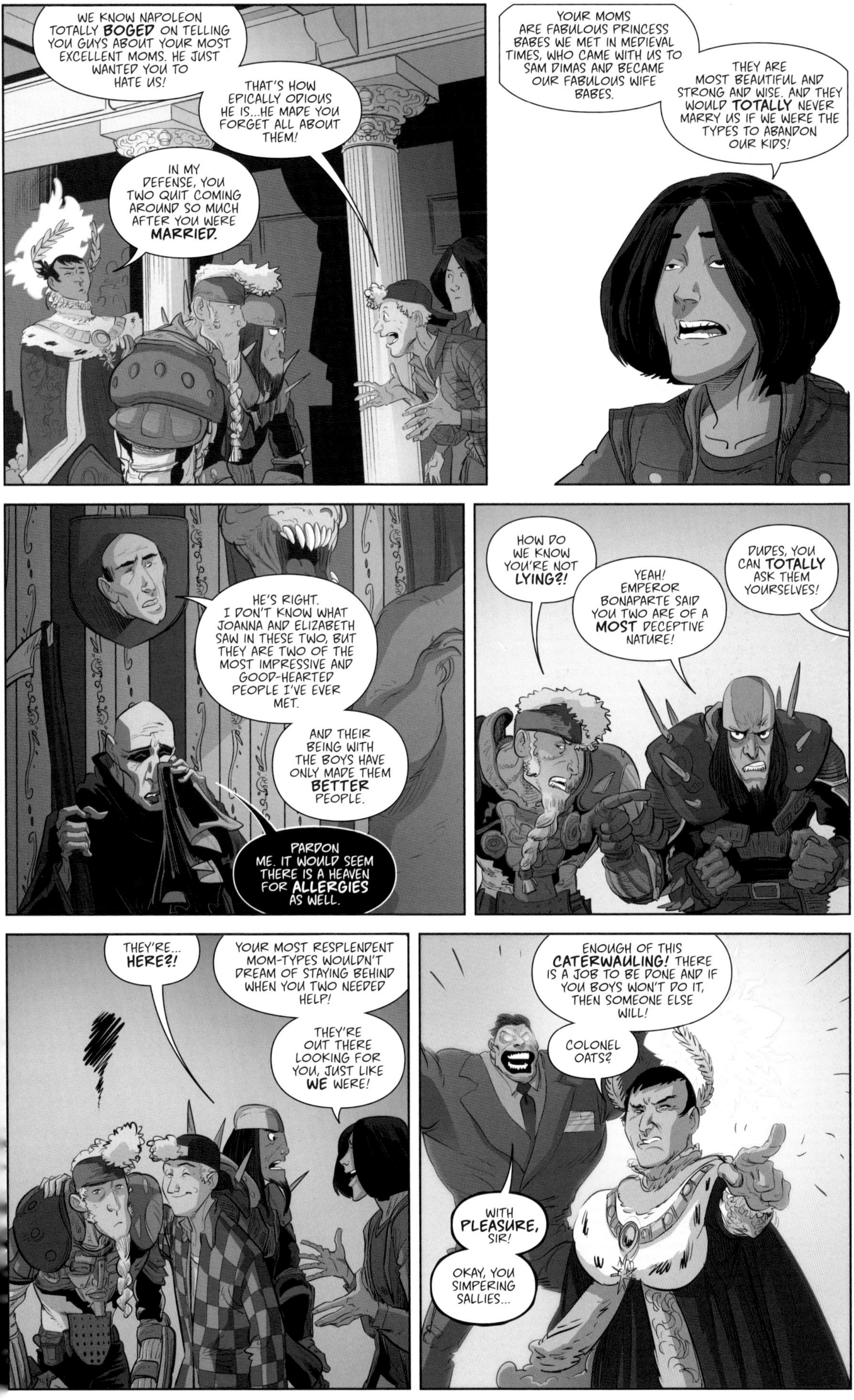
WE KNOW NAPOLEON TOTALLY BOGED ON TELLING YOU GUYS ABOUT YOUR MOST EXCELLENT MOMS. HE JUST WANTED YOU TO HATE US!
THAT'S HOW EPICALLY ODIOUS HE IS...HE MADE YOU FORGET ALL ABOUT THEM!
IN MY DEFENSE, YOU TWO QUIT COMING AROUND SO MUCH AFTER YOU WERE MARRIED.
YOUR MOMS ARE FABULOUS PRINCESS BABES WE MET IN MEDIEVAL TIMES, WHO CAME WITH US TO SAM DIMAS AND BECAME OUR FABULOUS WIFE BABES.
THEY ARE MOST BEAUTIFUL AND STRONG AND WISE. AND THEY WOULD TOTALLY NEVER MARRY US IF WE WERE THE TYPES TO ABANDON OUR KIDS!
HE'S RIGHT. I DON'T KNOW WHAT JOANNA AND ELIZABETH SAW IN THESE TWO, BUT THEY ARE TWO OF THE MOST IMPRESSIVE AND GOOD-HEARTED PEOPLE I'VE EVER MET.
AND THEIR BEING WITH THE BOYS HAVE ONLY MADE THEM BETTER PEOPLE.
PARDON ME. IT WOULD SEEM THERE IS A HEAVEN FOR ALLERGIES AS WELL.
HOW DO WE KNOW YOU'RE NOT LYING?!
YEAH! EMPEROR BONAPARTE SAID YOU TWO ARE OF A MOST DECEPTIVE NATURE!
DUDES, YOU CAN TOTALLY ASK THEM YOURSELVES!
THEY'RE... HERE?!
YOUR MOST RESPLENDENT MOM-TYPES WOULDN'T DREAM OF STAYING BEHIND WHEN YOU TWO NEEDED HELP!
THEY'RE OUT THERE LOOKING FOR YOU, JUST LIKE WE WERE!
ENOUGH OF THIS CATERWAULING! THERE IS A JOB TO BE DONE AND IF YOU BOYS WON'T DO IT, THEN SOMEONE ELSE WILL!
COLONEL OATS?
WITH PLEASURE, SIR!
OKAY, YOU SIMPERING SALLIES...

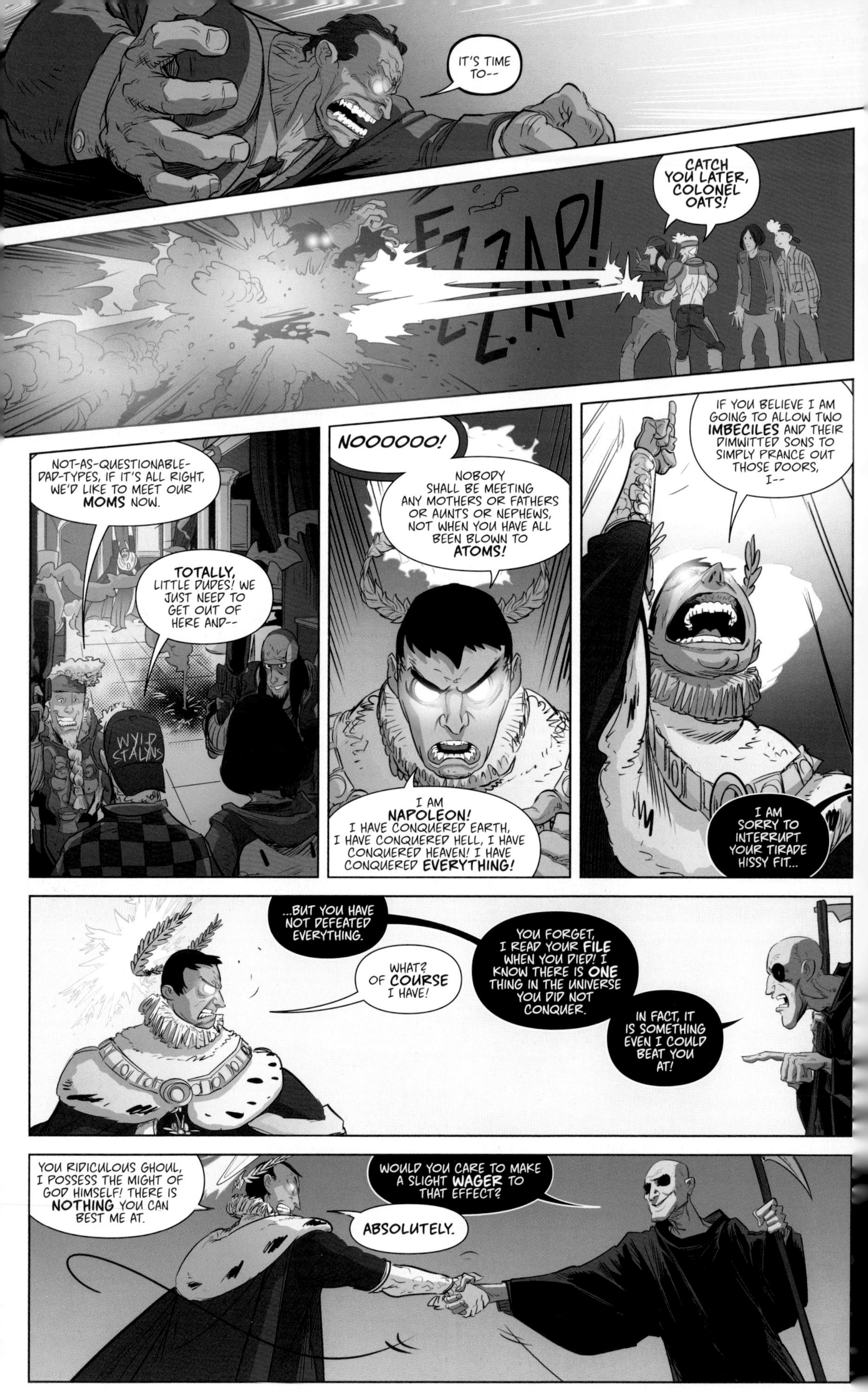
IT'S TIME TO--
CATCH YOU LATER, COLONEL OATS!
FZZAP!
NOT-AS-QUESTIONABLE-DAD-TYPES, IF IT'S ALL RIGHT, WE'D LIKE TO MEET OUR MOMS NOW.
TOTALLY, LITTLE DUDES! WE JUST NEED TO GET OUT OF HERE AND--
WYLD STALYNS
NOOOOOO!
NOBODY SHALL BE MEETING ANY MOTHERS OR FATHERS OR AUNTS OR NEPHEWS, NOT WHEN YOU HAVE ALL BEEN BLOWN TO ATOMS!
I AM NAPOLEON! I HAVE CONQUERED EARTH, I HAVE CONQUERED HELL, I HAVE CONQUERED HEAVEN! I HAVE CONQUERED EVERYTHING!
IF YOU BELIEVE I AM GOING TO ALLOW TWO IMBECILES AND THEIR DIMWITTED SONS TO SIMPLY PRANCE OUT THOSE DOORS, I--
I AM SORRY TO INTERRUPT YOUR TIRADE HISSY FIT...
...BUT YOU HAVE NOT DEFEATED EVERYTHING.
WHAT? OF COURSE I HAVE!
YOU FORGET, I READ YOUR FILE WHEN YOU DIED! I KNOW THERE IS ONE THING IN THE UNIVERSE YOU DID NOT CONQUER.
IN FACT, IT IS SOMETHING EVEN I COULD BEAT YOU AT!
YOU RIDICULOUS GHOUL, I POSSESS THE MIGHT OF GOD HIMSELF! THERE IS NOTHING YOU CAN BEST ME AT.
WOULD YOU CARE TO MAKE A SLIGHT WAGER TO THAT EFFECT?
ABSOLUTELY.

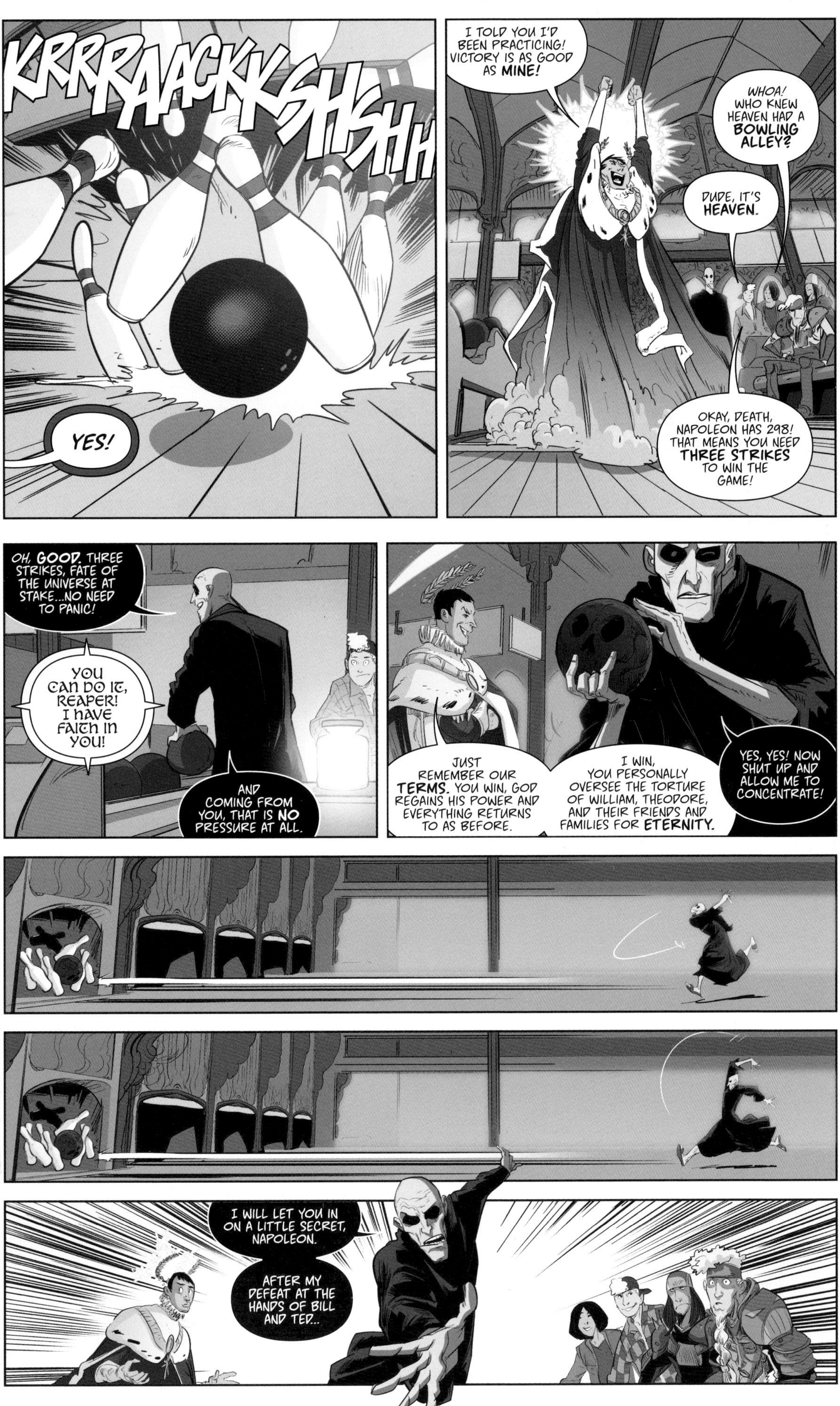
KRRRAACKKSHSHH
YES!
I TOLD YOU I'D BEEN PRACTICING! VICTORY IS AS GOOD AS MINE!
WHOA! WHO KNEW HEAVEN HAD A BOWLING ALLEY?
DUDE, IT'S HEAVEN.
OKAY, DEATH, NAPOLEON HAS 298! THAT MEANS YOU NEED THREE STRIKES TO WIN THE GAME!
OH, GOOD. THREE STRIKES, FATE OF THE UNIVERSE AT STAKE...NO NEED TO PANIC!
YOU CAN DO IT, REAPER! I HAVE FAITH IN YOU!
AND COMING FROM YOU, THAT IS NO PRESSURE AT ALL.
JUST REMEMBER OUR TERMS. YOU WIN, GOD REGAINS HIS POWER AND EVERYTHING RETURNS TO AS BEFORE.
I WIN, YOU PERSONALLY OVERSEE THE TORTURE OF WILLIAM, THEODORE, AND THEIR FRIENDS AND FAMILIES FOR ETERNITY.
YES, YES! NOW SHUT UP AND ALLOW ME TO CONCENTRATE!
I WILL LET YOU IN ON A LITTLE SECRET, NAPOLEON.
AFTER MY DEFEAT AT THE HANDS OF BILL AND TED...

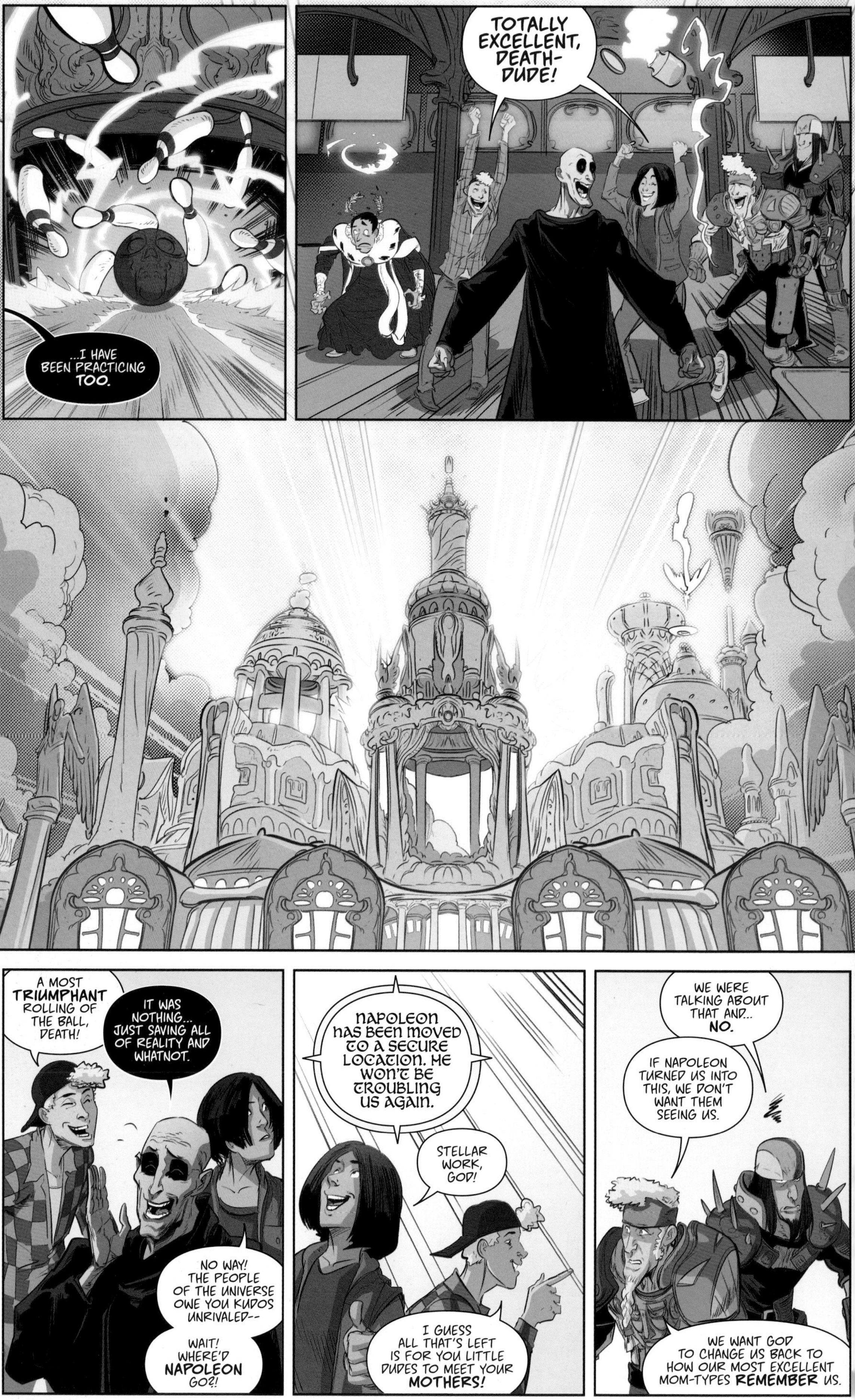
...I HAVE BEEN PRACTICING TOO.
TOTALLY EXCELLENT, DEATH-DUDE!
A MOST TRIUMPHANT ROLLING OF THE BALL, DEATH!
IT WAS NOTHING... JUST SAVING ALL OF REALITY AND WHATNOT.
NO WAY! THE PEOPLE OF THE UNIVERSE OWE YOU KUDOS UNRIVALED--
WAIT! WHERE'D NAPOLEON GO?!
NAPOLEON HAS BEEN MOVED TO A SECURE LOCATION. HE WON'T BE TROUBLING US AGAIN.
STELLAR WORK, GOD!
I GUESS ALL THAT'S LEFT IS FOR YOU LITTLE DUDES TO MEET YOUR MOTHERS!
WE WERE TALKING ABOUT THAT AND... NO.
IF NAPOLEON TURNED US INTO THIS, WE DON'T WANT THEM SEEING US.
WE WANT GOD TO CHANGE US BACK TO HOW OUR MOST EXCELLENT MOM-TYPES REMEMBER US.

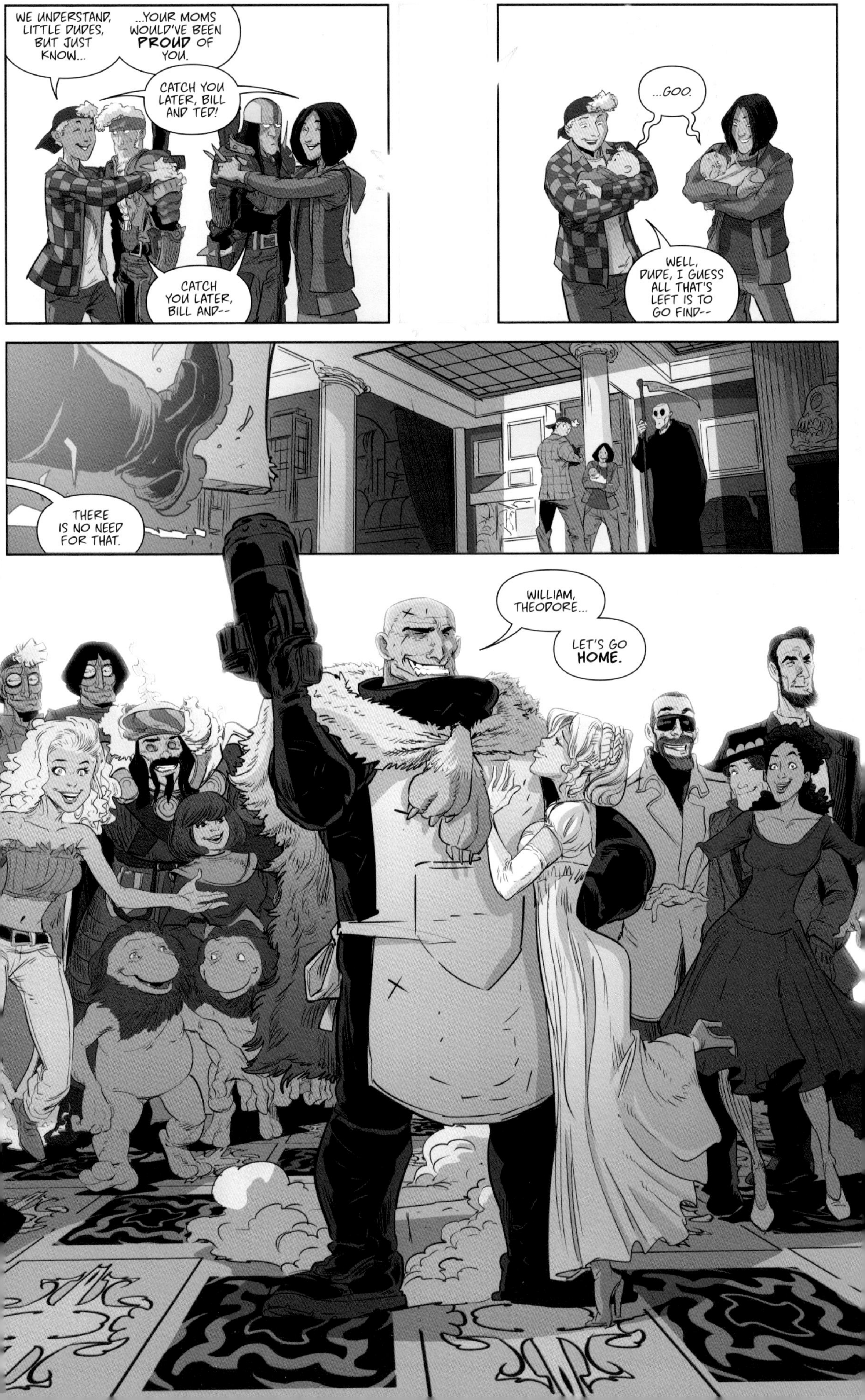
WE UNDERSTAND, LITTLE DUDES, BUT JUST KNOW...
...YOUR MOMS WOULD'VE BEEN **PROUD** OF YOU.
CATCH YOU LATER, BILL AND TED!
CATCH YOU LATER, BILL AND--
...GOO.
WELL, DUDE, I GUESS ALL THAT'S LEFT IS TO GO FIND--
THERE IS NO NEED FOR THAT.
WILLIAM, THEODORE...
LET'S GO **HOME.**

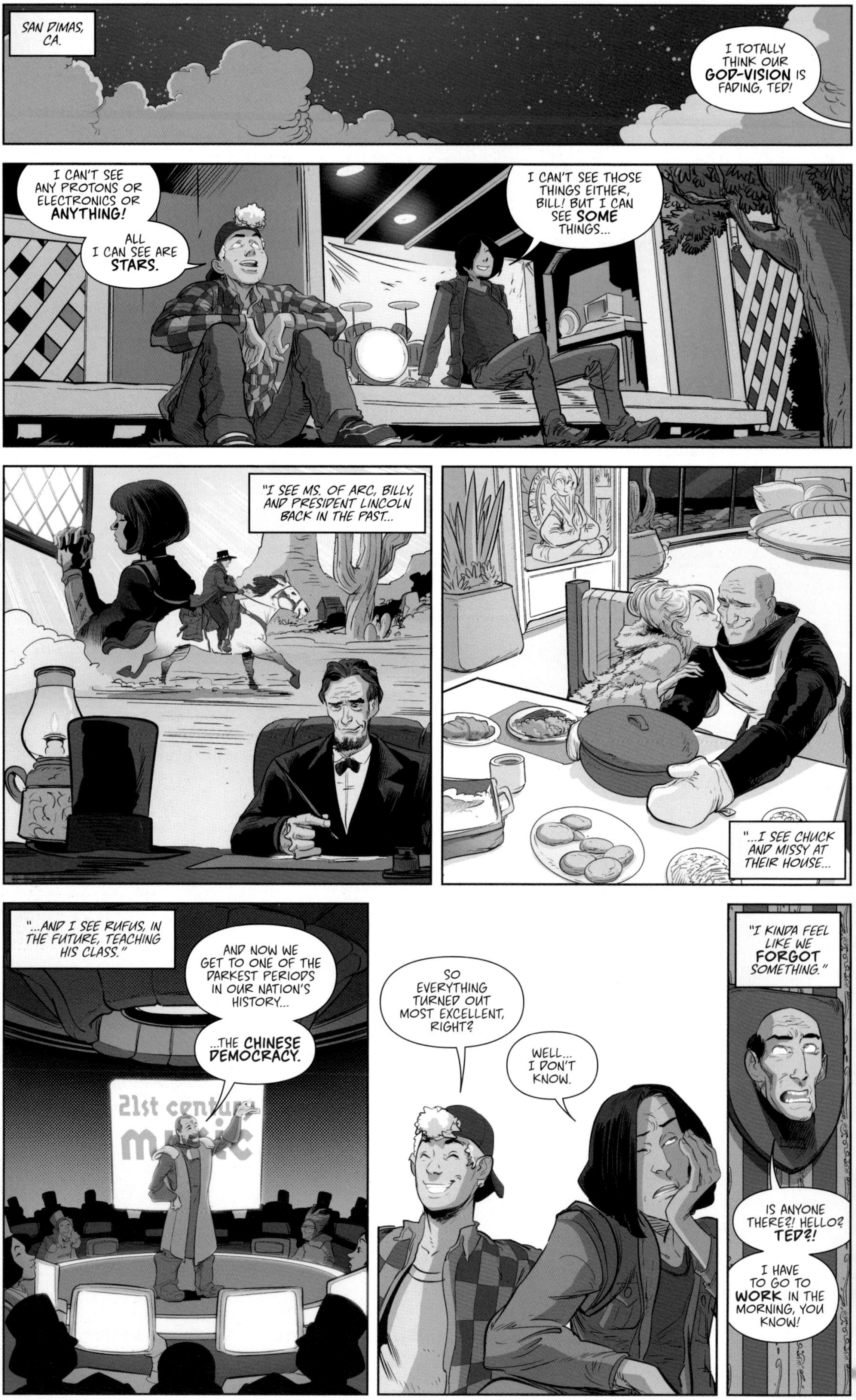
SAN DIMAS, CA.
I TOTALLY THINK OUR GOD-VISION IS FADING, TED!
I CAN'T SEE ANY PROTONS OR ELECTRONICS OR ANYTHING!
ALL I CAN SEE ARE STARS.
I CAN'T SEE THOSE THINGS EITHER, BILL! BUT I CAN SEE SOME THINGS...
"I SEE MS. OF ARC, BILLY, AND PRESIDENT LINCOLN BACK IN THE PAST...
"...I SEE CHUCK AND MISSY AT THEIR HOUSE...
"...AND I SEE RUFUS, IN THE FUTURE, TEACHING HIS CLASS."
AND NOW WE GET TO ONE OF THE DARKEST PERIODS IN OUR NATION'S HISTORY...
...THE CHINESE DEMOCRACY.
21st century music
SO EVERYTHING TURNED OUT MOST EXCELLENT, RIGHT?
WELL... I DON'T KNOW.
"I KINDA FEEL LIKE WE FORGOT SOMETHING."
IS ANYONE THERE?! HELLO? TED?!
I HAVE TO GO TO WORK IN THE MORNING, YOU KNOW!

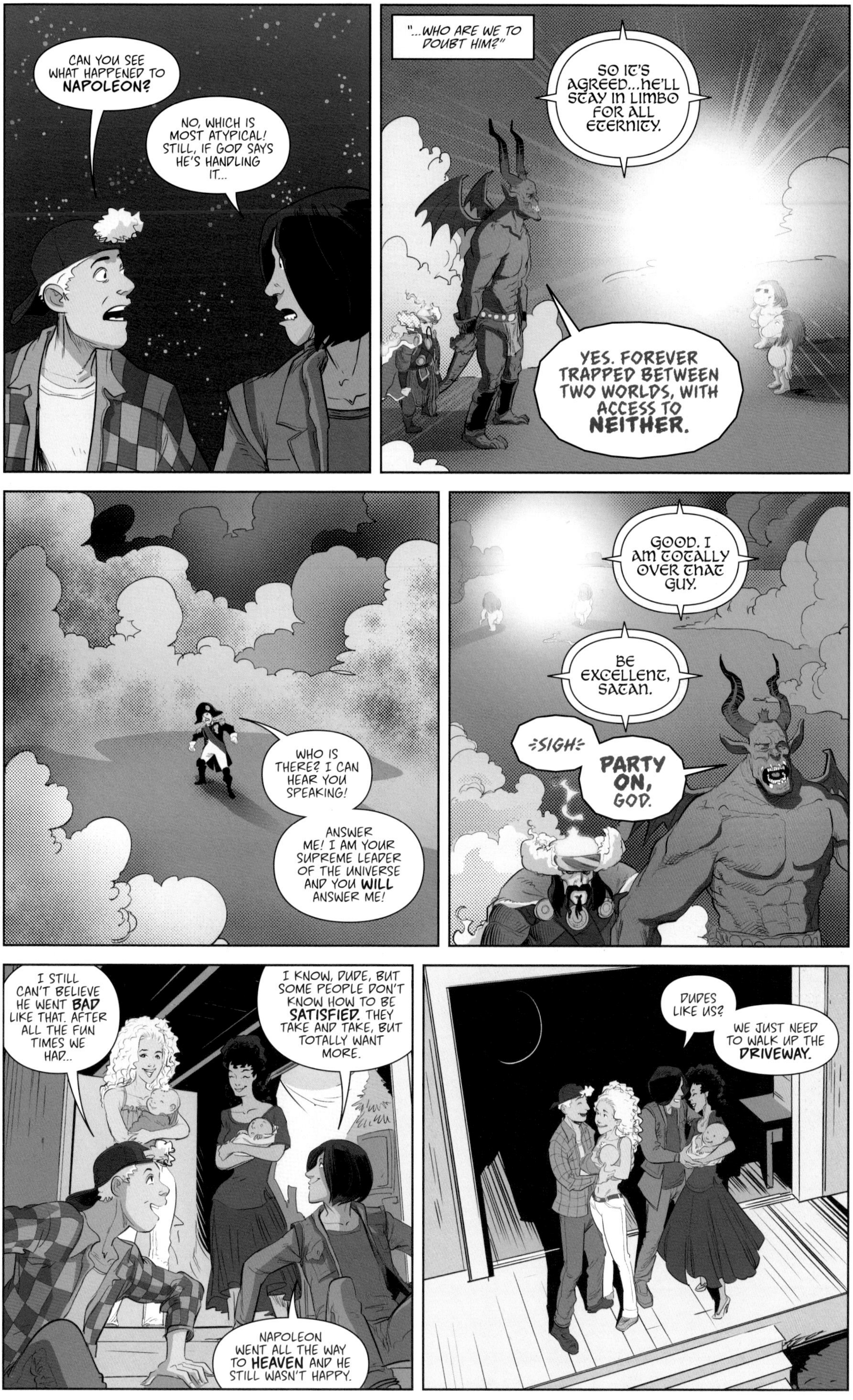
CAN YOU SEE WHAT HAPPENED TO NAPOLEON?
NO, WHICH IS MOST ATYPICAL! STILL, IF GOD SAYS HE'S HANDLING IT...
"...WHO ARE WE TO DOUBT HIM?"
SO IT'S AGREED...HE'LL STAY IN LIMBO FOR ALL ETERNITY.
YES. FOREVER TRAPPED BETWEEN TWO WORLDS, WITH ACCESS TO NEITHER.
WHO IS THERE? I CAN HEAR YOU SPEAKING!
ANSWER ME! I AM YOUR SUPREME LEADER OF THE UNIVERSE AND YOU WILL ANSWER ME!
GOOD. I AM TOTALLY OVER THAT GUY.
BE EXCELLENT, SATAN.
SIGH
PARTY ON, GOD.
I STILL CAN'T BELIEVE HE WENT BAD LIKE THAT. AFTER ALL THE FUN TIMES WE HAD...
I KNOW, DUDE, BUT SOME PEOPLE DON'T KNOW HOW TO BE SATISFIED. THEY TAKE AND TAKE, BUT TOTALLY WANT MORE.
NAPOLEON WENT ALL THE WAY TO HEAVEN AND HE STILL WASN'T HAPPY.
DUDES LIKE US?
WE JUST NEED TO WALK UP THE DRIVEWAY.

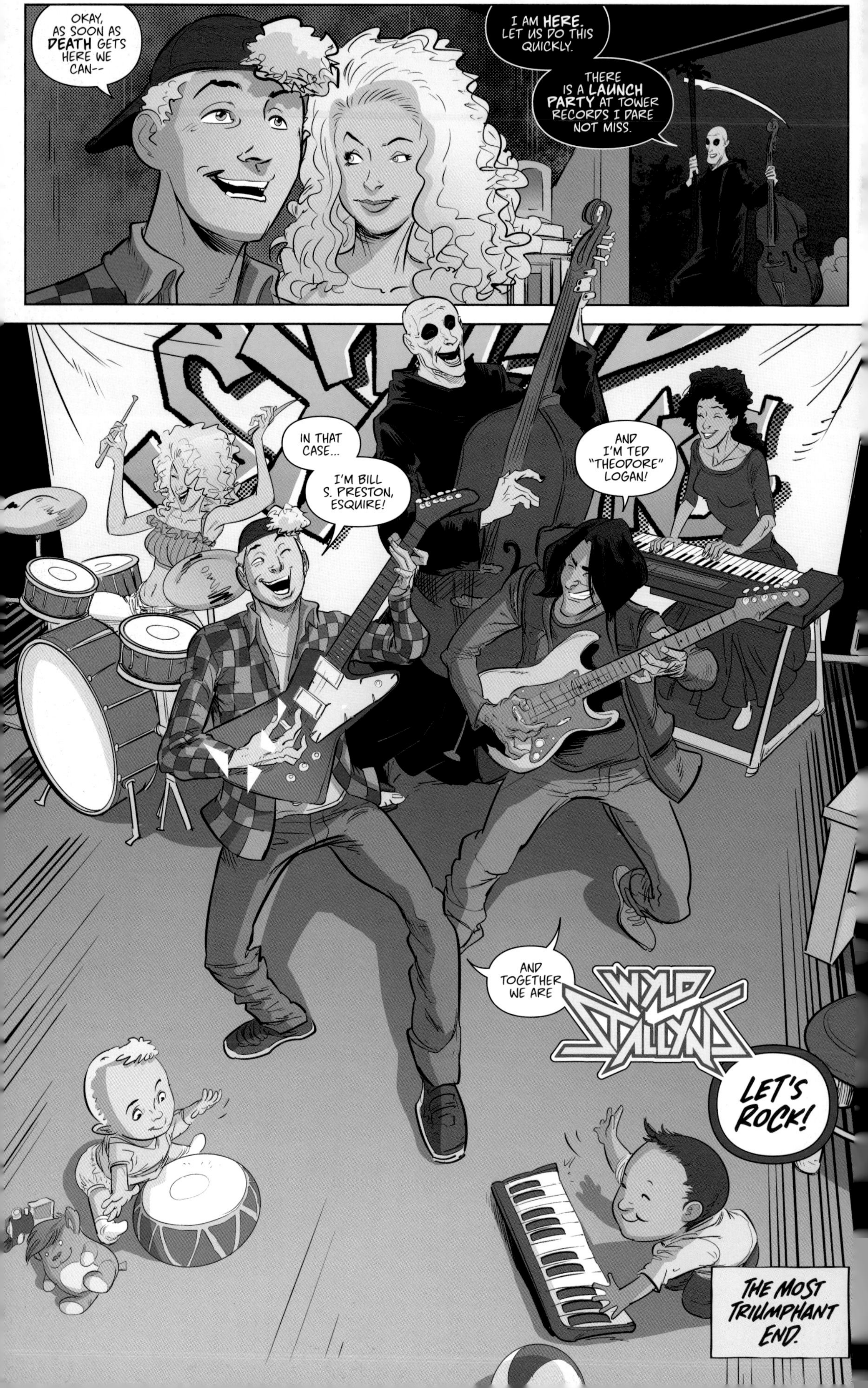
OKAY, AS SOON AS DEATH GETS HERE WE CAN--
I AM HERE. LET US DO THIS QUICKLY.
THERE IS A LAUNCH PARTY AT TOWER RECORDS I DARE NOT MISS.
IN THAT CASE...
I'M BILL S. PRESTON, ESQUIRE!
AND I'M TED "THEODORE" LOGAN!
AND TOGETHER WE ARE
WYLD STALLYNS
LET'S ROCK!
THE MOST TRIUMPHANT END.

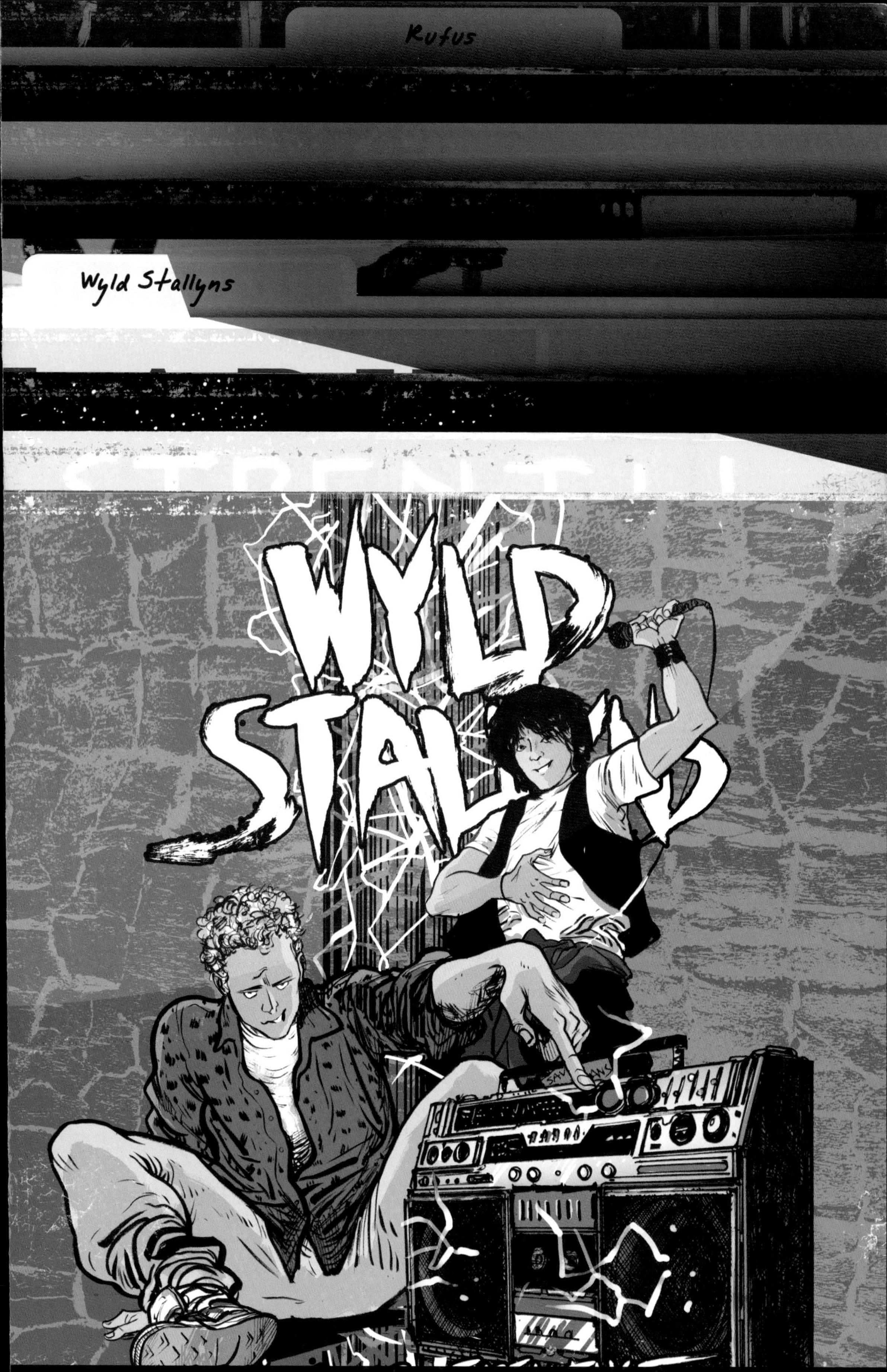
Rufus
Wyld Stallyns
WYLD

DANIEL WARREN JOHNSON ⚡ ISSUE FOUR SUBSCRIPTION ALBUM COVER

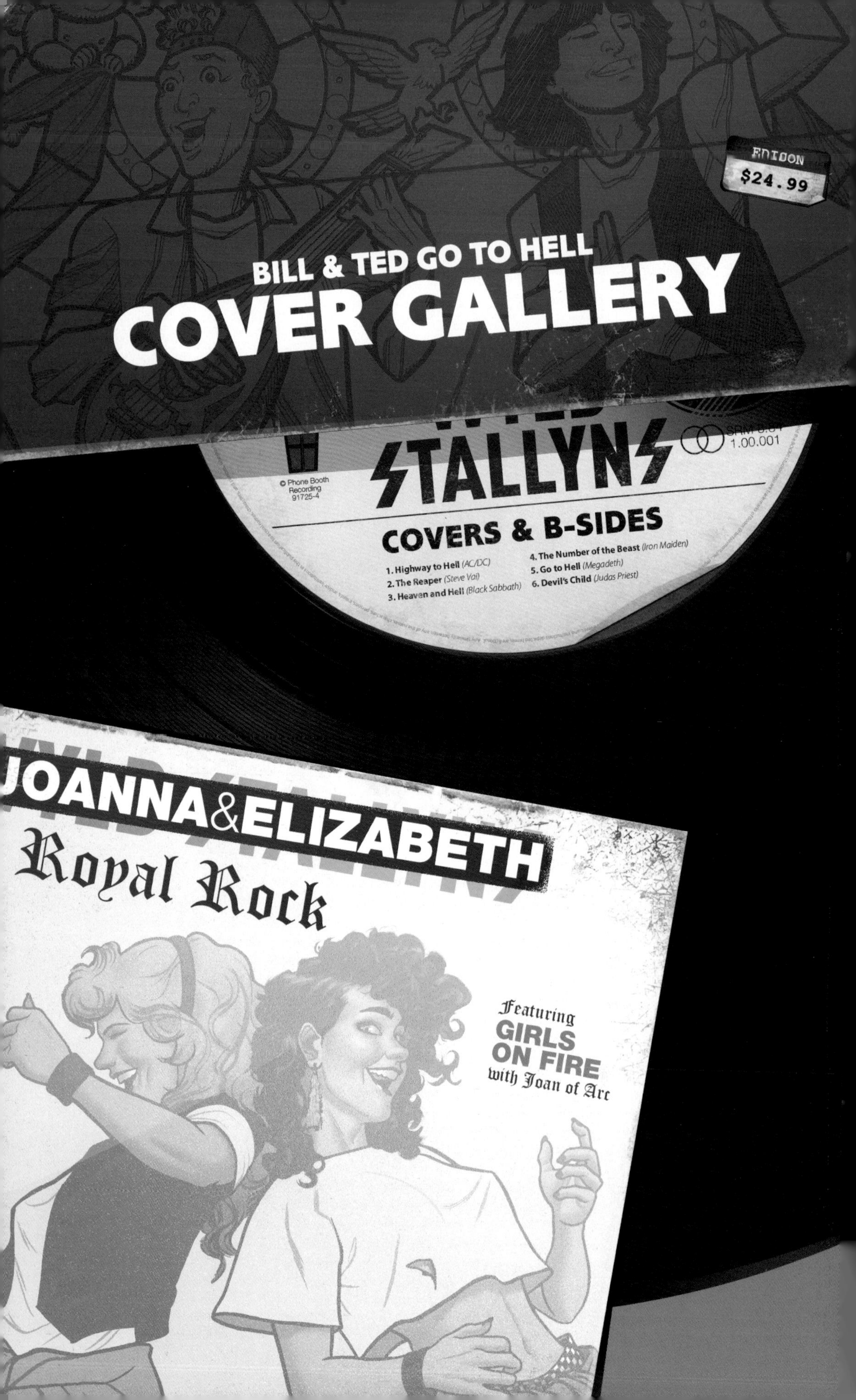
EDISON
$24.99
BILL & TED GO TO HELL
COVER GALLERY
STALLYNS
© Phone Booth
Recording
91725-4
1.00.001
COVERS & B-SIDES
1. Highway to Hell (AC/DC)
2. The Reaper (Steve Vai)
3. Heaven and Hell (Black Sabbath)
4. The Number of the Beast (Iron Maiden)
5. Go to Hell (Megadeth)
6. Devil's Child (Judas Priest)
JOANNA&ELIZABETH
Royal Rock
Featuring
GIRLS
ON FIRE
with Joan of Arc

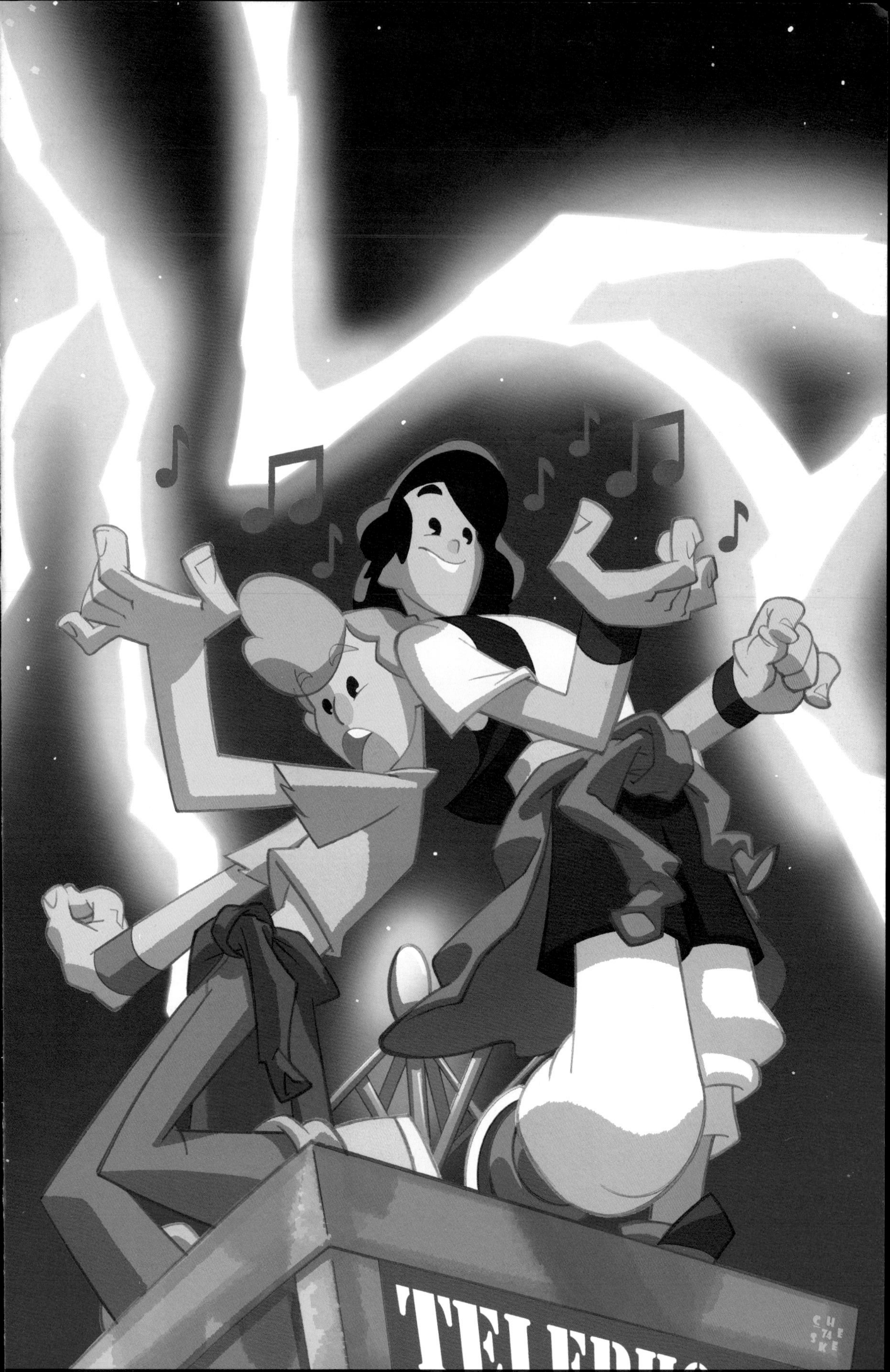

SEAN "CHEEKS" GALLOWAY ⚡ ISSUE ONE VARIANT COVER

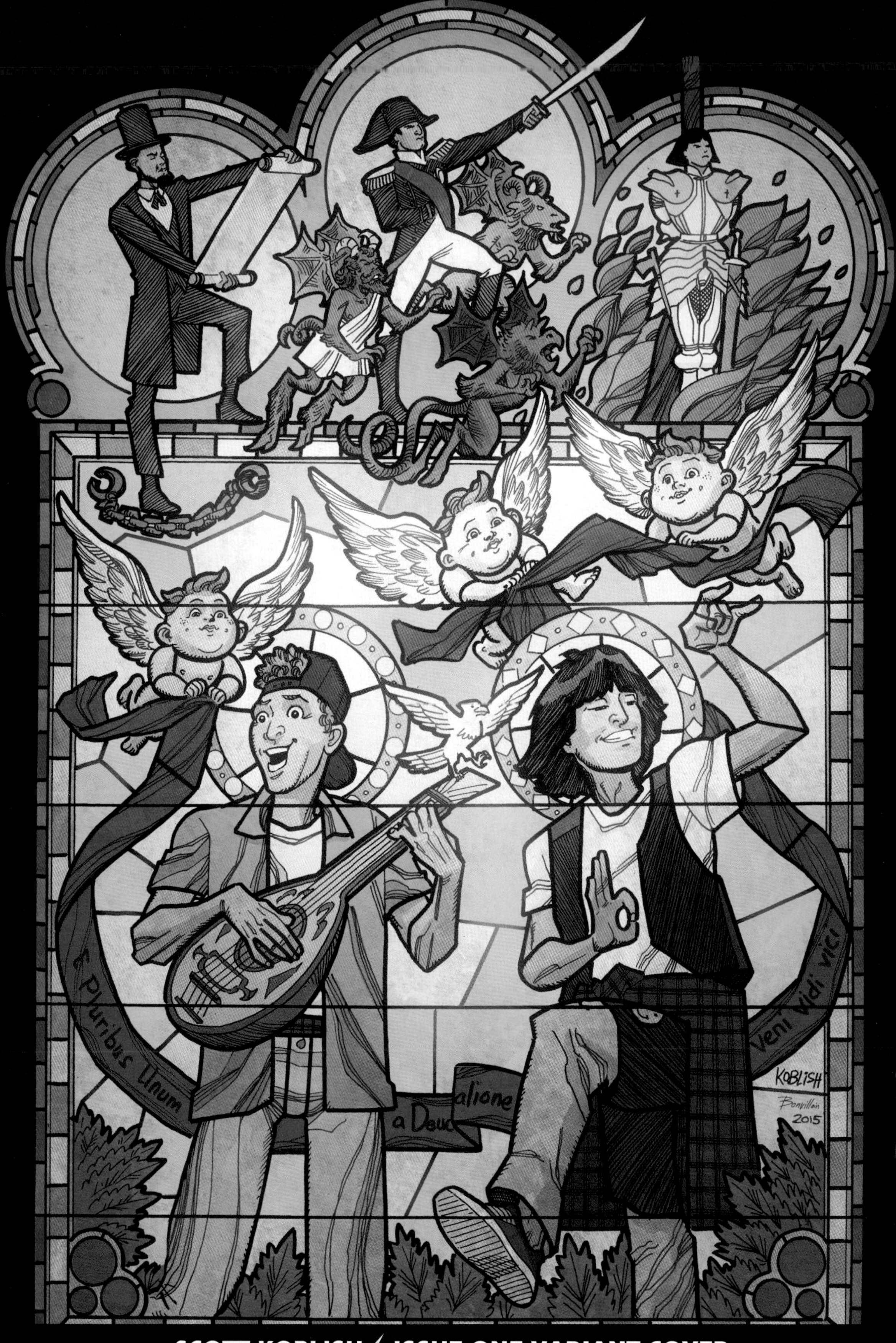
E Pluribus Unum
a Deuc
alione
Veni vidi vici
KOBLISH
Bonvillain
2015

SCOTT KOBLISH ⚡ ISSUE ONE VARIANT COVER
WITH COLORS BY TAMRA BONVILLAIN

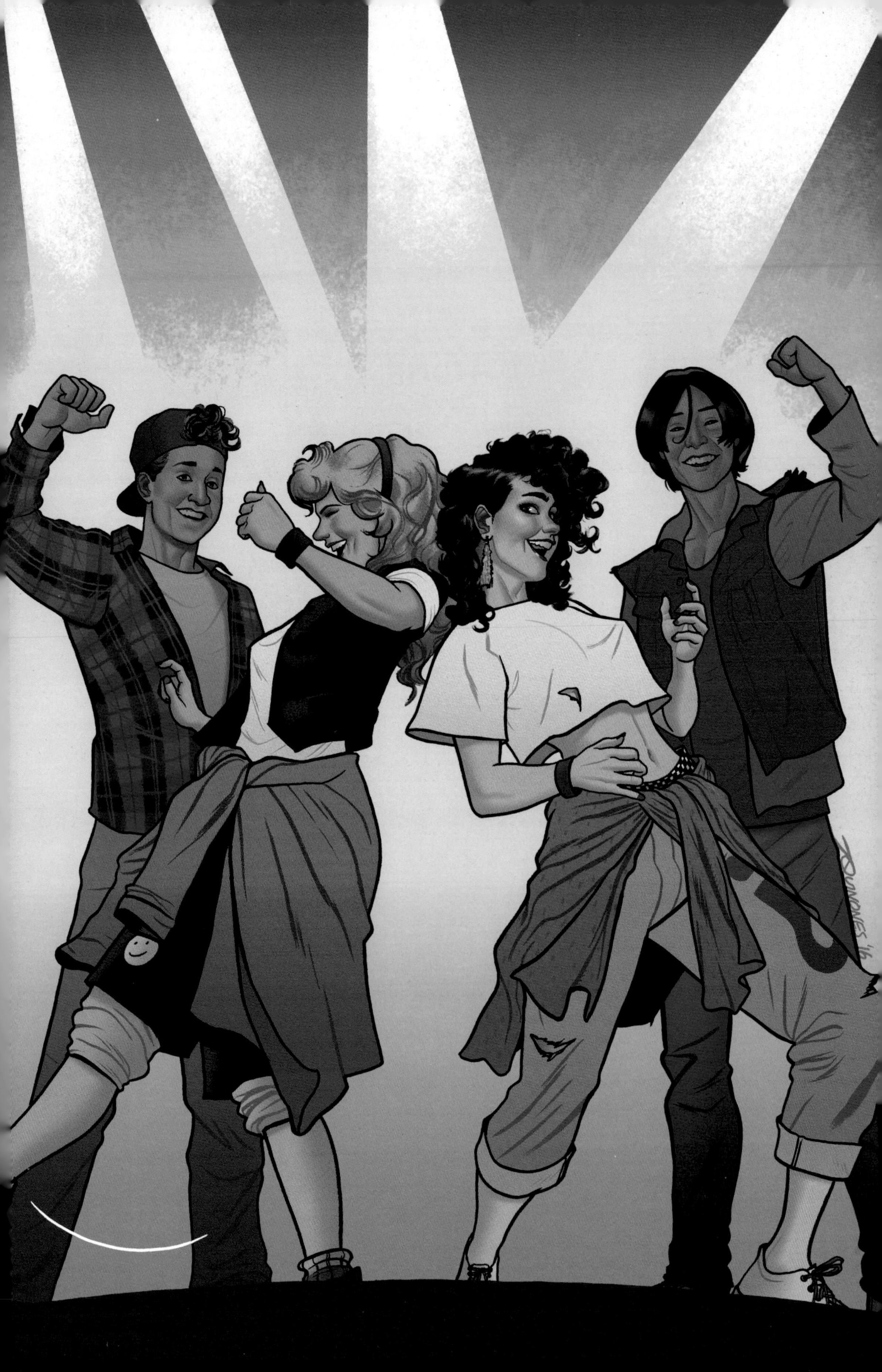

JOE QUINONES ⚡ ISSUE ONE NEWBURY COMICS EXCLUSIVE COVER

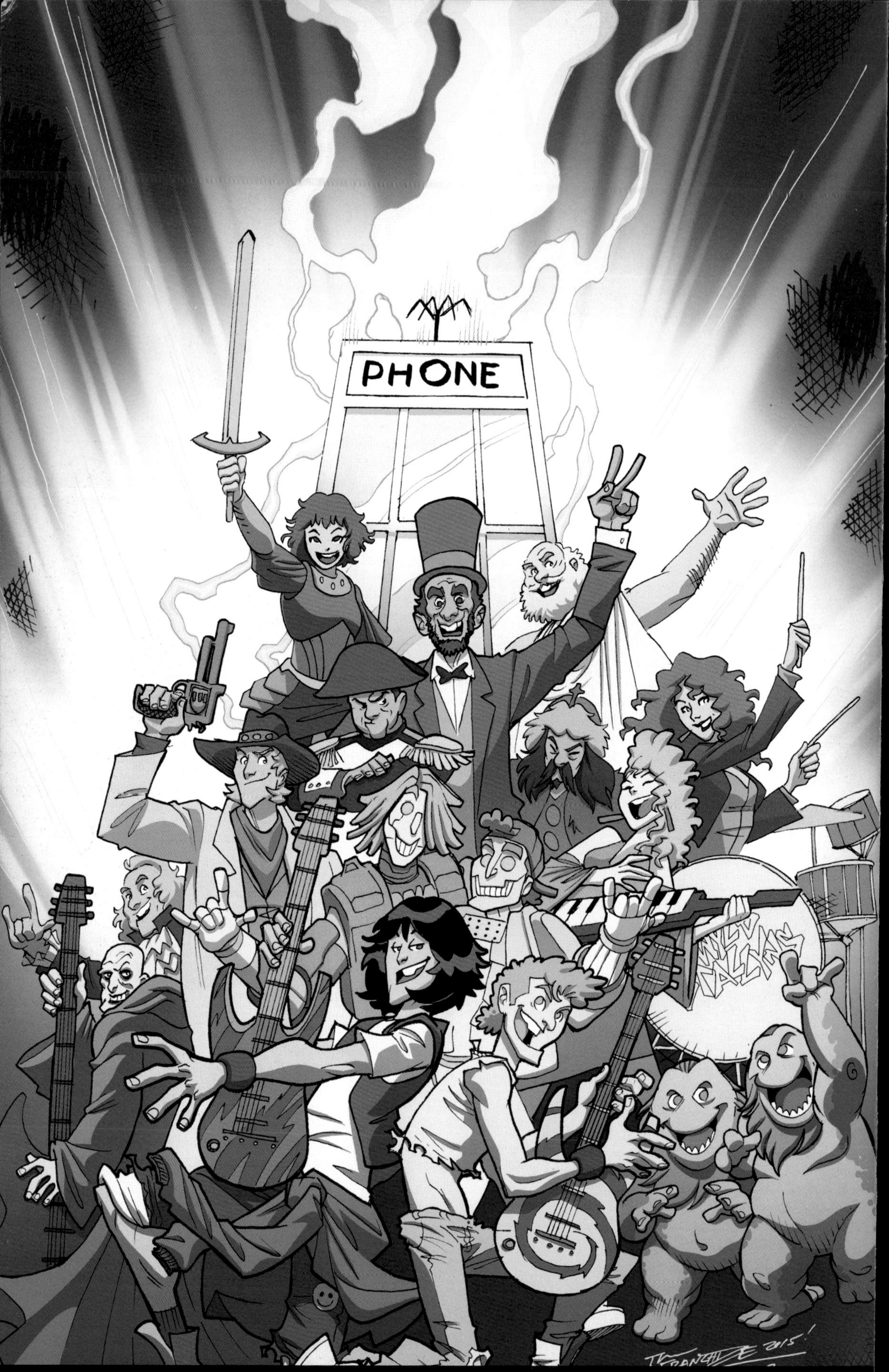
PHONE

JERRY GAYLORD ⚡ ISSUE ONE FRIED PIE EXCLUSIVE COVER
WITH COLORS BY WHITNEY COGAR

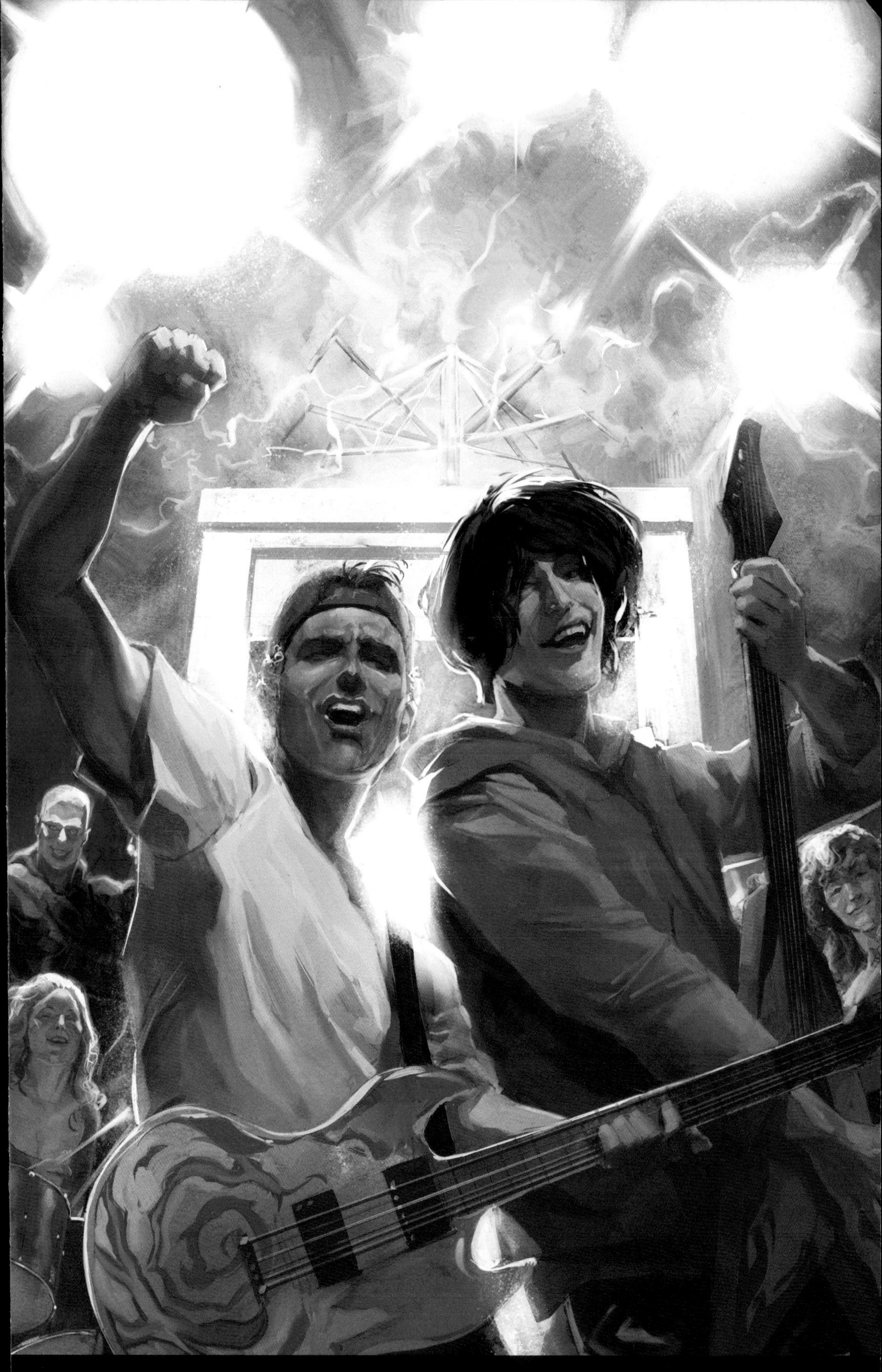

XERMANICO ⚡ ISSUE ONE TOUR POSTER EXCLUSIVE COVER

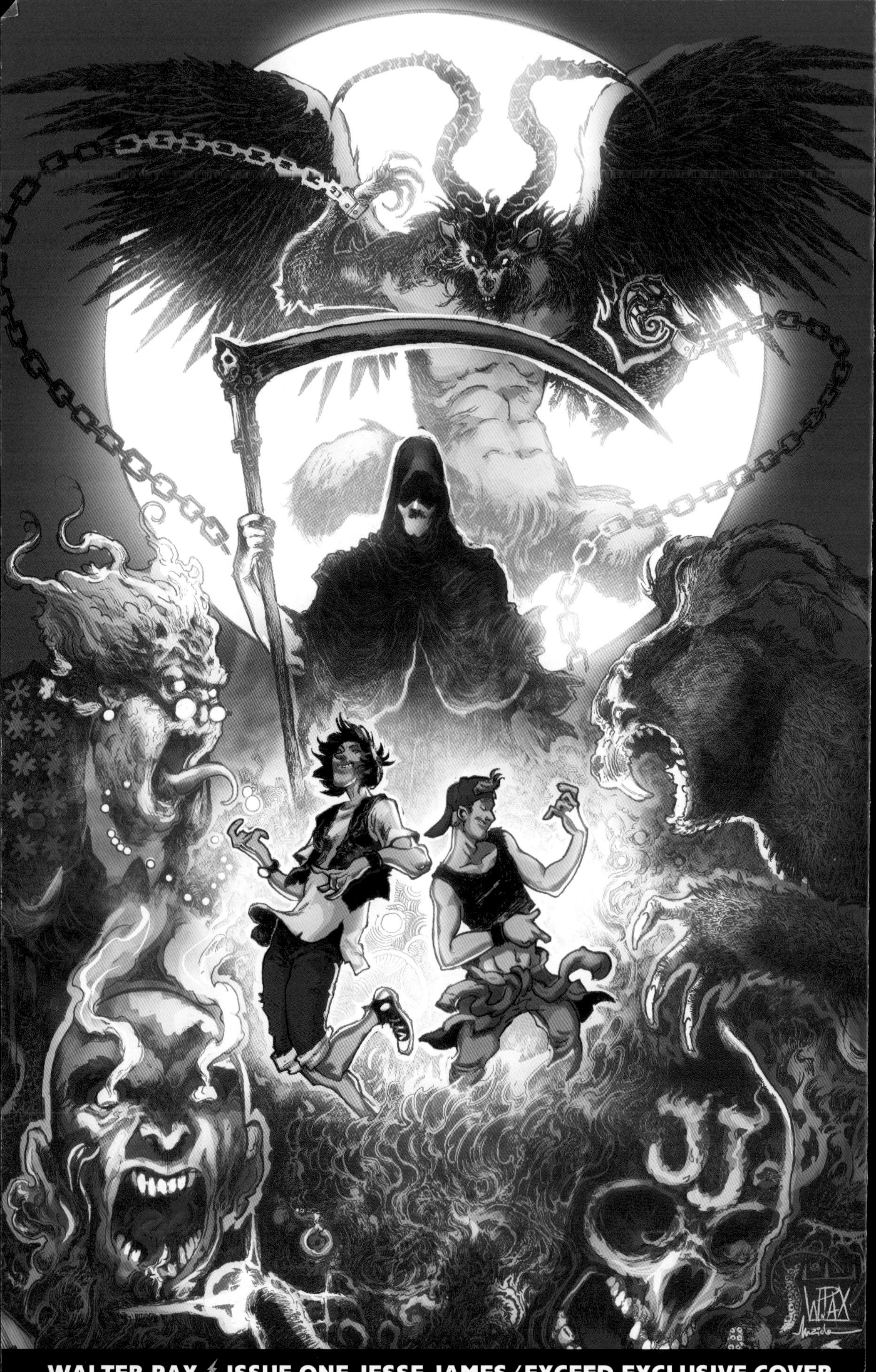
W.PAX
Maiolo

WALTER PAX ⚡ ISSUE ONE JESSE JAMES / EXCEED EXCLUSIVE COVER
WITH COLORS BY MARCELO MAIOLO

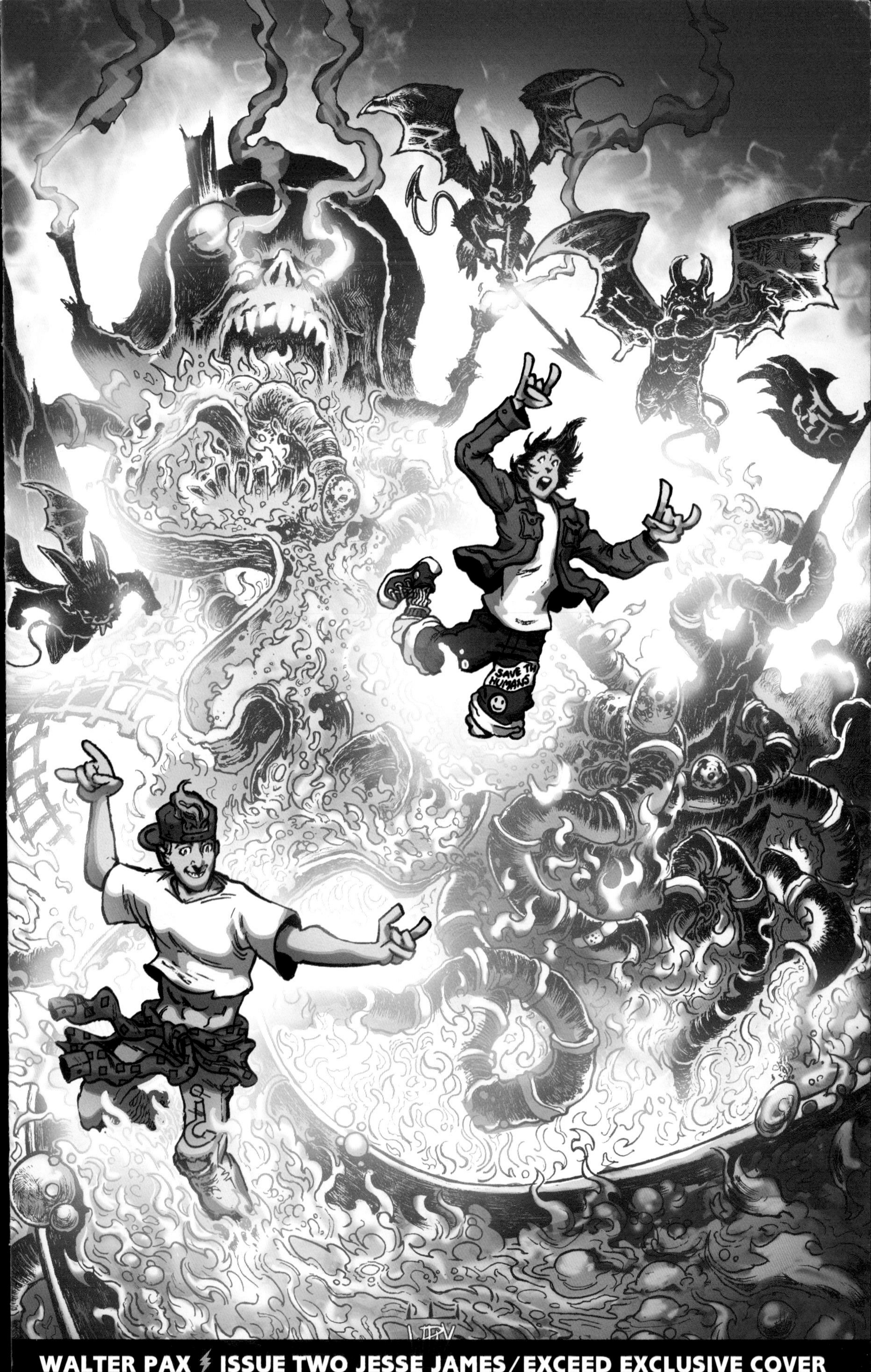
SAVE TH
HUMANS

WALTER PAX ⚡ ISSUE TWO JESSE JAMES / EXCEED EXCLUSIVE COVER
WITH COLORS BY MARCELO MAIOLO

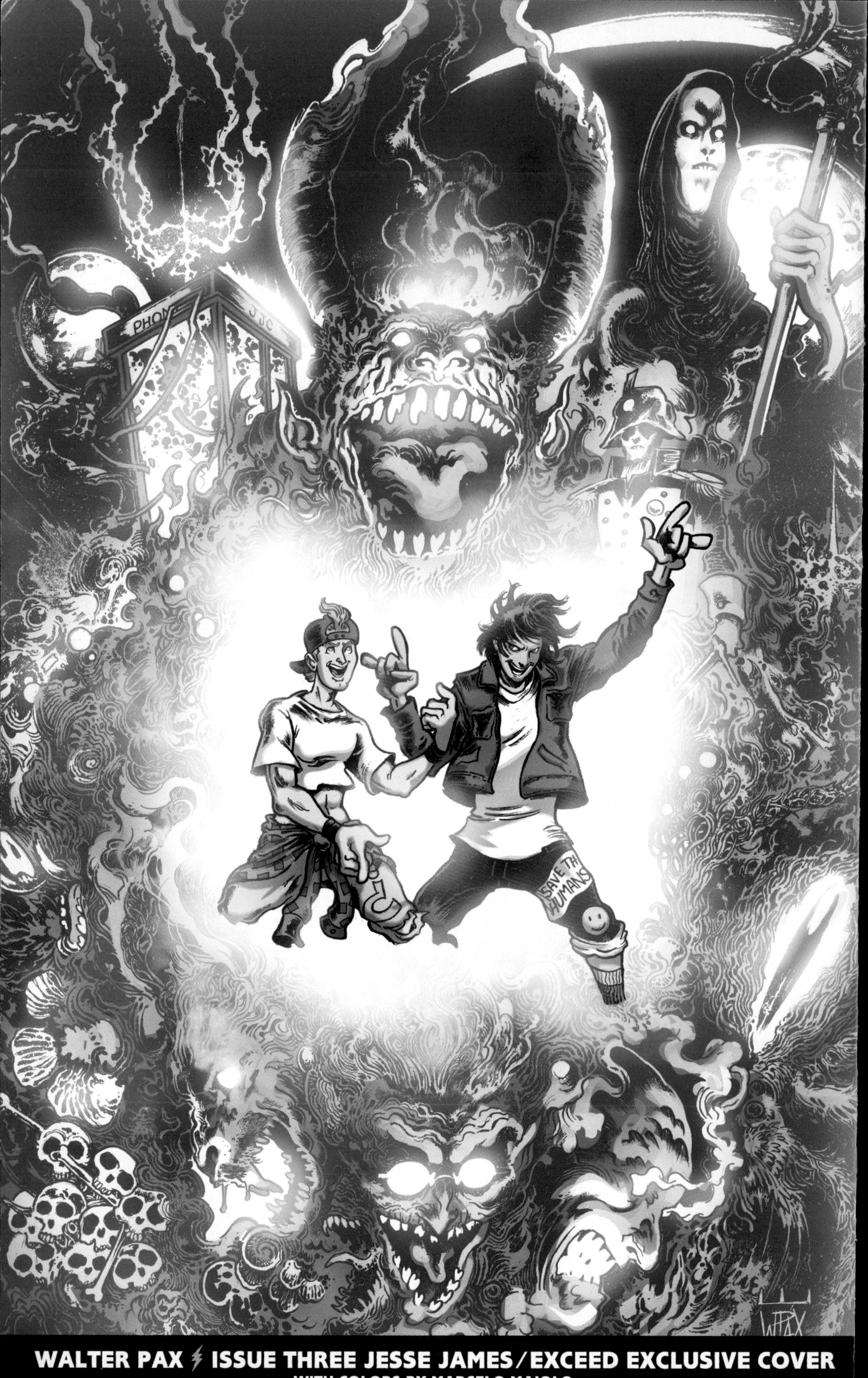
SAVE THE HUMANS

WALTER PAX ⚡ ISSUE THREE JESSE JAMES/EXCEED EXCLUSIVE COVER
WITH COLORS BY MARCELO MAIOLO

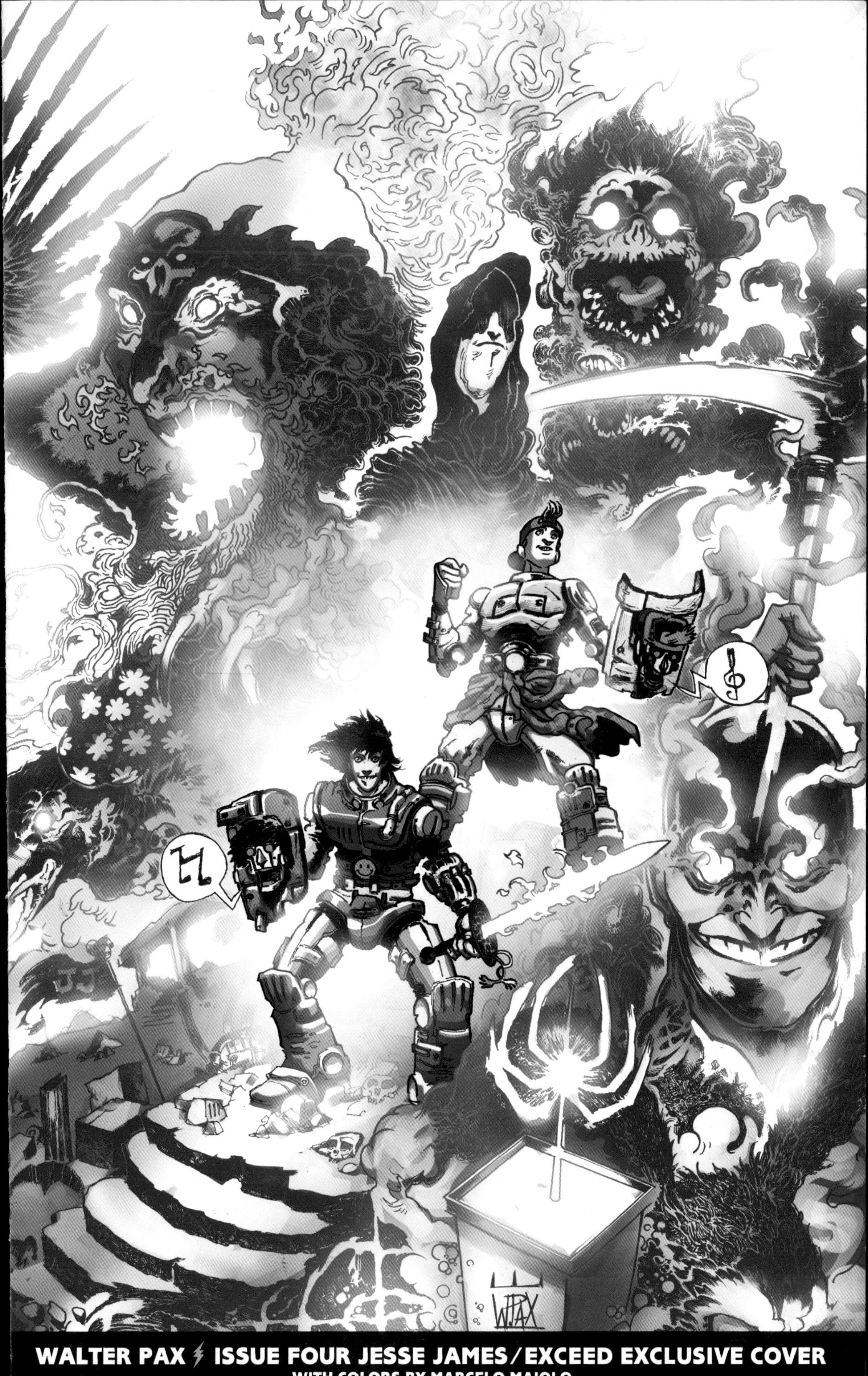

WALTER PAX ⚡ ISSUE FOUR JESSE JAMES/EXCEED EXCLUSIVE COVER
WITH COLORS BY MARCELO MAIOLO

WYLD STALLYNS

DANCE WITH THE REAPER

SIDE ONE

1. Electric Hell *(Wyld Stallyns Cover)*
2. Sympathy for the Reaper
3. Hell-O, Goodbye
4. Lucifer in the Sky with Diamonds
5. Trapper Reaper
6. Angle of Death *(featuring Station)*

SIDE TWO

1. Hades Man
2. I Love Lucifer *(featuring The Devil)*
3. Wishing Hell
4. Bogus Beelzebub
5. Hell Can Wait
6. Finders, Reapers

SRM 8.84
1.00.001

TELEPHONE

9 781608 869350

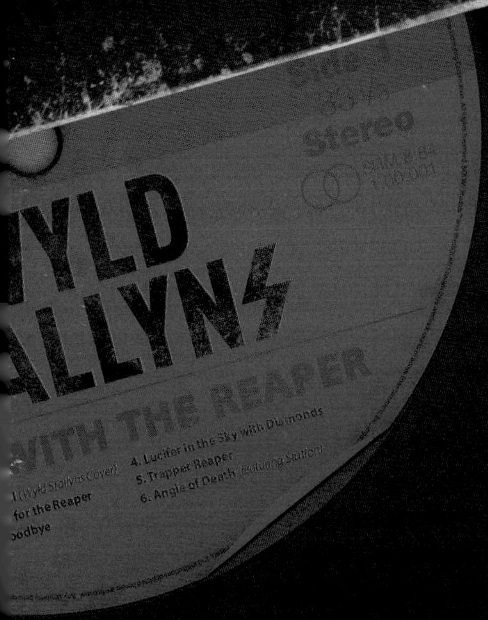
Side 1
33 1/3
Stereo
SRM 8.84
1.00.001
YLD
ALLYNS
WITH THE REAPER
l (Wyld Stallyns Cover)
for the Reaper
oodbye
4. Lucifer in the Sky with Diamonds
5. Trapper Reaper
6. Angle of Death (featuring Station)

A MOST EXCELLENT AFTERWORD

My relationship with most excellent dudes Bill S. Preston, Esquire and Ted "Theodore" Logan began in 1989, the year of *Excellent Adventure*'s release. I knew little about the film beyond "time-travelling high schoolers," hadn't heard of either Alex Winter or Keanu Reeves, and only had a passing knowledge of the great George Carlin. When I sat down to watch, I had no expectations. But as the lights dimmed and the first beats of Big Pig's "I Can't Break Away" filled the auditorium, I had a feeling I might be in for something pretty awesome…and I was right. The gray skies of Washington state felt a million miles away from the sunny climate of San Dimas, but as a high school senior who spent most of his time acing the classes he cared about (English and drama, for those keeping score) and turning his back on the rest, the fate of the universe resting on the graduation of two slackers definitely spoke to me. I left that theater with a sense of kinship to the duo…and, needless to say, I was happy when they returned.

My thoughts on *Bogus Journey* differ from most people as it's my favorite of the two. In this day where sequels or reboots are often recycling elements from earlier films, *Bogus Journey* is a marvel to behold as it sets out to be a completely different movie. Time travel plays a minimal role in the film, as Bill and Ted explore the afterlife and meet characters ranging from Station to the Devil to the Grim Reaper, with William Sadler playing one of the most underappreciated comedic roles in film (an opinion reaffirmed years later after viewing Bergman's *The Seventh Seal*). Between robot doubles, marriage proposals, battles of the bands, and a multitude of board games, *Bogus Journey* took the inherent idea of two regular dudes in extraordinary situations and went crazy with it. I was definitely still a fan.

Travelling forward to present day, when I was offered a chance to write new adventures for the boys I accepted without hesitation, viewing it as a chance to complete the love letter to the franchise I started writing in that theater. I wanted to build on elements of the films (as well as the previous series, *Bill & Ted's Most Triumphant Return*) while also making a "greatest hits" of everything I loved about them. So beyond immersing myself in the most resplendent lingo of the two leads, I got to touch on the impact fatherhood had on them. Princesses Joanna and Elizabeth recognized their untapped potential as main characters. De Nomolos's evolution continued via his relationship with Missy. Favorites from the films were brought back in various roles (including the surprise villain). And, of course, every opportunity to add to the glory of the Grim Reaper was jumped on. If I'd had a checklist of "wants" prior to writing the book, it would now be complete. The book was a tremendous amount of flashback fun to put together and hopefully it reflects that sheer sense of joy I felt in 1989…and still do today.

Be excellent to each other,
BRIAN JOINES
Portland, OR 2016

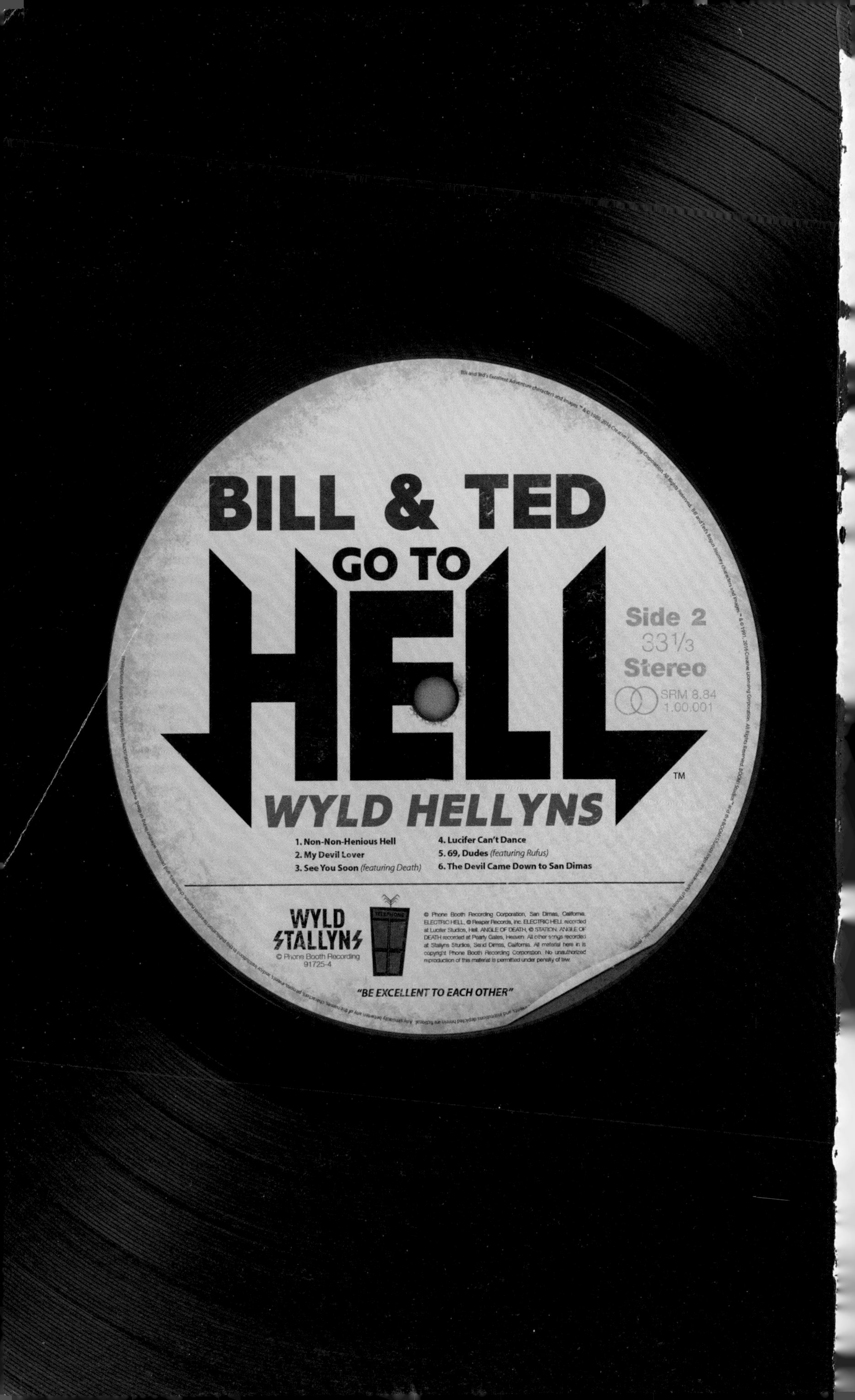

BILL & TED
GO TO
HELL
™
WYLD HELLYNS
Side 2
33⅓
Stereo
SRM 8.84
1.00.001
1. Non-Non-Henious Hell
2. My Devil Lover
3. See You Soon (featuring Death)
4. Lucifer Can't Dance
5. 69, Dudes (featuring Rufus)
6. The Devil Came Down to San Dimas
WYLD STALLYNS
© Phone Booth Recording
91725-4
TELEPHONE
© Phone Booth Recording Corporation, San Dimas, California. ELECTRIC HELL, © Reaper Records, Inc. ELECTRIC HELL recorded at Lucifer Studios, Hell. ANGLE OF DEATH, © STATION. ANGLE OF DEATH recorded at Pearly Gates, Heaven. All other songs recorded at Stallyns Studios, San Dimas, California. All material here in is copyright Phone Booth Recording Corporation. No unauthorized reproduction of this material is permitted under penalty of law.
"BE EXCELLENT TO EACH OTHER"